What Readers are Saying

"An invitation to reclaim the parts of ourselves that were abandoned, shamed, or stifled. Brimming with stories and ideas that illuminate and inspire, this book will help you take the sometimes terrifying steps needed to breathe life into a truer version of yourself."

~ **Jonathan Fields,** Founder of Good Life Project

"Inspirational, vulnerable, and insightful. Every story feels like a summoning back to wholeness. I was emboldened to lean into my truth despite how it may make others feel. This book offers several paths for creating personal change & contributions to the healing of the world."

~ **Shelley Adelle,** Performer/Maker

"I'm not sure what I was expecting when I sat down to read this for a friend, but the synchronicity that arose between what I read and where I find myself in this moment is undeniable. Just a few chapters in, I found myself feeling a range of emotions from inspired to gutted—it was incredibly beautiful and moving and so relatable. As I kept reading, in all the stories, Amanda's question, 'What is your story?', it just really resonated. I have felt like I 'should' be writing more academic, work-related stuff; but my heart hasn't been in it the way it needs to be to get that work out there. After a few chapters and a short meditation, I realized the story I'm supposed to tell right now and received the title. I can't imagine that any of this would have come up for me had I not read the chapters I did yesterday and spent some time reflecting on them—I'm so incredibly grateful!!

This compilation on the reality of what it takes to put a message out into the world offers a series of raw, insightful narratives. Exploring each writer's experience from internal and external perspectives, YCMTSU reveals the innermost thoughts of writers as they vulnerably navigate the insecurities of putting their deepest darkest thoughts out into the world for people to judge, while also learning to celebrate the little wins, and often finding joy and healing along the way. This book is a powerful reminder that behind every story is a flawed human being who makes the choice to push past the fear to share their message with the world."

~**Dimple Dhabalia,** Founder, Roots in the Clouds

"Reading through these stories, it is clear that Amanda uses several well-known and even researched approaches, whether she knows it or not. Polyvagal breathing techniques, centered and grounded mindfulness approaches, cognitive-behavioral modeling, and even some smatterings of psychospiritual methods are intertwined to provide outcomes similar to that of narrative therapy. (And don't forget the dark chocolate—there is research to demonstrate that it really does help us deal with dementors!)

From the perspective of 'deep psychology,' Amanda's process emulates that of an ancient, healing pedagogy of storytelling through writing. She encourages others to define what lies outside of our conscious awareness and may even illuminate that which an author may hold in an unconscious space: thoughts, impressions, and feelings which may not have not been previously admitted, even to oneself, including potential collective consciousnesses aspects with cultural and archetypal dimensions.

Amanda's invitation is in the tradition of depth work—one in which the participant may observe, grapple with, and consider what it means to really heal, and then share that journey with others who may find connection and even hope through the process."

~**Lonny R. Webb,** MSV, LCSW
Clinical and Forensic Social Work

"YCMTSU is a great read! It's a collection of stories written by writers from different walks of life who were encouraged to find a message in their messes and share it with others to make the world a better place. Each story is unique, authentic, and stands on its own. All together the book is a heart-warming compilation that reminds the reader we all have our stories and YCMTSU moments and their one purpose is to help one another not just survive but to thrive in this world. It inspired me to get busy and get my story out there. Thanks Amanda... and everyone!"

~**Kathleen Mizell,** Author of *Goo to Gratitude*

You Can't Make This St*ry Up

What If It's All Happening For Us?

Amanda Johnson & Her Rabble

True to Intention

You Can't Make This St*ry Up

What If It's All Happening For Us?

Published by

True to Intention

Prescott, AZ

www.TrueToIntention.com

Copyright © 2022 *by Amanda Johnson*

Cover Design by Lionheart Creations

Interior Design by Dawn Teagarden

ISBN: 9798792745865 (paperback)

Printed in the United States of America

www.TrueToIntention.com

Thank you for bringing my crazy out.

"Perfection is the enemy of the Good."

To the Creatives and Coaches who question your sanity...
May these stories help you realize you are one
of the sane ones, find your allies, build your own
cocoon, and become truer to your intention.

Aaron Johnson

Thank you for bringing your genius and levity to this project.

Acknowledgments

To the Co-Author that oh-so-perfectly inserts the plot twists and characters required to guide us home, and keeps it so damn interesting and fun.

To the partners and children who support us, we know it is not easy and we thank you for all of your support, even when it is messy.

To the team who worked tirelessly behind the scenes to make this book an experience. Theddee, the content is more powerful and true because of you. Alyssa, the cover is epic and captures every powerful message the stories in this book tell. Dawn, the interior is so wonderfully customized. Lori, Aaron, and Ciara, I would not be sane at the close of this project without you. (Wait. I'm sane, right?)

To the clients whose stories are not captured in this book, thank you for allowing me to witness your journey and for being part of my story and rescue mission.

With All My Love and Gratitude,

Amanda

Contents

Foreword

Karlyn Pleasants, Psy.D.

I let out a nervously hopeful sigh as I hung up from my first chat with Amanda and sent her the content I already had for review. She had explained her specialty rested in the non-fiction realm and she would most likely refer me to a colleague who works with fiction. But deep down, I already knew that I would not be able to ignore the magic that had crossed our paths at this point in my project.

The previous two years had been a mercurial blend of magic and frustration. I had sold my business—a unique treatment program for severe mental illness rooted in the values of community and shared responsibility—and found myself at a loss with what I was supposed to do next. My excitement for my newfound freedom had fallen flat. Instead, I was untethered and empty. I had lost my sense of purpose and was desperate for inspiration because one thing I knew: I wasn't done yet. But what would I do?

BOOM! Half-way through my new commute to my new job, out of nowhere, a clear idea landed in my mind. "A book," a confident version of my own voice said; and an image emerged in my mind's eye, showing me in a slow-motion instant the story I would be telling: two boys experiencing an awakening of special gifts and their search for meaning within a culture that pathologized them as mentally ill and ostracized them from their communities. I rushed into the office to tell a dear friend-colleague about my supernatural experience on the I-15 South, partly because it was so mystifying but also because I wanted to be held accountable. A grin spread across her face. "Of course you are! You're not done yet."

The following year felt like a magical journey. It was as if I had somehow accessed a mysterious databank of all things enchanting and dreamy. An open conduit where characters and storylines seemed to download directly into my brain along with creative plot twists and surprise discoveries. I traversed the endless maze of research rabbit holes where ideas unfolded and laid bare sparkling new paths to follow. I wrote fast and furious on restaurant napkins and the backs of boarding passes—whatever was available—as my mind wove together elaborate, stirring story lines.

Then, at nearly the same moment the pandemic shut down our world, my mind slowed and reached the inevitable *"download complete"* screen. I stared for weeks at hundreds of pages (and napkins) of content, wondering how to turn it into a novel. Then, two different friends, two days apart, both recommended the same book on writing. I picked it up and *AH HA!* I had my answer. Within days, I had at least a half dozen books on how to structure a novel. I basked in glorious flow charts and colorful bulleted outlines that spoke of acts, plot points, denouements, and climaxes. All I needed to do was place my content neatly into the well-defined formulas. Simple. One novel, coming right up!

Eight months into the structuring process, I had become a professional "plotter" with no novel to show. I was discouraged but not yet ready to throw in the towel and began wondering if there was such a thing as a book coach. As if on cue, an unexpected visit from some dear friends delivered. They graciously asked about my book; and when I embarrassingly confessed that I was stuck and had no idea what to do next, my friend shared that *coincidently*, his aunt had just published a book with the help of a coach and asked if I would be interested in talking to her. Um, yes please.

When we met again, Amanda shared that the timing was eerily synchronous: Something had recently happened with a person in her life that resonated strongly with my message. She wanted to work together and would send me a proposal. I was happy and also SCARED. How could that be? Wasn't this exactly what I was hoping for? While I reviewed the details, my mind scanned for all the reasons I should not do this. But I knew I would. Ready to send my contract back, I grabbed my trusty oracle deck for a final dose of reassurance. Shuffling the cards, one leapt out and landed face up, picking me before I could select my own card. *The Rabbit*... who offers the reminder to be wary of paralyzing yourself with all the ways things could go wrong... and release your fears to let your future unfold. Seemed mighty appropriate to me. I sent a picture to Amanda, freeing my fear that she would think I was a little too out there and revoke her offer. Her reply about floored me, and certainly assured me I was doing exactly what I was supposed to in this moment: "Just because synchronicity is the name of the game right now—my maiden name is Coelho, which means 'Rabbit' in Portuguese. You cannot make this stuff up!"

When I entered this project, I was looking to author a story with a message of hope. As a clinical psychologist, for two decades, I had helped guide a therapeutic community that offered belonging, belief-in, and empowerment to individuals with mental illness, most of whom had been written off as too sick or severe to get better. The profound healing and recovery I had witnessed over the years as a result of this approach was nothing short of miraculous, and

I wanted to write a story that would offer inspiration to those who might be questioning the possibility of having a life outside of a psychiatric diagnosis. What if "symptoms" are not always what they seem?

I joined the coaching and st*ry-healing retreats and enjoyed the work, even though I saw no *personal* relationship with the story. I enjoyed and appreciated the stories Amanda told about messengers realizing that the writing process was helping them uncover, heal, and rewrite a personal story; I simply just didn't think that part applied to me. In fact, as I began my writing journey with my new allies, unbelievable coincidences and breathtaking synchronicities appeared, leading me deeper into a mystical sea of infinite possibilities. The processes flowed. It was becoming a good story about *other* people, for *other* people.

Until the flow came to a screeching halt during a momentum retreat in the inspiring landscape of Mt. Hood, Oregon. After a day of wrestling with what I thought would be one of the coolest scenes to write, Amanda suggested I take a break and work on a different, easier scene. Next day, I churned out the most gut-wrenching chapter of the book, one that dragged me through nausea, headaches, back pain, and all sorts of physical ailments rare to me. My character had recovered a repressed memory of a traumatic, decades-old family secret, and her anguish ripped through me and onto the pages I wrote. At least I knew it wasn't mine; I was channeling her experience.

I returned home from the retreat and—YCMTSU— learned of a horrific incident that had been held secret in my family for nearly sixty years! A secret full of shame, rejection, threats, and loss. Despite my complete shock, so many puzzle pieces immediately fit together: generational family patterns and attitudes, bad blood and estrangements, addiction and illness, and plenty of other secrets. *Technically*, it wasn't my secret, but I had no doubt in that moment that I had absolutely been channeling something *real* and *personal* at the retreat.

Having released a generational story I didn't even know was binding me, the writing once again began to flow. For the next several months, I cranked out chapter after chapter in record time. Something had been unlocked inside and my doubts that this story had anything to do with me personally dwindled quickly.

Then I came to yet another skidding halt. I was approaching my last chapters but somehow kept getting caught up in insignificant details and any number of silly distractions. When Amanda suggested I was perhaps having feelings about bringing this story—*my* story—to a close, I leaned in. I'm a therapist after all. I make a living inviting people to consider alternative perspectives on interpreting their feelings and behaviors. And with that willingness, I pushed through the resistance, embraced the torrential and very unexpected meltdown of tears, and hatched the final, transcendent scene, aware with unprecedented clarity that this was indeed *my* story.

Something incredible had happened. On the page, around me, and within me.

I laugh and roll my eyes at myself whenever I think about my insistence that this fictional story was unrelated to my own. Much of my training as a clinical psychologist has centered on attachment and relational trauma, and I am both professionally and personally familiar with how stories influence healing. Even the research supports the fact that storytelling can serve as the voice for an experience that needs to be told and witnessed and that writing one's story broadens the path to healing.

No wonder the messenger's experience is full of starts and stops, and all the mess and mayhem that seems to emerge in between. No wonder so many people have brilliant ideas and never lay them to paper. No wonder authors write novels and never seek to publish, and dedicated students abandon years of academic study on the eve of completing their dissertation. It is the same reason a suffering individual may start therapy and drop out a few sessions in. The WHY is because the endeavor is usually associated with a story they don't want to revisit or tell.

Let's consider for a moment the psychodynamics of avoidance: We have a message to share, a magnificent idea for creating great change, a desire to teach our methods of success or healing so that others might be inspired to do the same. And then we get stuck. Disoriented and distracted by apparently-unrelated events in our life, confused and doubtful about why we started this project in the first place, we often find ourselves unconsciously sabotaging the very thing we say we want most: to share, create, teach, and inspire.

The key word is *unconscious,* as none of us are intentionally looking to hinder our own goals. What has happened underneath the surface is a serious collision between our new, shiny, and inspired self and our pre-existing self that unwittingly embodies the old stories, beliefs, wounding, and early programming that became hot-wired into our identity. Messages we received from the outside took up residence on the inside and became internalized truths that prevent us from achieving that which we are so eager to have. "Being seen is dangerous" or "Speaking the truth brings anger and rejection" manifests in procrastination of putting words to paper or avoidance of using our voices on stage, or any other number of behaviors that serve as inadvertent barriers to realizing our goals.

To release ourselves from the controlling grip of these invisible saboteurs, we must pull back the curtains of defense, bring our hidden and oft-forgotten beliefs into the light, and make some revisions to the old programming. This is no small endeavor; it can be painful to revisit the experiences that shaped our self-defeating beliefs. But it is exactly in the revisiting and rewriting of the old, outdated narrative where we find release from the powerful grasp of the past and the freedom to move forward, uninhibited, toward the actualization of our goals and the delivery of the message we seek to share.

In the narrative work of storytelling, Amanda is persistent in her press to tell and write our stories in great sensory detail. Writing fiction, I especially struggled with this in the beginning because after all, this story wasn't about me, right? But the reality was that each one of the characters in my "fictional" story held pieces of my own stories—truths and distortions, biases and blind-spots, adherence to terms of invisible contracts I wasn't aware I had entered into. In life and in writing story, it is too easy to abandon the parts of ourselves that we believe may threaten our status quo and (illusion of) stability. But our forsaken parts want to be heard, too. The neglected child, the forgotten sibling, the bullied student—they are the ones who hold our pain, fear, shame, and all sorts of other realities that aren't so shiny and bright. These parts have spent so much time isolated in those deep dark recesses inside, that when we exclude them—either intentionally or not—they don't like it and will find a way to show up anyway... and usually kick our asses in the process!

The opportunities for healing come in the rewriting of our underlying, highly influential narratives. By bringing all our parts forward to be seen and heard, we can see and feel our whole story from a fresh perspective and in a new light. It is here that we can begin the task of examining the old programming and hard-wired beliefs and decide where revisions and upgrades are needed. It is here where we discover the moments when we lose our agency and can instead pick up the pen and write a new response. It is here where we are empowered to release the roles we no longer wish to play and write into place new scripts and future storylines that support us in achieving our goals, sharing our messages, and living in alignment.

And, this work is so much more meaningful when we travel it with allies.

> *The meeting of two personalities is like the contact of two chemical substances: if there is any reaction, both are transformed.*
>
> ~C.G. Jung~

To bear witness to another's healing is a sacred privilege and one filled with abundant gifts and opportunities for professional and personal growth. Beholding the transformation that unfolds extends an invitation for us, as coaches, mentors, guides, and teachers, to reflect on our own roles and journeys in the spirit of healing.

If we believe that people come into our lives for a reason, that our paths do not cross by accident, that there are messages to hear and lessons to learn from each encounter, then it stands to reason that the people who come to us for mentoring, guidance, help, and support also have something to teach us—something that could, if we accept the invitation, facilitate our own healing and journey towards wholeness.

Jung posited that the mutual influence of two people offers the possibility of joint transformation. In fact, he believed this was the ultimate aim of the therapeutic relationship. But what if we extend this idea to all *helping* relationships—student and teacher, mentee and mentor, learner and coach? From this view, we might consider our helping relationships more like *working alliances*—a joining of forces with mutual goals that holds the potential for collective transformation.

As we seek to inspire growth, we too can be inspired to grow by the wisdom and gifts the people we work with offer. In supporting another in rewriting outdated narratives, we have the chance to examine our personal stories and do some rewriting of our own. When we lean in to the uncomfortable feelings that are brought up as we work together toward a common goal, we discover the wounds and patterns inside us that still need our love and attention.

As a therapist, I could write a book (ooh, another idea!) on the myriad of ways I have learned from and become a more integrated person from my relationships—*alliances*—with clients. I am often both humbled and heartened by their courage, perseverance, vulnerability, and strength. Their growth inspires my own through the opportunity to self-reflect and ensure I am aligned with myself and my message. It is not always easy, but it is always worth it.

This book presents 19 stories of the healing and transformation that can unfold if and when we decide we have a powerful message to share with the world, and surrender to the reality that any story we share is rooted in ourselves and blossoms when we share it with others. Plus, there is also the story of a coach who seeks to experience every magical and messy moment as an invitation to deepen her own healing.

It's all those stories and how they braid together that tells us who and what and where we are.

~Charles de Lint~

If we believe people come into our lives for a reason and that our encounters—the good, the bad, and the ugly—all contain important lessons that ultimately propel us forward, then we are poised to ponder the invisible threads of connectedness that link us together. Bell's Theorem, a principal in quantum mechanics, posits that once connected, an invisible stream of energy keeps objects connected, where they will continue to affect one another forever no matter where they are. Is it possible then that one of the goals of this elaborate nexus network that orchestrates our connections (and collisions) with others (and ourselves) is to let us know that we are not alone? That we are meant to belong, to be held and seen in both our trials and our triumphs, and to be supported in our efforts toward wholeness and purpose? The courageous, vulnerable, and inspiring stories in this book, to me, are the embodiment of this notion.

In this sense, we can more easily consider the possibility that events happen *for* us, rather than *to* us and hold the potential for growth, healing, and wholeness, even if it is difficult to understand at the time. A chance encounter, an out-of-the-blue idea, an unexpected rupture, a surprise discovery—if these things are happening *for* us, they could very well be invitations to tell a new story, or rewrite an old one, or help another do the same. Through the magic of synchronicity and the unfolding of boundless opportunities, we stand primed to create alliances, build supportive communities, and experience a shared transformation that has the potential to ripple out to support the healing and wholeness of others.

The only question left is: Are we ready to accept the invitation?

Introduction

You *Really* Can't Make This St*ry Up

"**A**manda, are you scared?" she probed.

"Not really," I answered, looking into the face of a client-turned-dear-friend on my computer screen. "I mean, I did feel a little unnerved when I walked into the grocery store and saw the bare shelves."

"Yeah, the fear is palpable," she started. "But I feel like an alien. I'm just not that scared."

"I suppose that's a good thing, right? People need hope and empowerment right now, and it would be impossible to offer it to them if we lost ourselves in the panic."

"Right. So, what are you thinking about the retreat?" She sipped her tea while she waited for my response.

"Well, honestly, I think that you *really* can't make this shit up..." I sat back in my chair and laughed out loud with her while I marveled at the synchronicities unfolding.

That's what last year was all about—preparation for THIS.

Nine months earlier, in July 2019—after six years of deep dives into my own st*ry loops, dissolving identities that had been placed upon me (or that I'd assimilated over time), and taking the terrifying steps to live my truth despite how it made others feel—I found my new realizations about myself, my Source (I call It my Co-author!), and the world being tested. Ridiculous lawsuits, changing relationship dynamics, and impossible work schedules forced me into sixteen-hour days full of travel, client work, retreats, study, and dozens of activities that I'd never have chosen for myself.

It was like a finals exam.

You see, even though I'd been witnessing it with my clients and preaching it for years, my experience and belief that "this is happening *for* us, not *to* us" had been challenged to its core right after I wrote my first book.

I mean, who wakes up to an almost-life-long abusive relationship and then says, "That happened *for* me"? Who moves to a new state to start their own life for the first time at thirty-six and leaves behind every person, situation, and credit card that had acted as a safety net? Who gets a part-time job at a grocery store, shakes their head the next day when three big contracts close, and keeps the job? Who facilitates the most challenging retreats of their life and shakes their head at the absolute perfection of what unfolded?

I'll tell you who—someone who has lost their damn mind.

Or... someone like me who has spent a decade marveling at the sacred magic contained in hundreds of personal stories *and* the timing of those stories crossing my own path.

I've spent more than a decade working with messengers who came to me for help in getting their story, expertise, and message onto pages and stages.

Inevitably, we arrive at a moment in our work together where the messenger sees the magic in their messy story. "Amanda, if that *(horrible thing)* hadn't happened, I would never have met *(important person)* and know what/who I know today. I would not have started searching for these answers. I wouldn't have experienced this type of connection with my *(Source)*, myself, and others. I wouldn't have realized my gifts. I would never have..."

I try to stay silent in these sacred moments and allow the truth they are speaking to fill the space because I know what usually comes next.

A health crisis, a financial fallout, a relationship breakdown, or some almost-unbelievable combination of these find their way into the client's storyline. And the plot twists do what they appear to be destined to do—make the client question everything they've come to believe: their message, their expertise, their capacity, their worth, and maybe even the magic they just realized led them to this moment.

That's when the work *really* begins.

You see, it's one thing to look *back* and see all of the magic in the mess; it's quite another to be *in the middle of the mess* and still trust that there is a sacred magic unfolding.

So, while the finals exam of the summer of 2019 looked like utter insanity to the people who love me and want me to be well and happy, I was present to and nearly (still human here!) enjoying riding the waves of very messy magic.

I *knew* the oversights in my calendar were happening with purpose, so I relished the unexpected hours of commuting with my son, who was about to start driving himself everywhere on his own... without me.

I *knew* that my car rolling across the parking lot while I was at the check stand was a gift, so I thanked my Co-author for showing me a false belief I'd had about my car without it costing someone's limb or life.

I *knew* there was a reason for the lawsuit, and I was listening for it when the lawyer said the six words that would lead to liberation in every other area of my life.

Of course, during this time, I was *also* witnessing similar events with my clients.

Magical moments of synchronistic meetups and connections were unfolding for some; and messy moments of car "accidents," running "injuries," and relationship "endings" were unfolding for others. And, because they had witnessed the magic in the mess of their past stories, even those dealing with insurance issues, surgeries, and heartache were sure of one thing: "There's some higher reason for this. It's going to make me stronger, wiser, and more WHOLE in the end. It's preparing me for what's next. I can already see the gifts unfolding in the conversations I had with the tow truck guy/medics/therapist..."

That's when the inspiration for this book struck.

Wouldn't it be amazing if I enlisted my past and present clients to share their magical, messy journeys of putting their message and mission into the world? To inspire other change agents to consider that maybe the inspiration to change the world is actually for us first—to help us become more whole and attuned to the magic that is at work around us all the time, even when we can't see it or believe it. And maybe I could share why or how their message crossed my path at the exact right moment for my own personal healing or business growth.

But this girl was busy. (Sixteen-hour days, y'all!) I wrote down my ideas and shared them with a few people whose eyes quickly lit up, but I didn't have time to really pull my thoughts together until November 2019.

By that time, the inspiration had expanded.

I'd had some tough conversations with clients about following the magic instead of The Messenger Matrix when it comes to growing their business. What if they could drop the idea that they "need" a funnel, a membership community, and a train-the-trainer program to "succeed" and just tune in and ask, "What is the right next step?"

I'd hang up and another would call. Of course, it "just happened to be" someone working in the same industry with their own enormous vision. I'd listen and ask them what matrix they needed to drop and what the right next step was, and then they'd hang up. And then someone else would call, and I'd realize that the three people I'd just spoken to needed to be connected because there was an incredible opportunity for collaboration and cross-promotion.

That's when I received a "random" referral to someone who needed some energetic support around a legal situation. After listening, and sharing some insights, I blurted, "It also sounds like you might need a better attorney. I have some lawyer friends in your area—I can find out if they have someone they trust..." I sent three emails and within a few hours, I had referrals in this person's neighborhood.

Evidence of the power of a trusted network of caring professionals with integrity.

Coincidence? No, that's what I call a YCMTSU moment.

So, what would happen if this group of clients came together to share their magical, messy stories of messenger-ing; and then we figured out how to start working TOGETHER to change the world more quickly and effectively?

A dozen people signed up to play at that level and another dozen committed to contributing their story to this book.

By the time we had signed all the agreements, made the deposits, booked the flights, and rented the Airbnb for our retreat, it was February 2020.

Weeks later, while everyone was getting ready to meet and co-create a new paradigm for the industries we serve, the corona virus showed up and the world was turned upside-down with panic as the news churned out one apocalyptic clip after another.

Hence the empty shelves and panic at the grocery store.

You can't make this shit up, right?

Just as we all committed to up-leveling our leadership and collaboration, the world was turned on its head. Travel bans. School and business shutdowns. People told to stay in their homes. Streams of revenue compromised or totally disappeared.

And here we were...

Our inspiration, messages, and beliefs about what's possible in the world—for people to truly reclaim their personal freedom and sovereignty over their bodies, minds, health, relationships, education, message, business growth, future, and more—were being tested.

And we had the choice...

We could look at the appearances and contract or drop this vision because it was so huge, because it seemed like everyone was too busy or upside-down to listen, or because it appeared untimely.

Or...

We could call this a test of what we've come to know by experience: The magic is always there/here in our personal and collective stories, and the plot twists don't just happen randomly.

What if this was the perfect moment?

What if the inspiration came when it did because our Co-author knew this pandemic was on the horizon?

What if we were called to be leaders and collaborators at this time because we have some answers and, more importantly, we have the practices to keep us present, mindful, and listening for more answers as they are revealed?

What if this was Leadership School?

Not the kind where you sit down, listen, take notes, raise your hand when you have a question, and then regurgitate what you've heard. No, more like what almost-doctors experience during internship. It's that moment when shit gets real. They're no longer safely observing, conjecturing, and postulating from behind their textbooks; they are interacting with real patients who need them to behave like real doctors, or else.

Shit was getting real, and we could no longer sit back and bitch and moan and criticize what's not working out there... in the systems that were built, good intentions or not, by people long, long ago. We were being called to the front lines of service to humanity. We were being asked to co-create the new way... fast.

And that's what we did individually in our homes and on the front lines in our own industries as opportunities opened up; it's what we endeavored to do collectively through this project.

Did we do it perfectly? Ummmm... no, not even close.

Did it all happen in the timing we believed it would? Nope, it didn't.

Did it turn out exactly like we planned? Of course not.

Did we all learn and grow and become more whole through the process? Absolutely.

In fact, as you'll see in the conclusion, we hit some turbulence individually and as a community. Some of us realized it wasn't the right fit and left; others had to renegotiate their time and method of contribution. Many of us disappointed each other—ripped some scabs off wounds that still needed healing—and worked together to create the salve. Most of us laughed and cringed and cried together. All of us became more whole, and the value of our stories and our work in the world became clearer.

Regardless of what happens with this project, we are already the better for it; and I believe it's because we brought all of who we are and everything we've learned, dropped it at the feet of the Co-author that we've come to know is conspiring on our behalf, and said, "We're listening. Give us the scripts. Insert the right plot twists and opportunities. Show us the way."

I believe the world needs more messengers like these.

Will you join us?

Well, actually, maybe you should take a look at what the process often looks like first!

Contrary to what many popular business and book coaches will tell/sell you, writing a book and launching a business to change the world is not as simple as following the formulas they offer so freely, especially for people like us. Those of who us are sharing stories and messages that are the direct result of overcoming and/or succeeding despite an abusive childhood or relationship, a deep betrayal or other tragedy, or a lifelong st*ry of not being enough (or being way too much) quickly slam into our old wounds and st*ries and struggle through the creative process. Most just quit. Not because they *decide* they don't want to rehash the past, but because their life goes upside-down every time they bring this project forward and they unconsciously (and quite accurately, in my opinion) connect the sudden physical symptoms, relationship ruptures, financial fall-outs, and other minor and massive disturbances with giving their attention to it.

More than a decade ago, I decided to use my own transcendent experience watching "magic eggs" turn into caterpillars and then butterflies as the framework for the journey I witness every aspiring messenger take. Watching caterpillars flip upside-down with absolutely no hesitation, I realized that this is the moment where most of us stop our journey. Our message (and the st*ries it brings up for us) sparks intense disorientation in our lives and we resist the very process required to transform into the beautiful masterpieces and messengers we are destined to be. But what if we knew how to co-create a safe enough space (cocoon) in and around us to allow all of those st*ries to be witnessed and dissolved and reorganized into the body and wings that would carry our message and purpose to the world? What if we had someone to tell us that it's best *not* to fly right away, but to strengthen our wings and learn to trust The Wind first? What if we were in a community (rabble) whose measure of success was wholeness instead of, or at least in addition to, the numbers of followers on social media or dollars in our accounts?

It's true that sometimes projects get stuck because the messenger has failed to clarify the core message, or chosen the wrong audience, or doesn't know how to organize their thoughts in a coherent manner, or is missing the storytelling skills that make content engaging. In fact, you'll find some stories in this book where one or more of these challenges brought a client my way. But more often than not, in my experience, projects and purpose stall and stutter because there is another reason the aspiring author, speaker, or coach has been inspired to write, speak, and support others. It's a divine conspiracy aimed at their wholeness, and writing a message or story is one of the most powerful ways to witness, embrace, and eventually accept their role as the co-author, narrator, and character of their story. But it's also one of the toughest.

What to Expect

Each chapter is written by one of the dozens of messengers I've supported over the last decade, all of whom are dear friends and three of whom are biologically related to me. I invited those who had the most powerful experiences and who represent many others who I either didn't invite or who decided this wasn't the right project at the right time.

At the end of each of their stories, you'll see that I've written "my side of our story," in order to inspire other coaches to consider the possibility that every client lands in our plotline with purpose and to explore what sacred contributions they bring. Even those who throw their hands up in frustration, throw some poop in our direction, and/ or walk away for one reason or another have a gift they leave with us. And trust me when I say, I've had plenty of those clients.

Some of these messengers catalyzed personal healing with their stories while others inspired and supported important expansions in my business. All of them arrived at the perfect time, and that means three of them have been delivering some of the most important messages I've received in my life since before they even knew they had a message.

Our collective intention is that you find at least one or two stories that help you to recognize that you are not alone in your experience of the upside-down creative and/ or coaching process. That you will consider the possibility that all those hot messes that blindside you when you start a project might just be opportunities for more wholeness. That there is a community of messengers and experts here that keeps it real and raw and safe and fun and is always embracing others who are willing to do this type of work to *become* the change we all want to see in the world.

So, let's get to it!

Ursula Mentjes is an award-winning entrepreneur, sales expert, motivational speaker, and author of four bestselling books. She was promoted from account executive to President of an international technical training company in just five years at the age of 27 when the revenue was in the tens of millions. Ursula specializes in Neuro-Linguistic Programming to help clients 2x their monthly sales while also releasing 10 hours or more hours off their work week. Her clients include Aflac, Ebenezer, Keller Williams, Fairview Hospitals, New York Life, Paychex, and more. She is on a mission to help millions of women business owners break through the 7-figure mark!

UpLeveling with Intention

Ursula Mentjès

"There's no way I can... publish this... right?" After attaching the document with the most painful story from my childhood, I hit send.

I know that story has been keeping me from my next level in every area of my life, but why would I print that for everyone to see? It's so... heavy.

Despite the churning in my stomach, I refilled my coffee cup to the brim and took a deep breath.

I need some air!

Plopping myself into the cozy chair on my deck, overlooking Lac Lavon, I imagined my readers and clients trying to digest that story.

There is only one reason to share that story.

The long-repressed hurt and anger were moving through my body, and I closed my eyes to breathe and remember what was true in that moment. I was safe and loved. I had worked for decades to heal from my traumatic childhood, and I had built a beautiful life with my husband and loved being a mommy to our son. My work was meaningful, and my business was growing steadily. And, I knew I wasn't alone in my journey.

I know I'm meant to do more and that this story is part of what's holding me back from helping the millions of entrepreneurs who need my message. I see it all the time in my own clients—how these old wounds create the limits of their impact and income. But do they really need to see my wound? Will it really help them?

"Yes..." The voice was a composite of my own and those of the last few coaches who had been saying this for a while now.

Well, I guess getting it on paper was the first step in bringing the wound into the light.

Buzz.

I glanced at my phone and saw Amanda's response: "Whew. This took my breath away. Where do you imagine putting this in the book?"

The lump in my throat returned.

Ring.

It was Amanda.

"Ursula, I'm... speechless... I'm so sorry that happened to you."

"I never told you that story, eh?"

"I mean, you've told me about some of the crazy stuff, but this is hard to..."

"Yeah, and I didn't include all the details there. I don't know how much of it to share or where, for the readers' sake, but I know it is time to share it."

After four successful books and more than a decade of personal and business expansion, I knew I had to do this; and I was grateful I had Amanda and our almost-fifteen years of friendship and coaching to help me sort through the process, and actually put it on paper.

The first time I saw her, she was sitting quietly at a round table at a networking event, in a loud room, politely listening to the business owner next to her. The look on her face said it all—she felt like she had just landed on Mars.

I like her already! I thought to myself, not knowing that she would become not only *my* book coach (I like to think she's all mine!), but also my favorite "quitting coach" and one of my best soul sistas on the planet. I had no idea that I would soon tell her all my stories, even the ones I was still too scared to write about (yes, there are many!), and that she would one day know me better than I probably think I know myself.

As I sat there, watching Amanda squirm, I had just finished writing my first book, *Selling with Intention* after realizing that speaking and training on the topic of sales did not give me the kind of platform I needed to help as many people as I desired to reach. I had founded a sales training and coaching company called Potential Quest (which became Sales Coach Now and is now Ursula, Inc.) with the mission to help salespeople and entrepreneurs discover that selling doesn't have to be hard. In fact, by experience, I knew it could be easy. Plus, I wanted people to know that the more money they made, the more freedom they would gain, and the more they could impact the world.

But then my inner critic had shown up to make a mess. *"Who am I to write a book? I'm not an author. How will I fill an entire book? I don't have that much to say!"*

Despite my negative self-talk, I felt the push and desire to keep going; and when I saw an advertisement for a class on how to write and self-publish a book at the Learning Annex in Los Angeles, I signed up immediately. A few weeks later, I attended the three-hour class taught by a woman who was an ex-felon that had not only successfully written and published a book, she had gone on to start a successful multi-million-dollar publishing company. Her message was, "If I can do it, so can you." I took on her belief and kept writing.

After I finished writing the first (bad) draft of *Selling with Intention*, I knew I had to find an editor because that's what the owner of the publishing company told us to do. (I am very coachable!) Handing the book over for the first time wasn't easy. It was like asking someone to tell me that my baby was cute, even when I knew, deep down, that maybe my baby really wasn't the most adorable kiddo on the planet!

I was also running at one of my first insane business deadlines—a launch party for the book where I intended to sell a companion workbook. The only problem was that I didn't have time to create the workbook. That's when my editor formally introduced me to the woman who squirmed through the networking event. A few days later, we met at a cafe at an outdoor mall to discuss the project and make sure she was the one to help me cross the finish line.

The original version of *Selling with Intention* still exists out there, with its bright red cover. I've seen it floating around. I have a couple of copies myself. As I continued to work and heal my own st*ries over the years, the second self-published version was born and then the third version, published with Morgan James, came to fruition. Each version was an evolution of who I had become, what I had been willing to heal, and how I was showing up in the world. The writing process, coupled with the entrepreneur journey, had forced me to confront those parts of me that were wounded: *I am not enough, I am not a writer, I cannot have that level of success. Who am I to make a lot of money? What if I become visible? Etc.*

Amanda held space for me when I was overwhelmed with old pain while challenging me, in the gentlest way possible, to look in the mirror and see what needs to be healed and cleared before I could write that next chapter or finish editing the one in front of me. For me, all hell always breaks loose when I am in the process of editing and requires piles of chocolate chip cookies and jugs of black coffee. Impatient by nature, I love the initial part of the process—being creative, writing, and tying the pieces together—but my inner four-year old comes out as soon as I realize it's time to edit. Over time, she talked me into building clearer outlines at the beginning, to contain the process, which has made the editing not-quite-as-painful. But, let's be honest, editing is a piece of cake compared to the inner work that I have to do as I write these books.

The biggest opportunities for healing did not come through writing my first book or the second or third. The opportunities for deep healing arrived when I wrote my fourth and fifth books. By that time, I had begun to see how Amanda's annoying insistence that I include my personal stories paid off with my readers and my clients. I really did not want to tell the stories of the financial disaster in 2008 and the moments I cried on the kitchen floor, wondering if I had what it took to come back from that mess. I wasn't excited to include the even more personal stories Amanda had witnessed as my friend while witnessing my journey of becoming a mother after so many years of wondering if it would ever happen. But she knew it was the moment that I began to apply my own message, which I had used to grow my business and help other people grow theirs, that I stepped into a new belief zone where pregnancy became inevitable. Enough people had thanked me for sharing these vulnerable stories that when this story of my childhood came up at the end of my fifth book, I knew it had to stay and asked Amanda to help me do it in a way that would be powerful for my readers but also safe for me and my family.

It took me years to get to the point where I was even ready to talk about some of the stories that I share in my fifth book, let alone put them in front of tens of thousands of people. And yet, there is a part of me that knows my resistance to telling my story, my truth, is a barrier to helping others. I have come to accept that I've kept a lot of stories on lock down to stay safe because a part of me believed that if I shared them, I might not be as credible, or people wouldn't see me the same way. And yet, the opposite is true: Sharing my story has been the exact thing that has allowed me to free myself, to free others, and to encourage them to keep moving forward despite the inner battles they might be facing.

In fact, as soon as I started this inner work around the story in my fifth book, *UpLevel Now,* I saw incredible shifts happen in my business and my willingness to be more authentic and vulnerable, which in turn gave my clients what they needed to do the same. In my marketing, I also became even more open and authentic which I know allows my ideal clients to find me even easier. In fact, as we got closer to launch time, I received a five-star review from Reader's Favorite. At first, I was terrified to read it—serious impostor syndrome! But then, over a steaming cup of coffee, I opened it up and, with one eye open, began to read. Let's just say that the gentleman's five-star review made every challenging moment of writing this book worth it. Two sentences even made me smile out loud: "In *UpLevel Now*, Ursula Mentjes's writing style is no-nonsense, matter-of-fact, and feels like she is talking directly to you. On more than one occasion, I had to look over my shoulder to see she wasn't peering directly into my limiting beliefs that UpLevel Now will bust through." My direct sign from the Universe to keep writing, keep going, and never listen to that voice that says I can't.

Amanda's Side of the Story

I was too overwhelmed to close my computer and simply walk back into my life. I had to do something first.

Ursula!

I quickly dialed her number, knowing that if anyone was going to understand what I was experiencing, it was this client-turned-sista-friend who was all about powerful intention.

"Ursula…" My breath caught in my throat with excitement when I heard her voice.

"Yes?"

She always sounds like she's smiling on the other side of the phone—like she already knows what I'm about to say. I imagined her angelic face, smiling blue eyes, and wavy blonde hair draped down her back.

"I figured out my One Great Goal," I started, using the language I'd been learning from her as we worked on her second book. "I'm going to write a series of children's books with a parenting manual to help them raise happier, healthier children. I was talking to my mentor earlier today and…" I finished my story, including the part about mapping the content out and realizing that I was made for this project.

"Wow! Amanda, that is awesome! What can I do to help?" Her enthusiasm was palpable.

"Well, I left out the craziest part..." I paused.

OMG, if I say this out loud, she might think I'm nuts!!!

"I saw myself attracting a teacher from *The Secret,* and working with them. I mean, these teachers are out there showing people how to use the Law of Attraction to work on their own dreams and self-image. Why wouldn't they jump at the chance to offer their audiences an opportunity to help their children learn and benefit from the Law of Attraction while they are young?" I held my breath.

"Amanda, that is BRILLIANT. And I know you will do it. How soon do you want this to happen?" she asked.

"As soon as possible..." I blurted. "I outlined all of the content, and I'm going to ask a friend to help me with illustrations."

"Fantastic! I am going to hold this intention with you while you take that next step," she declared before telling me she had to run into a meeting. But right before she hung up, she said, "I'd love for you to join this One Great Goal mastermind I'm starting next week."

"Wow, thank you. Yes..."

"Awesome, I'll send you the details when I get home. Amanda, this is an incredible idea, and it *is* going to happen." And with that, she was gone.

As I hung up the phone, I grinned from ear-to-ear, feeling her belief infusing every cell of my body. If there was any doubt that this could happen before that moment, it was gone.

This is just one of the hundreds of scenes in my life where Ursula has been the first person I call, the first person to believe, and the first person to offer support because the message she had just delivered and I had just edited had arrived in divine time. Four months after this scene, after reading the autobiography I had written for an application to join a training program with The Secret Teacher I had met magically only three months later, Ursula said, "Amanda, as I was reading this, I saw this vision—it was Aaron (my son), leading an army of angels to come help you..."

If that's true, Ursula was one of the first angels he called in, and it happened at the absolute perfect time.

It was 2006, the year after I'd abandoned my dream of being a teacher and begun working as an online writing instructor for a dear mentor's new enterprise. My marriage was falling apart. My health was spiraling. My financial situation was more of a disaster. The only bright spot in my life was this little boy who had come to help three years earlier, and I was terrified I was going to damage him beyond repair.

When Ursula had asked my mentor/boss for help in developing the workbook for *Selling With Intention* (in two weeks, cuz that's how she rolls!), she quickly referred her to me. I remember where I was sitting the first time I heard her tell me what she was up to in the world, and I can still feel the tingly sensation that traveled from my heart to every cell of my body. Her sentiments about potential, the capacities of the conscious and subconscious minds, and power of intention quickly knit together previously disparate parts of my education and experience and made me realize that I was the perfect person to support her. More importantly, it called all of my own potential, capacities, and intention forward. In that moment, I had the opportunity to use my curriculum development chops from my teacher training and all that I had learned from my dad about the power of the subconscious to help Ursula and everyone who would experience this workbook.

I joke with a lot of people in Ursula's community that most people think of her the way our history books think of its most talked about figure. There's Before and After Ursula. The moment someone meets her, that's it—life as we know it changes... forever.

When I turned the workbook around in a few weeks, she not only gave me more work and asked me to take a second look at *Selling With Intention,* but she started referring all of her entrepreneurial friends to me. She quickly turned into one of my biggest cheerleaders, referral partners, and friends. And working with her has taught me A LOT about how many messengers operate and what we *all* face on this journey.

First, I learned how easy and common it is for messengers to leave their true "secret sauce" out of their message. The thoughts, feelings, and behaviors that come so naturally to them are treated like assumptions, when those are truly some of the most valuable gems they have to offer. After watching her interact at networking meetings and her events, I knew exactly what had been left out of *Selling With Intention* and was able to help her make it an even more valuable offering to her readers.

Second, avid readers and writers like Ursula have this funny little habit of trying to pack several books into one. And even after I spend a whole manuscript keeping them focused, they still start writing the next book before they finish this one. Every time we've worked on a book, she's heard me say, "That's the next one," at some point in the process.

Third, the journey of a messenger is a spiritual-emotional one that is designed to return us to wholeness. For many years, I was one of the first people Ursula called to share her "wild" ideas for events and programs; and I had the backstage pass to the realities of the journey—the self-doubt and second-guessing, the fears, the old st*ries and wounds, and the natural rollercoaster of emotion that is entrepreneurship. As a client, as a coach, and as a friend, Ursula modeled honesty and grace through all of it, even when she didn't think she did.

And she knew how to stretch me like only the best coaches, mentors, and friends do. When I'd state a goal that she knew was too small, she'd ask a question to expand it. When I'd give her the number for what I could see charging for one of my programs, she'd say, "Okay, but what's the *most* you would ever charge for that program?" When I shared the offer for people who would purchase ten copies of my first book, she asked, "And what are you going to give those who purchase twenty?" Gulp. Always the stretch. And now that I think about it, I'm certain that she and Aaron have been in some sort of spiritual cahoots this entire time. Right after she stretched me to twenty copies, he asked me what I would give to people who wanted to purchase fifty! I knew it!

Of course, it helped that she always received the message I needed right before I needed it.

Selling With Intention reminded me of the God-given power I had to create a new story for my life. I wasn't concerned with sales at the time, but the universal principles she shared brought my heart and mind together in a way they hadn't been able to attune before and opened me up to possibilities, dreams, and inspirations I simply couldn't access before then.

One Great Goal showed up right before my own lightning bolt message inspiration, and I'm sure it's what allowed me to see and own the huge vision that came through and take the scary steps of signing up to work with a teacher from *The Secret.*

Selling With Synchronicity was handed to me right in time for me to take action when the vision for my first huge event and inspiration for new offerings to support my messengers came in, leading me to my most exciting and profitable year in business.

The Belief Zone dropped in right after I had taken the biggest step to reclaim my power and my life and then found myself wondering if I'd made a huge mistake and how I was going to do it all on my own because business was dwindling. In addition to editing that book, I worked through all of the exercises and saw the bigger picture that my Co-Author had already been trying to show me—that I needed to offer message and st*ry-healing strategy, not just book strategy, so messengers could see from the beginning that we are doing way more than writing incredible books over here. It definitely expanded my own belief zone.

And this latest book, *UpLevel Now,* arrived as inspiration during a time where my Co-Author was demanding deeper integration between my professional and personal selves. I shook my head in awe and gratitude when I saw that this book was going to offer the most personally and professionally integrative message to date.

Every time she brings more of *her* to her work as a result of more vulnerable stories, more acknowledgment and leading with her obsession with quantum physics and woo, or more intensive personal healing, she infuses more magic into her writing and people get the opportunity to experience her the way I have—intention, coffee, chocolate chip cookies, and plenty of belly laughter as we marvel at the YCMTSU moments that connected us and continue to unfold in the most divine ways.

Jenée Dana graduated UCLA in 3 years in spite of having ADHD and she still had a blast. Her book, *Have Fun & Get It Done,* became a #1 bestseller back in April 2012 and has won multiple national and international awards. Her first award was the Gold Medal in Education from the Readers' Favorite International Book Awards. Today, she is a web application developer, Salesforce Consultant, and writer at HaveFunGetItDone. com. She lives in San Diego, CA with her husband and two cats, George and Jane, and loves weight lifting, hiking, Peloton riding, Netflix binging, fur-babies, traveling, and snorkeling with sharks. Yes, snorkeling with sharks.

Fun and that Other F-word

Jenée Dana

Sitting around a table with a few other messengers, I found myself struggling to answer Amanda's questions about the core message and market for this book while trying to listen to what the others were sharing.

Focus, Jenee. On them. Amanda will help you figure this out.

When it was my turn to share, I put it all out there, "Amanda, I have to tell you. I'm struggling with this. You know that I want to write a book to increase my credibility with my market for this My Focus Book life planner that I created, but I haven't really been able to get any traction with the female entrepreneurs and professionals who would benefit the most from this product."

Amanda nodded her head thoughtfully for a moment while my mind served up one frustrating moment after another.

Two days before I'd met Amanda, I was at a networking meeting trying to get the word out about my new business and the paper planner I published. I was just out of college and had enough unearned confidence to think, *Why not publish my own planner since no one else makes a planner I want?* Oh, and even though I was very much old enough to drink, I looked like I was still in middle school. I knew this because I worked at a middle school and teachers often mistook me for a student. Real confidence booster.

So, I was at this networking meeting, trying to be one of those boss bitches everyone keeps talking about, and a woman there approached me with a really concerned look on her face. "Excuse me, are you supposed to be here?"

In my head, I was thinking, *Excuse YOU, rando lady;* but I didn't want to get escorted out by men in uniform so I said, "Um yes, I'm registered."

And this woman had the nerve to respond, "Shouldn't you be in school? It's 10 a.m."

Now I realized what this bitch meant. *First of all, Karen (although we didn't have that fun term just yet back then), you can go fuck right off.*

But right under all that anger was a whole lot of concern. *No one is ever going to take me seriously. Why do I even bother trying to impress these people and wear suits? I just look like a frumpy sixteen-year-old in a suit. *sigh* Not even the nerdiest of nerds would ditch high school to show up to a business networking meeting. Just... why?*

I have no control over my facial expressions, so I either looked like a deer in headlights or like I was plotting her demise.

Finally, I mustered up the courage to speak, "Oh no, I'm not in high school. I graduated from UCLA and I just started my own company."

"Oh gosh, you just look so young," she said before walking away and leaving me to awkwardly find a seat *not* at her table.

At that point, I felt hopeless. I had just invested a couple thousand dollars, with a small loan from my mom, to manufacture my first planners and I didn't know how I was going to sell them if no one was going to take me seriously. I had somehow created a great product, and I already had amazing testimonials from my beta users achieving incredible results in a short amount of time. Yet I could see the dismissive, "Awww, what a cute lemonade stand" in these ladies' eyes and I knew that I needed to figure out a way to work around that. But how?

Just then, a woman announced the guest speaker was about to take the stage. She started reading his bio and when she mentioned that he is an author, everyone in the room said, "Oooooooo." When he spoke, I noticed that the room treated him so much differently and hung on his every word.

For real? Okay then. I guess I have to be an author.

But how? I don't know how to write a freakin' book. Words are hard! In school, I had struggled to learn how to read. I'd felt like the dumbest kid in class. I was watching Hooked On Phonics on repeat at home. On repeat! I have word recall issues to this day and I stutter sometimes.

And then, two days later (You can't make this story up!), I met Amanda at a conference. She asked me what my business was and I showed her the daily planner I'd published. She smirked and said come with me and introduced me to a lot of people.

She never looked at me with that dismissive, passive-aggressive, plastic "What are you doing here?" face. She genuinely cared about what I had created and wanted to help me show it to others. When I asked her what she did, she told me about this pilot book mastermind she was thinking about doing, and I immediately got chills. You know when you just know you are exactly where you are supposed to be with exactly who you're supposed to be with? Everything in that moment felt right.

She knew how to write books???? *Whaaaaaattttttt?*
Universe, you sly minx, you.

"Amanda, it's a real problem," I shook my head, wondering what the others in the room were thinking of me... if they thought I was too young to do this too. "Just two days before I met you, I had a really tough wakeup call around this..."

When I finished telling her the story of the networking event, she smiled at me and asked the question that changed everything: "Jenee, where did you become a productivity expert? What's the story of you having to figure out a better way to plan your life and work?"

"Oh, well, I had to figure it out in order to graduate UCLA a year early with ADHD," I answered matter-of-factly. Everyone in the room leaned in and I continued, "Yeah, I was completely unwilling to sacrifice my social life for good grades, so I had to figure out a way to have fun and get it all done."

Everyone gasped.

"That's it! That's the name of your book!" Amanda exclaimed. "That's the story!"

Goosebumps and raised hair confirmed that she was right.

Amanda applied her genius at structuring the outlines and flows of books, and I had an outline that excited me in no time at all.

Now, it was time to write. But, I couldn't.

For months, I churned a heaping pile of shit every time I sat down to write that first chapter. I wrote it over and over again. And, shocker, it was still crap. Sometimes I wouldn't even write; I'd just stare at a blank page on the computer questioning all of my life decisions up to that point. I was trying so hard and getting nowhere.

Finally, I called Amanda, admitted that it wasn't just a busy schedule keeping me from writing, and shared my writer's block frustration. "I can't write this stupid book because I hate sitting and typing. I'm so used to writing academic papers for school, and I want the reader to feel like I'm sitting across from the table and talking to them. I don't know how to type like that."

"Well, why don't you just speak your book? There is software that can type out what you say for you."

That night, I researched the software and bought it. Back in my day (funny how that makes me sound old!), it wasn't freely available on our phones and computers. And you got the software... in the mail. Not the email... the snail mail. *angrily shakes fist*

Amanda, having learned that I have ADHD and knowing how much I loved my topic, reworked my outline into a series of questions and instructed me to give myself short increments of time to answer them. She said this would help me avoid rabbit trails and also keep me from spending too much time on parts of my message that I love and not enough time on the other parts.

Sitting on my couch at 10:30 p.m., I pictured a friend (my reader) sitting across from me, drinking coffee, asking me these questions. Then I just answered the questions out loud and the computer typed it out for me. I was able to write until 1:30 a.m. when my mind turned to mush.

It wasn't perfect, but I was getting all my thoughts out on the screen. I planned to clean everything up at the end.

I repeated that process the next day. Sat down at 10:30 p.m. to write, because my brain, like a child, decides to have a party at night when it's time to go to bed. *"Psssst. Hey. Hey there. Waaaaatcha doing? Hey, you remember that time you farted in class in 6th grade and tried to cover it up with a cough? Me too."*

I finally gave in and thought, *Why fight it? Just embrace it.* And it was the best thing I ever did. (Guess what time I'm writing this chapter at? *wink, wink*)

That second night, I spoke my book from 10:30 p.m. to 1:30 a.m. again. I was shocked when I realized I had just finished answering all the questions on my outline.

How on earth am I done?

The next day, I spent a couple hours cleaning up what I'd typed and then sent it off to Amanda.

Hot damn!

Once that part was done Google became my BFF. I'd ask her things like, "How do I get a barcode?" because I had no clue what I was doing but I knew books had barcodes on the back cover.

It took a couple months, but I got everything aligned to self-publish with Amazon and Barnes and Noble.

"Jenee, this book looks amazing!" Amanda exclaimed when she saw the draft of the cover I'd sent her. "And actually, I have a proposition for you. Would you be willing to apply your productivity expertise and your newfound knowledge about publishing to a partnership with me?"

In the pilot program, I was one of four authors, but I was the only one to finish my book within the program. This made zero sense to me because her program was beyond amazing. She gave us everything we needed to finish our books, but I know how life can get in the way.

She continued, "I have this event that I'd like to put on in March and a few authors who want to publish their books by then and speak. Could you help them through the self-publishing process and maybe be a 'productivity buddy'? I realize that there is some serious upside-down transformation going on with these folks that's keeping them from finishing, but I don't want them to become too disconnected from their books in the process. Maybe you could schedule time with them and help them get it done and still have some fun?"

I started with accountability coaching to help get authors to write their books on time. Writing is an intimidating process, especially if you've never written a book before. So, with zero judgment, we individually talked through what was causing writer's blocks and brainstormed workarounds for each cause. And if authors didn't want to speak their books, I'd have them promise me that they would write for forty-five minutes. Even if all they were writing was, "I don't know what to write," they had to keep writing. Sometimes, if they didn't have anything completed by our meeting, I would ask them to use that time they'd blocked to work with me to write and send me an update at the end of the writing session. When they would report back to me that they got four pages or even a whole chapter done, we celebrated. That year, every single author in the program finished their books. The accountability coaching, coupled with the approaching deadline for a big book launch event that Amanda was hosting, was just what they needed to move through all that sticky author st*ry and get it done. I also guided them to complete the post-writing production checklist.

Eventually, I decided to run a bestseller campaign... a few months after moving 2500+ miles away from family and friends to a remote island, because you know, why the hell not? I planned the date and told everyone I knew. Since I was out in the middle of the pacific ocean, my mom offered to throw a book launch party at her house for friends and family. I was so grateful for all of the support I received, but I was a freaking wreck watching my book climb the ranks and then stall in the afternoon. I thought we weren't going to make it; but in the evening, we pulled through and hit #1 Bestseller on Amazon in several categories. I was floored, but I still felt like a fraud. Imposter syndrome is a nasty bitch.

Then, I pitched my book for an award and... I got a five-star review and then a Gold Medal in Education from the Reader's Favorite International Book Awards. This meant so much to me because they are respected within the larger publishing house community, but they let indie publishers submit too. I still remember when I opened the email. I screamed and then I cried a little and then did an obligatory dorky happy dance. And to think I almost didn't apply because I was afraid of being rejected.

With all of this experience, I was able to help some of Amanda's clients with their bestseller campaigns, too. Aside from the real stress that comes with a best-seller campaign (#whyauthorsdrink), we really were having fun and getting it done.

In 2013, when Amanda stepped away from her business to work on a personal st*ry, I found myself getting ready for a new chapter in my life with a husband and an idea to turn my planner into a web app.

I was invited to pitch my web app idea at a Hackathon. My idea was selected to participate and I recruited zero programmers onto my team. Zero. In case you were wondering, the entire point of Hackathons is to see what you can code in 48 hours. My team was amazing. And since we didn't have developers, all we could do was create mockups of what we wanted to code and plan our presentation. I got up there in front of 250+ people and 5 judges and all I could see were the judges' "judgey" faces. If you've never had 5 people on a panel look at you with utter disapproval—you haven't truly felt that level of shame yet. Their unimpressed faces screamed "Dafuq?" and had me blanking on what I needed to say next. So, I just proceeded to shakily say "Ummmmm" over and over again. I felt like my stomach was hitting the floor. My kick ass team ran, and I mean ran, from the back of that giant warehouse room, onto the stage and took over the presentation, saving me from myself. I'm still so grateful for them to this day.

A few weeks later I had an interview with one of the judges and another woman to get funding for my web app idea. I acknowledged that epic, and very public, failure and said "Well, I can only go up from here, right?" I moved onto the next rounds and was awarded the funding.

In case you haven't noticed yet, I didn't know what I was doing. Once I finally managed to recruit developers onto my team, I discovered I was the worst manager of developers. I'd ask for something and get back something else. Even though communicating with my design team was a breeze, I knew my developers were not the problem. So, I started to learn how to code so I could communicate better with them.

Then the startup ran out of funding because, well, developers are EXPENSIVE. My tech savviness at that point equated to barely being able to turn on my TV, which led me to make expensive mistakes creating a web app. Even though I was so grateful for the experience and the mentorship, I felt like a total dumpster fire—filled to the brim with regret and sprinkled with shame on top. But then I thought, *"Hey, developers are expensive."*

So, I got a job as a claims rep for an insurance company and studied programming online classes at night. (Just in case you were wondering, I got two self-paced online classes on sale for $10 each. So much better than $100k in student loans without a guarantee of a job to pay off those loans.) There were so many times I just wanted to throw my computer out the window. But I kept going. After countless brutal interviews, I got a job as a web developer working as a contractor with NOAA and PMNM. I know my book had a small part in them taking a chance on me, which then led me to be able to go on a research expedition for twenty-six days in the most remote part of the world... and get paid for it. I snorkeled with sharks, y'all! And that wasn't even the coolest thing I got to do there. Don't get too jelly, I also worked 13+ hour days through weekends, landed on a jellyfish, and got stung in the vicinity of my vajingo. Sooooooo... yeah. Adventures were had.

But still... pinch me.

Then I started getting contacted by recruiters to be a Salesforce Administrator because supply was low and demand was high. The pay they were offering was a lot more than what I was getting paid, so I started studying for my exams. I failed those twice. *Whah-whahhhhh.* Those exams were written in a way that made me feel like I was forced to take five shots before being presented with Rumpelstiltskin riddles. But an amazing woman who was also studying for her exams DM'd me from a Facebook group and asked if we could be study buddies. We lived in different states and time zones, but we made it work and studied almost every single day together for more than three months. We passed that next exam, and then got two additional certifications on the first try. I couldn't have done it without her.

I started a blog at HaveFunGetItDone.com and created a few brands on Etsy. I even randomly made a bean bag chair cover with a poop face and sold one to someone I didn't know, because who doesn't love a good poop joke, or turning their blanket storage into their very own pile of shit?

Now, I work for an amazing human-centered organization where everyone works 100% remote and has amazing benefits. It's because of this amazing flexible job that I have good enough benefits to be able to afford IVF since... I have scrambled eggs, but that's another story for another time.

Along the way, after each failure, I sometimes wondered...
Why did I do all that work on that book?
What is the point?
Have I failed? Am I settling?
Did I take a wrong turn?
Shouldn't it look like...?
What do people think of me?

But every time I go there, I remember: This book has indirectly opened doors for me all these years and in ways I never expected. Even though I'm not where I ever imagined I would be, every single thing happened just as it was supposed to—lily padding me to each opportunity. Whether I was jumping off of a success or a failure (lots and lots of failures), I kept adapting and moving. Sometimes my anxiety or ADHD would flip me around like a pinball machine, but I kept moving and would eventually get back on track.

I set out to create some fun brands and shops on Esty with stuff that makes me laugh. Gusty Bitch has funny and empowering gifts that show your girlfriends you get them. Turds & Taters—we just sell turds and taters. I said what I said. And I rebranded My FocusBook to Have Fun Get It Done. Now I'm developing my planner into a digital and printable planner for people who own iPads and the GoodNotes app. I know I'm not done failing. I never will be. If you take anything away from reading about this experience, I hope it is this: Failure is a good f-word, so keep f-ing up.

Amanda's Side of the Story

"Amanda, I'm done!" the brilliant and bubbly young woman exclaimed.

"Oh my goodness, Jenee, that's amazing!" I congratulated her, stunned that she had finished her book so quickly.

I guess that question-based outline worked! I chuckled to myself and wondered how many more times in my career I would be celebrating a good outcome of a total experiment. I had no idea that I was about to find out.

"What's next?" she asked.

I gulped. *What's next? Ummmmm...*

"Jenee, I... uh... you're the first one to finish. We're going to have to figure this out together. I can do the final edit on it, and we have Dan to work on the book cover design, but I'm not sure about anything else..."

My messaging expertise had helped Jenee establish more credibility by telling her incredible story of finishing her university degree in only three years despite her ADHD, identify a reader that would glean the wisdom from her story, and also make those biased older folks listen to her. I mean, why would they tune out someone who said they'd just figured out a way for them to save a whole year's tuition for their child? When I handed her the message matrix, she immediately saw that this could be a whole lot easier than she had imagined.

Looking back, I'm *really* grateful that Jenee was the first client to finish a manuscript because she is all about adventure and figuring shit out. Having also been coached by Ursula, she was an eager partner in answering the question: "What is the quickest and fastest way to publish this book?"

About the time she was ready to do this, I was inspired to put on my first big Dare to Dream event. The vision was to put new authors on stage next to a celebrity speaker I'd worked with for several years, and coach them through the process of sharing their story on stage and creating small offerings to sell at the event. There were two other clients who were close to finishing their manuscript and quickly agreed to jump in. But how in the world was I going to help them through production when I hadn't done it myself?

I asked Jenee to partner with me and become the book production support person for all of my clients. She gave me a "hell yes" and we got to work because we didn't have a whole lot of time.

It didn't take long for her to find a designer who could format the interior or learn the ins and outs of Amazon's self-publishing arm, known then as Create Space. She helped my clients get their books done with as little muss and fuss as possible, and she delivered an amazing presentation at the event. But she didn't stop there. She went on to adapt Ursula's approach to launching an Amazon Bestseller and was a bestselling *and* award-winning author in no time at all. Pretty soon, we were working together to help people stay on track with their writing, the production, and bestseller campaigns... and having a ton of fun getting it done.

Then, life happened.

Right after I'd decided to slow down the business to figure out which st*ry was sabotaging my big moments, Jenee got married, moved, and started working on an app. From the outside-looking-in, it appeared she'd lost her desire to push her message forward as other parts of her life vied for her attention. But every time I've talked to her since, it's become more and more obvious that Jenee is far more concerned with living and modeling her message than she is with sharing it with others. Even as she's navigating one of the most emotional challenges a woman can face, she's embodying her message of setting goals aligned with one's values, staying positive, and making sure to schedule in the fun and laughter.

She's doing the only thing all of us can really do— following the inspiration to the next step and trusting that it's taking her to the next right experience. I couldn't have written in better timing of the inspiration for writing her book and its fast completion, and my inspiration to expand my services beyond my expertise. Every time I get stuck— trying to see too far ahead, figure things out, and move it all forward—I remember how she showed up at the exact right moment with exactly what I needed... and I look for the fun!

Theddee Rheyshelle is a hungry heart dedicated to knowing God so she can know who she truly is and the Love that she is meant to be in her world. At sixty-two, she's decided to honor her introvert and spend her golden years sharing her hard-earned wisdom by writing children's stories and adult storybooks for the child within. According to Theddee, "It's never too late to give our inner child the love and affirmation needed to become all we are meant to be!" Her first children's book, *The Invisible Magical Matter-Ring That Makes You Matter,* reminds the young and old that we all matter.

The Invitation to Heal a Story
I Didn't Even Know I Had

Theddee Rheyshelle
(formerly Tami Dempsey)

"What I want you all to understand is that you have just said 'yes' to a transformational process. Over the next week, you may find yourself triggered... maybe even badly enough to want to back out. I'm asking that you remain committed and simply pay attention to what comes up for you. While it can be really uncomfortable, it's a necessary piece to sharing your story," Amanda explained as she finished the pre-retreat conference call.

Sharing my story? My stomach knotted.

I had just finished writing my first fictional book and imagined it to be a beautifully illustrated story book for adults... one that would sneak in a back door and open a Christian's mind to a concept that had transformed my life. As a teacher and one who loves writing curriculum, I had tried—unsuccessfully—to share this information in a way that was easily understood. And then I had received, what I call, a Divine Download... a story based on truth but fraught with half-truths, out-right lies, and a whole lot of fairy-tale. I loved watching the mind—especially the Christian mind—struggle and fight its way through the story. The brilliance of it fascinated and inspired me. I couldn't wait to make it a reality!

So, everyone else is going to write their own personal story? Ugh. I don't fit in already. I felt my first twinge of resistance.

Over the next week, I was indeed triggered. The first two events were easily overcome with my tools and training. The third event took me a day, maybe two. (Seriously, I mean, since when does a person doing your nails completely ignore what you ask for and do something totally different?!? Not only different—but something I hated—while I was sitting there with tears streaming down my face?!?)

The fourth event was still bothering me when the fifth event knocked me for a loop. Each incident involved my words, feelings, and/or my "no" being ignored, discounted, or totally disregarded. Each time, I felt violated and betrayed.

The last situation happened at work. I had, with the agreement of the HR Manager, written a letter to our payroll service provider stating that our new (expensive) system still wasn't working for us, what we needed it to do, and that we would not be investing in anymore new software to get this done, as we had been promised that what we had purchased would meet our needs. I requested they meet with all their departments, figure out the solution, and schedule a conference call with everyone necessary to make this happen. The letter was adamant and clear: No further investment and no new equipment! They needed to fulfill their commitment or we would cut our losses and move on.

The conference call was scheduled for mid-morning on Friday since I would be leaving early in the afternoon for my retreat. The first words out of the representative's mouth were, "We've all met together and have decided that the best solution to your problem is..." another investment for an additional piece of software.

My eyes widened. The blood drained from my face. I lost my voice. I couldn't think. I couldn't speak. I looked over at the HR Manager for help, and I could tell by the look on his face that he could see what was happening to me. My entire body was shaking uncontrollably as if in a state of shock. Tears were threatening to spill over my lower lashes. As the representative continued to talk, my panic grew. I was shaking my head, and the only words going through my mind were, "No! No! Please! No!"

I hugged myself and put my head down on my desk trying to control the shaking, willing myself not to cry, while the HR Manager finished the call... agreeing to the investment.

WHAAAT?!?

I was furious. *They all just totally ignored me... ignored my "plain as day" boundaries. Nobody is listening!!! Why can't they hear me??*

Again, I felt violated and betrayed... forced to do something I did not want to do. Still unable to speak and humiliated that all my professionalism was disappearing right before my boss's eyes, I grabbed my purse and left the office—a little earlier than planned—and headed for the retreat center. On the way, I was trying to analyze what I was feeling...

I feel like I've just been raped! But... how would I know what that feels like?

I parked and rolled my suitcase toward the Guest House where a stranger was standing at the door to greet me. *Oh my God! What have I done?!? I've agreed to come to a retreat with people I don't know?!? What was I thinking?!?*

Without introducing myself—or even a *hello*—I blurted, "Can you tell me where my room is?"

Amanda asked, "Are you Tami?" I nodded and she simply pointed and quietly said a room number. I made it to my room and had a total and complete, ugly cry meltdown.

How do I get out of this? I can't leave... my boss paid for this as a gift. I have to stay...

And the rest of the retreat was tortuous for me. I could not participate in the activities or answer the questions because my brain was simply not functioning. There was one interaction in which Amanda cornered me in front of the group and asked me, "Would you be willing to go back?"

Go back? Are you freakin' kidding me?!?

I had no idea what she was talking about, but I instantly knew I wasn't willing and gave an adamant, "No!"

"Why not?" she asked, pressing the issue.

Oh my god, woman! What part of "no" don't you understand?!?

My good girl's middle finger itched and threatened to do something it had never done before. I was livid. *How dare she?!? Why should I go back? Haven't I suffered enough already?!?*

The last straw was when this *leader lady* let us know that Saturday evening and Sunday morning would be spent with each of us sharing our story with the group.

Whaaat? Sharing my story? What story? I don't have a story!!

My mind spun out of control. Panic set in. I felt like I was on the floor, on my back, trying to crab crawl away, but I had run out of floor and was now trying to climb the wall... keeping my eyes on this thing that was out to get me. My insides were kicking and screaming. The only words making any sense were, "No, no, please, no!"

Finally, about 1:30 a.m., I had a sane thought. It was simply a song that I had written many years prior. That's all I had. *Well, Lady, you said, "Go back," so I guess this is what "back" looks like for me.*

The next day, I waited until I couldn't put it off any longer. The last one to share, I stood before the group and began to sing, "My heart, O God, hungers after yours, I wanna know you... I wanna know you..." When I finished singing, my personal story poured out of me...

My Story

It took a bona fide "laying on of hands" miracle to usher me into this realm of form and time. Mom had a physical ailment that would not allow her to become pregnant. Ten months after being prayed for by a faith healer, I was born.

My mom and dad were "Apostolic Pentecostals" and they prayed the way Apostolic Pentecostals pray—if you know what I mean. Dad would get up a little before 5 a.m. each day, change my diaper, wrap me up like a papoose, and carry me down the block to the church for his morning prayer. He would lay his little "Pocahontas" on the altar and feed me a bottle while he talked to God. I would go back to sleep to the sound of my daddy praying.

I would wake again about 9 o'clock; and Mom would change my diaper, lay me on the bed where she knelt, and feed me a bottle while she talked to God. I would go back to sleep to the sound of my momma praying. They say that, within about two weeks, I refused to go to sleep unless somebody was praying.

As a toddler, I began experiencing absolutely-no-way-around-it miracles as a result of the prayers I prayed. I knew, without a shadow of a doubt, that God was real and that there was power in prayer. And yet, as a young adult, I had been in emotional pain from as far back as I could remember—in spite of my prayers... begging God for relief.

I told God on numerous occasions that I felt like He was this huge vending machine up in the sky with no price tag on the buttons; and I was a hungry heart gazing longingly through the glass at delicious-looking packages of everything I needed to heal my heart and nourish my soul. "Desperately, I keep putting in my quarters and pushing the buttons, fasting and praying, and then fasting and praying some more, hoping against hope that You'll have mercy on me and let *something* drop down the hatch—anything to relieve this aching hunger in me. My good days are so few and far between..."

My daily prayer was, "Papa God, I know that in Your Spirit is everything I can possibly need for this journey. Why can't I access it?" I begged Him to tell me the secret to His vending machine.

And then, I heard about a thing called *Listening Prayer...* where one dialogues with God, asks questions, and listens for the answers. Novel idea, right?!? I couldn't wait to ask my Papa God about the vending machine.

"So, tell me... what is the secret to Your vending machine?" I asked the next morning in the stillness and quiet of a darkened living room, lit only by a globe of the world emitting a rose-colored hue.

"Tami, the difference between your good days and your bad days is whether or not you hear the counsel of My Spirit. Daily I speak peace into your life, but you rarely ever hear Me."

"Why don't I hear you?"

(smiling) "You're making too much noise—kickin' and screamin' and throwin' a fit on the throne room floor."

(chuckling) "You mean... all the time I've been travailing for answers... You've been talking to me?"

"Tami, every time you enter into My presence, I scoot over on the throne, pat the empty space beside me, and say, 'Come, sit with Me. Let Me speak peace to your storm, truth to your tormented mind, and healing to your hurting soul. I have the answers, the ideas, the wisdom and the inspiration you need, right now, today—in this very moment. Shhhhh. Be still and know Me.'"

"Oh my Lord! All that time—through all that pain and all that struggle?"

"Yes, Tami. All that time—through all that pain and all that struggle."

(deep sigh) "I feel like I've missed out on so much life I could have been living..."

"I am Word, and I am always speaking. If you will listen, I can restore the years the cankerworm and the caterpillar have eaten."

The Story is Not Over Yet

I summed up my story by saying, "This conversation was the beginning of my healing journey. For years, I had been leaving frantic thirty-minute messages on the answering machine of heaven. Learning to dialogue with God changed everything. His truth began healing my life, setting me free from my emotional pain, one lie—one trigger at a time."

I curtsied and headed back to my seat.

"Wait!" Amanda instructed, reminding me that it was now time to listen to feedback from the group. Over in the kitchen area, there was a lady sitting at the dining room table working on her book. She wasn't a part of our group, but she asked if she could share. She said that, while listening to my story, a song came to her. She wasn't a singer, but she wanted to share it. She began to sing a song that I had been "known for" as a teenager. (You can make this st*ry up!!!)

I started singing the song with her; and before I could finish, I fell to the floor sobbing uncontrollably. That song had taken me back to a place I did not want to go—a place of *suffering.* I hadn't felt that kind of emotional pain in a very, very long time.

And now, here I am on the floor in unbearable pain. What lie am I believing?

It came in an instant. *You have to be willing to live a life of suffering in order to be used by God.*

I knew immediately this was no longer true for me. While this belief may have been my reality back then, it certainly was not Truth—from Papa God's perspective. The pain lessened, and I stood to my feet and faced the group. As I did, I noticed Amanda standing *waaay* across the room by the exit door...

Oh my God! What have I done? I have just made a total fool out of myself in front of a group of strangers. Amanda is even trying to get as far away from me as possible...

She rejoined the group and began facilitating the feedback. The parts of my story that had stood out to them were about me being "hungry for God" and referring to Him as a big, huge vending machine in the sky...

Diving Deep

While others left the retreat that day with outlines to the story they were meant to share, I left drained, feeling totally humiliated, and knowing that I wanted to teach others how to dialogue with God.

Because I had missed out on all the exercises and was leaving without an outline for my book, I volunteered to serve at Amanda's next Jumpstart Your Book retreat. I followed along from the sidelines; and at the end, while cleaning up, I showed her the outline I had come up with on how to hear the voice of God.

She took one look and said, "Where's your story?"

"My story?" I questioned, my stomaching knotting up again. *What's up with this lady and 'my story'? I just want to write a book!*

"Yeah. This is great information, Tami, but where did it come from? How did you learn it?"

"I learned it by dialoguing with God."

"Do you have an example of that?" she asked gently.

"Well, yeah. I have lots of prayer journals..."

"Can I see one?" she probed.

What? Show you my prayer journals? White, hot fear shot through me.

The next week, I forwarded her a few of my conversations with God. Her emailed response was, "Oh my God, Tami, this is your book!! I think you should tell your story by sharing your prayer journals..."

Share my prayer journals? Are you kidding me? No way! That's like asking me to get naked on stage. I ain't doin' that.

"But," she continued, "you're going to have to wrap the dialogues with the background story so the reader can get the full picture."

After a few days of resistance, it dawned on me, *What better way to teach people how to dialogue with God than to model it for them and let them witness the power of it?*

Once I said *yes* to this preposterous idea, I understood what the "going back" was all about—going back to where I was, how I was feeling, and what was going on when I had each of the conversations with God.

Going back was not fun. And not easy. However, I now had the tools Amanda had shared about creating a safe place, cocooning, and "surrendering to the upside-down." I playfully changed Willie Nelson's "On the road again" to "Upside down again... just can't wait to be upside down again..." And this became the soundtrack of my life while I spent the next several months eating lots of chocolate and reliving the pain and suffering of my younger years by going back and filling in the details, the emotions, and the background story behind each divine dialogue.

My first prayer journals were the one-way conversations, cries of desperation and longing, and then the rest were full of the healing and transformation that took place as I learned to hear the voice of God and dialogue with Him. I was amazed at the story that unfolded...

Willing to Upside-Down

Just as I was getting the hang of surrendering to this "upside-down thang," I jumped into book production and right back into the fire. *Mercy of the Lord!* Not only was I Amanda's first retreat *challenge*, I became the problem child in every aspect of the production process: dressing for success, makeup, pictures, design cover, and interior design.

Nobody is listening to me!! I'm being forced to do things I don't want to do and accept things I just can't live with!!! When am I ever going to matter?

My uglies surfaced. Big time. I was not pleasant to the experts—or grateful. Old beliefs and old st*ries were being exposed left and right. I felt like a tube of toothpaste that someone was stomping on—determined to get out every last bit of ugly in me. My attitude and behavior stunk to the high heavens, and I felt powerless to stop it.

I'll never forget the day that Amanda called and said my first book had arrived. She was so excited and asked me to stop by her house to see it. The moment I flipped through the pages, my heart sunk. *Un-freakin'-believable!!* The one thing I had stated was an absolute must—a non-negotiable—hadn't happened.

When I am shopping for a book, I always look at the size of the print. If it's small, I immediately put the book back on the shelf. Therefore, I requested that the print be a little larger than typical. So, when I personally had to struggle to see the print in my own book, the devastation was real. Again, my words and feelings hadn't mattered. Again, something was being forced on me that I didn't want, something to which my "no" had been adamant.

And now it's too late. I have to live with something I said I couldn't live with! I felt victimized. Betrayed. And hopeless. *My dream of becoming an author is all yucked up now and my book is forever-ruined!*

I'm not sure exactly how I made it through to the book release and the standing ovation that occurred after my keynote, but what I can tell you is that my story didn't end there.

I had said "yes" to my first retreat in March and experienced my week of triggers. One year later, I received and powerfully launched my *forever-ruined* book. (Not really, but it certainly triggered a story in me that was crying out to be healed.) The next year, at the same time, an old memory started picking away at me. I kept remembering my fourth birthday party and being very angry with my mom because she had made me sit next to a girl that I did not like. With the little memory came a lot of intense feelings toward my mother. My book had basically shared the story of healing the angst toward Mom, and we were finally at a place where I could be in the same room with her without being triggered.

I am not in the least bit interested in re-opening THAT can of worms!

However, the memory was relentless. It wouldn't leave me alone. One night, about two o'clock in the morning, I finally surrendered to this invitation to go upside-down and found myself remembering backwards, from the party...

Why was I so upset?

*Oh yeah... Mom brought this girl in and sat her down right next to me, squeezed my shoulder, pointed her finger, and hissed, "Be nice!" I remember trying to get really small so that no part of that girl could touch me. Wow... such anger towards my mom. My little mind saying, "I hate you, hate you, hate you!"
What the heck was that all about?*

Ahhh... Mom asked me if I had invited "the girls," and I nodded... cuz I HAD invited them... just not HER. When she asked about HER specifically, I'd dropped my head. She'd admonished me for lying by saying, "All liars shall have their part in the lake that burneth with fire! You've got a spanking coming when we get home. Get in there right now and invite her!"

She had *forced* me to invite this girl. I remembered trudging up the steps to the church thinking, *I can't do this. I can't do this.* I felt sick to my stomach, gagging on my own saliva. And then I had another thought—a thought that wasn't mine, *"Talk to her mom, baby girl. Talk to her mom."*

I ran inside, talked to her mom, and ran back outside before SHE could see me.

Oh yeah... Mom and I had argued, big time, about inviting this girl. I was adamant that I didn't want her at my party. Mom had said, "We're Christians. We don't treat people like that. We can't invite all the other girls from church and not invite her."

Ohhh, I remember now... When she asked me why I didn't want to invite my "best little friend," I felt sick to my stomach, had a horrible taste in my mouth, gagged, and couldn't swallow. The only words my four-year-old had come up with was, "Cuz I hate her!!"

This, of course, had not been acceptable language for a Christian, and once again, I had been punished for bad behavior. After a few back-and-forths, I had crossed my little arms, stomped my little foot, and declared, "If she has to come, then I am NOT having a party!"

"Young lady!" Mom had said, finally putting her own foot down, "You ARE having a party, you ARE inviting her, and you ARE going to be nice!"

Whew. The rage and anger of that four-year-old is off the charts. I feel her pain, her nausea, the gagging.

I tried to think of a four-year-old I knew... to imagine that child feeling what I was feeling. I couldn't think of one. And then I realized that, as a Court Appointed Special Advocate, I had spent the entire morning in a classroom of four-year-olds the day before. You seriously can't make this st*ry up!!

I tried to imagine the little ones at my table feeling the rage I was feeling, and it made me weep for the child in me.

Where is all of this coming from?

Almost as soon as I asked, I had the answer.

Ohhhhh nooooo! That's right... I spent the night at that girl's house, and she tricked me into playing "big girl games" with that man...

Honestly, at that moment, the betrayal, rape and molestation didn't really register an emotional charge. What was coming through loud and clear was the role my mom had played in the ordeal. She had *forced* me to include this girl that had betrayed me, *forced* me to invite her, *forced* me to sit next to her, *forced* me to be nice to her—and she had continued to *force* me to do things I didn't want to do, things I felt like I just couldn't do, things I knew I couldn't live with... all throughout my childhood and even into my adulthood.

Oh man, Mom became the face of my rapist—the person who ignored my "no's," the person who had forced me to do things I didn't want to do... couldn't do!!! I forgot all about him and focused all my anger and hatred on her!!

As I lay on the couch cocooned in a safe space, I could see that, after that fateful party, I never again sat on my momma's lap, never hugged her, and never told her I loved her.

That four-year-old child in me has been resenting and resisting my mom my whole life. Lawd a' mercy! No wonder it has been so hard to be in the same room with her...

I had completely blocked out the violation. I only remembered hating my fourth birthday and not wanting *that girl* there. I didn't remember why—until my fifty-fourth birthday. Fifty years later...

The rape that I could feel in every cell of my being—and yet of which I had no conscious memory—had happened in March... just before my fourth birthday. I had been hating my birthdays... resisting them, and becoming physically ill to escape them... all of my adult life... with absolutely no clue why this was happening.

Oh, this is what a Cocoon feels like.

I was able to move through the emotions of that horrible event, journal it, and continue my healing process because I had learned how to go upside-down and give myself permission to cocoon—without judgment. Each March since 2011, a different element of that horrific experience has surfaced—a part of the story that was ready to be re-written and healed.

In March 2019, I woke up one morning with my mind already writing a poem. I got up and sat down with my laptop and in minutes, I had a children's book entitled, *You Matter! A Book About Feelings.* Days later, I realized I had written the book the child in me needed to hear. For the next few weeks, I read it aloud to her each morning. I did this until I could hear it playing softly and continuously in the background of my mind.

The past two years have been spent letting my Younger Me know in every way possible that she matters by paying attention to and honoring her feelings—even when they don't make sense to me. Even when... and especially when... honoring them appears to be un-Christ-like or dishonoring to another. (Like not calling my 86-year-old mother for months because the child in me didn't want to. The adult me could have easily taken myself by the scrap of the neck and "done the right thing," but I chose to honor that precious child that kept saying, "No! Please, no. Don't make me do that.")

I do believe this old st*ry has finally been completely rewritten because I now know, without question, that everything I am willing and not willing to do, allow, and let exist in my life is based on (and determined by) how much importance I place on my own mattering—and I am 100% responsible for my mattering. I don't have to be mean or ugly, adamant or argumentative, whiny or pouty. I simply need to be resolved.

These past few years have been about learning this truth and coming to the realization that not everyone is going to care about my feelings. This does not change their value or importance. Not everyone is going to agree with my ideas, opinions, and beliefs. This does not lessen or weaken their ability to effect change. Not everyone is going to recognize or applaud my skills, genius and talent. This in no way diminishes their power to bring joy or alleviate suffering. I matter. Every part of me matters. I am the answer to somebody's prayer. They are waiting for and needing me to show up in all my God-given glory. I am THAT important.

Consequently, this birthday season was my smoothest ever. As a gift to myself, I decided to publish *The Invisible Magical Matter-Ring that Makes You Matter!* and the adult story book I had originally set out to publish in 2010, *Perfectly Formed, Flawed, and Filled: The Tale of a Potter and His Very First Vessel.*

The journey of healing my story—a story I didn't even know I had—all started the moment I said "yes" to writing a book, and then "yes" to sharing my prayer journals, and then "yes" to sharing the "mom" aspect of my story... all of which were key to healing the event that had become the software secretly running and controlling my life.

Seriously, you can't make this st*ry up!

Amanda's Side of the Story

The day arrived, and my heart fluttered while I set up the Guest House and waited for my very first retreat clients.

What if I can't do this? What if they just paid me all this money and they don't get what they are coming to get? It had been a tough few weeks leading up to the retreat, and I was doubting myself. Relationship challenges. Allergies emerging out of nowhere. And my grandma had fallen in the middle of the night earlier that week and had to be hospitalized. As soon as they'd told me she was being discharged that day, I'd made the decision to move forward with the retreat, but geez.

What if those were all signs that this was a bad idea? I was in the middle of talking myself off the emotional ledge when Tami burst through the door. She was the only participant I didn't know very much about. At the very last minute, one of the other participants had called to see if there was room for Tami and worked out all of the details between us.

Looking up, I caught my breath. Tami was clearly upset—wide-eyed, red-faced, and breathless. "Where's my room?" she asked without so much as a greeting.

I glanced at my notes and pointed in the direction. "It's number five, second door on the left." I bit my lip with concern as I watched her drag all of her stuff to her room and shut the door behind her. [Tami, tell the truth, you slammed that door! :)]

Oh my goodness!

I pulled myself together enough to greet everyone else as they walked in, and we got started.

The whole weekend was amazing, except that Tami seemed paralyzed. She probably said a total of ten words the first two days, and wasn't completing any of the exercises or interacting with the others.

What am I going to do? She's not going to get what she came for. I'm not delivering on my promises. Maybe this was all a bad idea!

I'd even called the healer I was working with at the time, the second morning, to ask her for some support with the anxiety that had kept me up all night. After reassuring me that it was Tami's anxiety, not mine, she helped me release it; and I got back into the facilitator game.

It was the last day of the retreat, and the others had already had some massive breakthroughs through the exercises, conversations over meals, and in the labyrinth. We were finishing up the last exercise in the bright living room of the guest house, and Tami was the only one left. All eyes on her, she walked to the front of the room, as everyone held their breath and silently prayed for a breakthrough.

"My heart, O God, hungers after Yours..." The tears welled in everyone's eyes as she sang a song that had clearly been conceived in pain. Time stood still. When the song was over, she shared her story and the message she wanted to share with the world.

Everyone in the room was stunned into silence. Finished and suddenly uncomfortable, Tami curtsied and sat down. Quickly wiping the tears from my cheek, I snapped back into my role and asked her to stand back up, and the others to reflect back what they'd heard. One of the ladies said that while Tami was singing another song had come to mind, and asked if she could share it. Tami nodded, and when the woman finished the first verse, Tami took over. When she finished the song, she dropped into a heap of tears in the middle of the room. Face down in child's pose, she wept. And the room wept with her.

I leaned on the wall in front of me. *What am I seeing right now? This doesn't look like people needing to write books. It looks like the transformational workshops I spent years trying to learn how to facilitate!*

"Amanda, this is your real work... It's not about the books. It's about them. They need a safe space and someone to walk with them on this journey, so they can heal as they write their stories."

There was a pause, and the room was silent, save Tami's quiet sobs.

"But Amanda, you are standing by the door. You can say no if you want to."

I looked up and was shocked to see that I was actually standing right next to the door. *When... how... did I get over here?* I shook my head and looked at the woman on the floor. *I can't leave. There's a woman in a heap of pain. I have no idea how I'm going to do this, but I'm not leaving.*

"Just keep listening. I prepared you for it. I've brought you here. I am not going anywhere."

Tami had no idea that her willingness to stay there in all of her discomfort and share her story catalyzed a breakthrough and healing for me.

It had been a decade since I'd heard the Voice that spoke to me while she was on the floor. It was One I had listened to and been guided by in high school but lost my access to when I went to the university and began questioning all of my religious foundations.

Of course, in what would come to be known as YCMTSU Style, her message of dialoguing with God reignited mine.

Months later, when we were going through book production, her experience of feeling unheard by the designer and apologetically requesting many revisions, and then being in a tizzy about the photo shoot, confirmed and solidified my emerging realization that every single step of this message development process requires us to face an old st*ry that must be healed (witnessed at least) for us to keep moving forward.

It is completely impossible to try to capture all of the YCMTSU moments I've experienced with Tami, now known as Theddee. We share many of the same childhood wounds, personality traits, strengths, kryptonite, and challenges as a result of all of that. Every one of our interactions since that day she landed on the floor have made me a better facilitator, CEO, and person.

When she asked to volunteer at my retreats, "to try to soak in the whole experience and process," I welcomed her support and all of her questions about why I chose to respond to various experiences in different ways. Her inquiries expanded my awareness and increased my confidence and she quickly became a trusted confidant who helped me to process all of my "facilitator st*ff" during breaks and between retreats.

She became my biggest cheerleader and one of my dearest friends, saying YES to every program, retreat, and course I have developed since because she is just THAT committed to her own healing journey. In every great memory associated with my business, I see this woman's face. She learned with me. She taught me so much. She co-facilitated with me. She trusted me. She even, at my

request, agreed to call me on all my stuff and hold me true
to my intention in my writing, business development, and
eventually my personal transformation with my family. I
can't count how many times she's turned my own stuff on me
with love [and a devilish little giggle].

In 2013, when I lost access to that Voice again, she walked
beside me as I dove into the deepest darkest depths of my
st*ry. She stepped in to help me with my ailing grandmother
while I supported clients at their retreats; and she was
the one who woke me up to the reality of my toxic family
system and literally saved my life with her gentle but firm
observations. She listened and supported as I processed
and healed and took the first steps to my personal freedom;
and she even went so far as to care for my grandmother
when I left. In my darkest moments, when my "good little
codependent" tries to take over, Theddee is the one who
reminds me with her words and her being: "You and your
feelings in this situation matter."

In the same way that her message of dialoguing with
God opened my communication channels again, as I have
supported her in clarifying her message, healing her st*ry,
and reclaiming her power, she has been a pivotal part of me
doing the same.

Lisa Arreguin is a songwriting coach, musical artist, and business entrepreneur. She is author of the book *The Crazybrave Songwriter: A Spiritual Guide to Creative Songwriting (Balboa Press, 2018)* and the critically-acclaimed jazz album *Timeless (2000)*. She holds a master's degree in psychology and is dedicated to working with musicians to blend solid songwriting technique with keen musicianship and heart-felt expression. Lisa offers songwriting courses and educational pieces at LivingCrazybrave.com and, along with her talented family, owns and operates LoveandLaughterMusicGroup.com—a full-service recording studio in the heart of Anaheim, Ca.

The Crazybrave Labyrinth

Lisa Arreguin

It was a chilly Southern California night and I was being asked to walk a labyrinth. The labyrinth before me was one of those twisty, rocky ones that might seem fun to walk at first but, if done with intent and purpose, can yield a deeper personal mystery.

I was attending a 2010 book writing retreat led by my new friend, Amanda, and our assignment was specific. We were to think of a personal question, place that question metaphorically in our right palm, and do a pledge of allegiance move by covering our hearts. We were then instructed to walk the labyrinth by suspending thought and letting our hearts work out the answer. The labyrinth was serving as a mindful meditation, a prompting of sorts, and a means of finding an answer to a burning question. Amanda had suggested that our hearts would speak the answer when we got to the middle of the labyrinth. And I believed her.

The difficult road of attempting to write a book had taken more than six years. I had started, stopped, and abandoned the idea of writing a book so many times that I was now paralyzed by the prospect of getting anything done that was remotely good. Signing up for the book writing retreat was a last resort and a place to hopefully jump start my desire once again to actually write.

And now, here I was, at a retreat for writers, walking a labyrinth in the middle of the night, looking down at the tops of my shoes, vaguely aware that it was past my bedtime.

The question came to me clearly as I stood in the dirt at the door of the labyrinth: *Why am I having such a hard time writing this da*n book?*

This seemed like an obvious question. Probably one that the other participants were asking themselves, too. I hoped for a simple answer.

My brain: No thinking, Lisa. Just concentrate on your first step.

About fifteen of us walked in silence, struggling to see ahead in the dark and to follow where the road was going. Our gracious host must have known the road would feel difficult and had carefully placed soft fabric butterflies and colored lights along our path as a reminder to remember to unfold and trust in the process. The movement of the curves seemed to defy realism as I circled back and forth in no apparent pattern. Out of my side eye, I noticed that one of the participants who began walking the labyrinth just ahead of me, was now curiously behind me, and then a few minutes later was moving away from me once again. I was acutely aware that suspending my thought and yielding completely to my heart impulse was a different sort of feeling altogether; and it was clear we were all separate but equal in our walking attempt to navigate the mystery of the labyrinth experience.

I trusted that the wisdom of my heart was working on the question.

As I squinted to see ahead with uneven rocks digging into my feet, I felt time suspend as I walked down through the moments in my life that had brought me here.

In 2008, our family-run music business was hit hard by the economic downturn in America. I was a vocal coach with a bustling business and had come into the music industry first as a songwriter and then as a recording artist. Our talented family members were deeply involved in all aspects of music publishing, songwriting, recording, and music production. Despite the struggle of entrepreneurship, I always considered myself one of the lucky ones who was blessed to live an entrepreneurial life of creativity and music. When the recession hit, we did everything we could to push back on the brink of collapse and we vowed to use our collective creative minds to solve this tough problem. We downsized, relocated, changed our business model, sold our home, and did our best to hang on to our lives and our business. But it was a painful time and we wondered why we were in this predicament since we had always worked so hard to maintain an honorable business that helped and encouraged others.

Two years later, my back and hips began to hurt and I just chalked it up to the stress of it all and did my best to use my hero-like skill of emotional repression to deal with the pain. A nice doctor suggested rest/rehab but finally validated what I already knew, that I had deteriorating discs in my lower back. My economy was deteriorating, my back was dissolving, and my stress level was sky high.

Signing up for Amanda's retreat was a promising outlet for me. I could immerse myself into a new creative venture; and I knew it would help me to re-focus, distracting me from the problems at hand. Creative people live in the joy of creating something from nothing and, like creating beautiful music, I was reaching for my happy place of writing—a place to gain some sense of equilibrium in my life again.

Coming back to the present moment with the lighted labyrinth in front of me, I began to see the center of the labyrinth come into view after what seemed like eternity.

Unexpectedly, the answer to my question popped up—from my heart to my head. It was profoundly simple and very clear.

My heart's answer: You are having a hard time writing this book because you are scared. We know this to be true. All you need is some time and some support. You are in the right place.

My brain (sarcastically): Well, now... that's a big revelation. Scared? Really? What's there to be scared of?

It's really an interesting thing to observe your brain and your heart in a back-and-forth confrontation reminiscent of the rapper battle in the Eminem movie *8-Mile.* Your true heart feels like it has a deep center of wisdom that feels quiet, strong, and honest. Your thought brain, on the other hand, can spin a rational argument with lawyer-like precision— even when it is dead wrong. By the next morning, I had convinced myself that I wasn't really scared at all, but instead had put off writing the book because I was simply too busy with my music business.

At breakfast, the participants shared their labyrinth stories and I listened to insights while learning a lot about how powerful the heart is when you need an answer. After that, Amanda shared an outline from a book intro and talked about how best to capture the beginning of a story. She talked about reader engagement and how *the hook* works to capture the reader's attention.

And there it was! A stroke of lightning. *The hook* of a song, commonly called the chorus, is the theme we sing repeatedly and is typically called *the hook* because it helps "hook" us into the song's theme. I would work out the chapters of my book based on the structure of a pop song. How incredibly simple!

And I thought writing would be easy.

The *high* of the retreat left me feeling giddy with inspiration and ready to get busy writing. I immediately bumped out the chapter outline based on *the hook*, and began to build my chapter ideas. I wrote and thought and wrote some more, eventually feeling like my inspiration engine was starting to dim after months of trying to cram my story into a pop song format. As I tried to untangle the ball of yarn, it began to feel more like I was shoveling dirt into the same bottomless hole each day. I was running out of steam and quickly editing my way to nowhere.

In order to solve a problem, or figure out a life dilemma, I typically engage in a kind of weird hybrid cross-thinking action that involves some imagination, some intuition, and a combination of emotional stuff. At times, this creative approach had backfired, launching me straight into the dishonorable position of becoming a graduate from the School of Hard Knocks; and at other times, it had worked wonders as I pursued entrepreneurial ideas and creative endeavors.

I knew instinctively that writing this book was necessary and important—I could feel it in my bones. My creative thinking helped me connect, with deep reciprocity, to musicians about the courage of self-expression, perseverance, and the importance of believing in themselves. I wanted to let them know that it was all going to be okay and that all they needed was some attention and some love on their journey. As my labyrinth experience had so eloquently shown me, perhaps I was also fearful of doing something that I was afraid wouldn't work out. I feared that I might miss the mark, or tell the wrong story and risk not resonating in the right way with musicians who needed guidance and direction. Although I considered this option of fear as a real thing, I still hoped I could step up to the challenge of writing a book that would deeply support other musicians.

Meanwhile, with pain resonating down into my left hip, my back was getting worse and making it hard to walk without limping. My husband would drop me off in the front of restaurants and stores so I wouldn't have to walk across the parking lot; and those motorized carts at Costco started to look like tantalizing candy carts, the kind I used to chase down the street when I wanted some ice cream. Thankfully, despite my worsening physical energy, our music business was bouncing back and in full swing.

I dove into business workaholic mode and powered through physically. Telling myself that I needed to work more to help sustain our fast-paced company, I put the book off for another time. It was 2015 when the book finally caught my attention again.

An Opportunity Sparks a New Focus

I ran across an internet ad for a new writer's contest hosted by one of my favorite book publishers, Hay House Books. I'm not normally a contest kind of gal, as I keep some sense of healthy cynicism nearby about my chances of winning such things; but I also instinctively knew that a contest would give me built-in deadlines and help to re-energize my goal of writing a book. I was very familiar with Hay House Publishers for their focus on all things metaphysical like books, tarot cards, holistic healing, meditation, and for the brilliance of introducing the world to great teachers like the incomparable Ms. Marianne Williamson and Mr. Wayne Dyer. I was such a huge fan, in fact, that I probably had every Hay House author on my bookshelf at one time or another.

The Contest Offer:

1. Fly to New York and attend a weekend writer's workshop

2. Submit a book proposal

3. The Grand Prize Winner would receive a full ride as a published Hay House author

4. The 1st, 2nd and 3rd prize winners would receive a host of gifts from the Hay House independent arm, Balboa Press, that amounted to thousands of dollars of content review, design, and formatting

The timing seemed just right, and I felt excited at the idea of finishing a book and perhaps getting a new perspective on the process. I pulled together my pennies and asked my daughter if she would fly to New York with me. My daughter was familiar with New York City since she had attended school there, and one of her friends was gracious enough to let us stay at her place in downtown Manhattan.

In true Hay House fashion, I made a vision board, hung it on my wall, and plastered affirmations, pictures, and notes to help me focus on the prize. In a big oversized font, I wrote *1ˢᵗ PLACE WINNER* on my board and looked at it every day for months as I set my intention to win the whole thing.

The New York City conference was a wonderful circle of like-minded, creative energy. As focused as I was, my hip was coming to a grinding halt; and it was tough to stand and walk, especially through the streets of New York. I hadn't anticipated that it would be that tough, and I did my best to minimize pain by eating in close proximity to the conference hall and walking only when necessary. Even though the pain was a nagging, unbearable companion on the trip, my resolve was steady and focused. I wanted to win the prize.

On day two, I was sitting in the workshop with other wide-eyed writers; and the speaker was clear: "We've done these workshops all over the country, and we know that only about a third of you who attend today will submit your book proposals to us."

I immediately did a visual room count, estimating that there were about three hundred attendees. If only one-third of the conference attendees submitted their book proposals, that narrowed the group nicely, giving me much better odds.

They opened the room up for questions.

Question #1: After I write my book, how many social media platforms should I be on?

Question #2: What's the best way to write my first book? How do I start?

Question #3: How much does it cost to edit and format a book?

I got an eerie feeling, from head to toe. *Have I heard these questions before? What is so familiar about this scenario?* Then it dawned on me that after years of working with new singers, songwriters, and musicians, these were the kind of questions they asked when they were beginning the creative process. Their fears would surface as they anticipated entering the unknown; and I knew, first hand, about artistic fear and working hard to figure out what to do next. It was at that moment I had a knowing. I knew I had a real chance of winning this thing.

The night before we left New York to fly back to California, there was to be a great celestial event over the skies of the city. A rare supermoon and lunar eclipse was expected to appear in late evening and the skies had cooperated nicely by giving us a cloudless sky, perfect for viewing. New Yorkers poured out onto the midnight streets to witness the gradual disappearing of the moon as the ominous shadow swallowed light, leaving only a thin bright ring surrounding the moon's edges. I was in awe of the moment; and I thought about the gravity of the conference, the wonderful time traveling with my daughter, and the deep connection to life's purpose that are reflected in the moon and the stars.

I came back home with yet another surge of inspiration to get going and, with gusto, jumped into the process of writing. I discovered very quickly that writing an effective book proposal was tough and super confusing. I couldn't seem to google my way out of this one, although I tried on multiple occasions. A feeling of impending doom loomed over me like a disappearing moon or a familiar déjà vu moment that felt like shoveling dirt into that proverbial hole once again. I got a pit in my stomach. and it was clear that I needed help. I had spent good money to fly to New York and putting this off again was not an option. My strategy now was to check in with my deeper self by putting a question into my palm and covering my heart—a useful habit that I had learned from my labyrinth training.

Question: What do I do next?

It wasn't long before a memory returned. I remembered that at the New York City conference I had briefly spoken with one of the speakers, and she had given me her business card. As a book editor who worked closely with Hay House Publications, she seemed like a good person to call. I hired her on the spot and jumped in immediately with a tight writing and editing schedule for my book proposal. I finally felt good about my prospects and submitted the final proposal hours before the deadline.

And then I waited.

Orthopedics and Destiny

A few months later, I had an important meeting with an orthopedic surgeon to discuss my crumbling hip. And the news wasn't good. If I wanted some relief from daily pain and to have some normalcy again, I needed a full left hip replacement. There is nothing like major surgery to leave you feeling out-of-sorts and vulnerable, and I left the doctor's office knowing that there wasn't really a choice in the matter.

It was April 26, 2016, and I was only vaguely aware that my bone doctor appointment had landed on the same date that Hay House would be announcing the winners of their contest. While sitting in the parking lot of the doctor's office early that morning, feeling odd about the inevitable surgery, my phone rang.

It was a representative from Hay House calling to tell me that I HAD WON THE CONTEST. I couldn't believe what I was hearing. I had been selected as the Grand Prize winner, just as I had envisioned. The nice lady on the other end of the phone congratulated me, then paused, and kindly asked me to hold on for a moment while she clarified something.

I started to cry.

The simultaneous one-two punch of life events colliding at the same time made my whole body shake, and I took a deep cleansing breath to gain some control. Then she came back on the phone.

She immediately apologized for getting it wrong. I was NOT the Grand Prize winner after all. I had actually come in as the 1st place winner instead. Tears of joy continued, and I thanked her profusely for the call. The richness of the full moment didn't escape my consciousness as I sat in my car. I had just received a reality check that required major surgery almost at the same moment I received the best news of my life. Somehow, I knew these two things went together as the synchronicity of the moment sunk in.

When I got home that day, I looked at my vision board. Amazingly and incorrectly, I had written down 1st PRIZE WINNER in a big clear oversized font; and for months now, I had been looking at that phrase and thinking GRAND PRIZE WINNER. The interesting reality was that not only was I confused, Hay House was momentarily confused as well about which prize I had won. Weird and so very interesting! You really can't make this stuff up!

What did I learn that day?

Be careful what you write on your vision board.

Now that I had won, I went into a high gear and called Amanda immediately. When she picked up the phone, I screamed something like "Help! Help! My hair's on fire!" or something equally unintelligible. Soon after, we jumped into the deeper editing and rewriting process together. Over the six years that had passed since we had worked together at the retreat, I had developed a series of chapters based on topics that were important to my audience. What I couldn't do on my own was see how they could all flow together in a cohesive whole. Fortunately, that's Amanda's genius, and she reminded me of the original magic of the song structure. When she showed me how all of the separate pieces I had written fit into this structure, I was excited. It required setting up each phase of songwriting and weaving the themes through the pieces of writing. It was hard work and, at times, I wondered if I would get through it; but I felt that my writing was changing and that a new, more honest voice was slowly emerging—a voice that was more straightforward, vulnerable, authentic, and deeply connected to my first love of songwriting.

We worked on this for about six months; and I wish, in hindsight, that I had purchased a better writing chair. My hip didn't appreciate the lack of attention, and pain was par for the course on any given day. I had intentionally postponed my surgery on purpose, so that I could remain *on purpose* to finish the book before going into a lengthy recuperation period after surgery. I was happy that the writing flowed easier, and I began to feel a new voice emerging as I wrote. The pressure of wanting to finish before my surgery was an ever-present motivation to get it done.

The surgery was successful and post-surgery flew by with a little help from my lovely family and my two new friends, Percocet and Advil. I was thankful that the manuscript had been completed and there were only a few items to take care of before the launch. Almost exactly two years, to the day of receiving the happy call, my book launched on April 27, 2018.

Carlsbad, CA

The years since the book release have been wonderful. I was able to market my book by talking to small groups at bookstores, sharing ideas with songwriting groups, and speaking to anyone else who wanted to listen to me discuss the spiritual side of creative songwriting.

At the end of the crazy year we will all remember as 2020, I was settling into a new chapter of living and wondered what might be on the horizon. The closing of one chapter prompts another door to open, and I was keenly aware that a transition was on the horizon. But what exactly did that mean? What would a new life look like?

In order to have some introspective time alone and to get some needed rest, I took a solo trip to Carlsbad, CA, a beautiful California coastal town and a perfect place to find some solitude from a busy life. This four-day trip was set aside for a specific purpose—to reflect on my book journey and to ask God and the universe about what I should focus on next.

After I had rested for a few days and had filled up on the cool sun and clean air, I took a leisurely drive around the gorgeous hills of Carlsbad. As I admired the quiet communities, my phone rang; and I recognized the number. It was an independent book manager who had called me on a few occasions, but we hadn't had the opportunity to chat on the phone yet. I gently pulled over to the side of the road to accept the call. We had a nice conversation about the publishing world, and we hung up after vowing to talk again in the future.

I took a breath and looked around. I realized that I had no idea where I was, completely lost in a community of gorgeous houses and manicured lawns. Thank God for iPhones and a Global Positioning System to lead the lost to their final destination. I looked up at the street sign to get a starting point. Ironically, the street I was on was Hemingway Drive. As I drove down the hill, I turned onto Tolkien Way, and then Dickenson Drive, and then Whitman Way... all successful authors who had made a difference and created legacies with their creative pursuits. I pulled over to absorb the fullness of the moment. Perhaps this writing thing was something I should pursue. Perhaps I would buy a home in Carlsbad one day and pay for it through my writing ventures and live at the top of the hill in this beautiful neighborhood. Yes, my imagination rarely has limits. Once again, synchronicity was speaking; and I thanked the universe for the conversation with the book publisher and for the street signs that seemed to be giving me a clue.

Question: But what now? What do I want to concentrate on?

The twists and turns of my labyrinth journey continue to ask me to make a decision between holding back because of fear or reaching forward because of love. As I walked the labyrinth on that night in 2010, I made a choice to leave my senses open to receive an honest answer to a simple question and the deeper answer concerning fear came in a barrage of questions that took years to unfold.

My heart's answer: Remember the creative calling to write a book versus the stress of dealing with a failing business in 2008? The crumbling hip or the trip to New York? The vibrancy of the sun or the lunar eclipse of a supermoon?

I think life has been asking me, in small ways and large, to let go of the pain, to detach from the outcome, and to center on the process of creating something wonderful just for the love of it. The labyrinth metaphor has helped me remember that there are no simple answers to anything. Life is, and will continue to be, uneven, dark, light, and multilayered; but I get the awesome opportunity to create a new reality every day based on my heart's guidance.

The choices have always been mine to make.

I think I'll be smarter the next time around, with the lessons of the labyrinth crisp in my thoughts. This time, I'll expect good things by looking ahead for fabric butterflies, colored lights, and teachers who share their skills. I'll let the mysteries work themselves out and trust that tough times will work out in the end. This time, I'll loosen up, let it flow, and have a better time as I smile through the shadow parts and enjoy the triumph of doing.

I have now let go of portions of my old life, although I still work to build our family business. I've gone back to being a writer, a songwriting coach, and a teacher. In some ways, I've spiraled back to my original self, reflecting the power of the labyrinth lessons; and I've come back to some quiet honesty and to what my heart knew to be true all along.

I am fortunate enough to have witnessed some remarkable stories from many of my clients over the years as they moved through the process of self-expression and transformation. But without my own experiences, the painful ones and the satisfying accomplishments, I couldn't be a light for anyone else—and perhaps that is the reason for it all anyway.

Amanda's Side of the Story

"The hook!" she exclaimed as she shot out of her seat and bolted for the door.

I looked up from my computer in time to see her smile and turn without an explanation. Glancing at the other startled expressions at the table, I smiled and shrugged. "Maybe it was inspiration?"

I'd just been explaining that the introduction of a book has to hook a reader in—deeply engage their heart and their head—when this extremely quiet woman had surprised everyone.

When they all continued eating their lunch, I began reading the introduction I'd worked on for my first book, which still wasn't even close to done more than three years after the inspiration had changed the trajectory of my life. It was okay, though. I'd accepted the fact that I needed to heal my life and feed my family, and my Co-author was definitely supporting me in both of those endeavors.

An hour later, we found Lisa back at the Guest House, putting the final touches on her message matrix. She was glowing.

"Amanda, look! It all fits... perfectly! It's like my whole life has been... a song!"

As I perused the poster full of post-it notes, I was overcome with wonder.

Damn. I knew it would be awesome for her to structure the book like a song, but this is next level. Her life... a song.

Goosebumps covered me from head to toe.

I wonder...

This was the first of many gifts that Lisa brought to my life—the affirmation that one's story and expertise are divinely woven together so perfectly that when we map it out, it's overwhelming. All of it—the triumphs and the tragedies—when witnessed as a whole narrative, told a story of love, grace, and redemption. It was what I'd experienced when my own inspiration struck; and as I stepped into the role of coaching others to share their stories, something told me it was true for them, too.

Of course this songwriter's story is framed like a song! Just like my butterfly approach emerged from those two weeks of witnessing the metamorphosis process with Aaron.

Lisa's beaming smile not only confirmed my suspicion, it radiated the awe that I had felt just a few years before.

If only everyone could see the sacred at work in their story.

That experience with Lisa deepened my faith in my work and purpose during a time of much uncertainty professionally and personally, and I'll be forever grateful.

So, you can imagine what happened inside me when Lisa began to wrestle with and eventually walk away from this framework that had downloaded so divinely. It was the beginning of my realization that just because *I* can see and hold this vision of their story, message, and future possibilities, it doesn't mean *they* can... or should. And yet, there is something about it that is extremely important.

We stayed connected while she addressed some of the other important things emerging in her life; and we even found ourselves in a women's entrepreneurship mastermind together, which also led me to another client who dramatically changed my life with a powerful message. Then, it was quiet for almost a year.

When she returned after years away from the project and brought me a series of chapters she'd written, I knew exactly why she hadn't been able to finish it. The book still wanted to be organized like a song, but without her personal narrative being the thread that wove it all together. She was not easily convinced until I laid it all out in front of her, but her beaming smile told me we were back on track with the true intention for this book.

Because my Co-author put Lisa in my path, I walk into every project with messengers, waiting for the sacred to reveal itself in the story and knowing that the creative process will help us to determine what is truly necessary to meet the needs of the reader.

Marlia Cochran is a Pastor, Transformational Speaker, Author and Recovering Perfectionist. She received her BA in Christian Ministry with a Minor in Psychology (Azusa Pacific University) and an MA in Pastoral Studies with a Youth Ministry Emphasis (Haggard Graduate School of Theology, APU). Marlia currently resides in Southern California, where she serves as Associate Pastor in Covina and lives with her best friend and husband Josh, their three children, and their dog Reesie Joy. She loves spending time with her family, watching a good movie, and laminating her stresses away.

The Good Girl Gets Her White Picket Fence

Marlia Cochran

We sat in a tight circle, a little dazed because of the earliness of the morning. Two of the ladies sat cross-legged on the floor, and the rest of us snuggled down on beanbags. "So, how's everyone doing?" Amanda smiled at the group.

On the drive out that morning, I had been wrestling with my own set of "What Ifs." *What if God punished me with this disease? What if I hadn't left the ministry? What if I hadn't been so stubborn*? And the one that always caused the greatest angst was the "What if I had just listened to God in the first place?" Even as I sat and listened to the other women sharing, I struggled to stay present to what was being said because the "What Ifs" played over and over in my mind.

When the circle had wound its way around and it was my turn to give my weekly update, all I could do was tell them the story that started all the "What Ifs" in the first place.

"It was about six months before I became ill, and I was standing in my office, frantically pulling papers together for a meeting that I was already late for. I don't even remember what the meeting was about or who it was with; but at the time, it seemed to be the most important meeting of my life. I prided myself on being able to keep dozens of plates spinning without dropping any, but I had a sense that they were teetering on an unknown edge that could destroy me.

"I was a PTA mom, house church leader, growing two businesses, training for a marathon, and essentially running from God. He and I had a bit of a falling out after Savannah was diagnosed, and I couldn't grasp why He would do that to her, to us, to me. I thought I had fixed most of it, but there was still a deep-seated and bitter wounded-ness that kept Him at arm's length, and kept me on the move.

"Just as I shoved the last stack of papers into my leather attaché case, pushed my hair out of my eyes, and grabbed for my car keys, there came a soft but firm, 'Do you hear Me?'

"My heart raced as I spun around, dropping my purse and everything in it. I looked to see who was in the room, knowing full well that no *physical* person was there. As I stooped down to quickly stuff everything back into my purse, feeling angrier that I was now running even later, He said it even louder, 'Do you hear Me?'

"Still trying to ignore that I even heard anything, I gathered up my things with shaky hands and set them on the desk to rearrange them before bolting out the door. Again, but with a gentler and almost pleading tone, He questioned, 'Do you *hear* Me?'

"Irritated, I shot back, 'Yeah, I hear You,' and then snatched up all that had distracted me, leaving the room and God behind."

I looked up at the women in the circle, thankful that all eyes were full of love, not judgment. Taking a deep breath through the tears, I felt ready to continue.

"Okay, so fast-forward to six months later, I get sick; and one of the things that goes through my mind again and again as I sit in the hot tub is that if I had just listened to Him, if I had just been obedient, if I had just been a good girl, He wouldn't have had to punish me like this. That when He asked if I heard Him, He was telling me I'd better listen up, or else, and I ignored Him instead. I knew He was calling me to focus, slow down, and ultimately come back to my calling, but I wasn't ready to let go of how I felt He had failed me. And so, He broke me. He made me sick so that I would have to listen. It's all my fault! The pain, the fear, the trauma for Josh, Savannah, and my family... the financial devastation, no more babies... all of it is my fault! What if I had just listened?"

The ladies sat quiet for a moment, the room heavy with emotion, allowing my words to settle in. I could feel my muscles tighten as I struggled not to run out of the room. The "ugly cry" was just waiting to come out. When it had come to the point of almost feeling awkward with silence, Pastor Tami finally spoke up, "I know you think that this has all been a punishment, but what if it wasn't a warning that He would 'break you' at all, but a loving warning meant to save you?"

The hair on my neck and arms stood up, "Huh? What are you saying?"

Her voice soft, she said it again, "What if He was warning you to save you, not to punish you? What if he was trying to tell you that something bad was happening in your body, and if you didn't slow down, then you would become sick? Isn't that who He is, our salvation? Isn't that what He did as our Father—sent His Son to die for us so that we could experience His saving grace and unconditional love? Couldn't He have been making you aware of what was going to happen or what could be coming, trying to prepare you for it, or even prevent it?"

I was stunned, and if I could have fallen down, I would have. It felt like an atomic bomb of restorative understanding had just exploded in my brain and in my heart! I was outwardly speechless at the thought of what she had just verbalized; but internally, a barrage of questions flowed one right after the other.

Could that actually be true? Could He have been warning me to save me? Could it be that all of this isn't a punishment, but just What Is? Could He actually be the Good Father He claims to be? Is it possible that I have two degrees in theology, and yet had my picture of God and me all wrong this whole time?

I had lived the past six years feeling condemned and abandoned, missing one of the best parts of my Abba Father—His real and true love for me. Suddenly, I saw God for who He had been all along, but my bitterness had kept me from accepting—a Daddy trying to protect His girl... and not because I was a good girl, but just because I am HIS girl!

The God-Matrix: Redefined

Still trying to figure out how all of the pieces fit together, I pained over the concept of God truly being a good Father who gives good gifts. For so long, I had seen Him as having given me this awful disease, failing me by allowing Savannah to be born with microcephaly, and forgetting about me when I felt that so many people were "abandoning" me as a child. There was still a question that I just couldn't shake and would always rise up in my mind, heart, and even out of my mouth: *If He truly is a good Father, then He wouldn't let these things happen. Good Fathers protect their children, and don't allow pain and suffering, right?*

I decided to say it out loud one morning in another breakthrough session with Amanda and my developing sisterhood.

"Okay, so I'm seeing my body healed, and I can see the spiritual growth happening. We're even getting into a groove with our new normal, but I still can't quite reconcile the disparity that I feel between who God says He is throughout scripture and who I feel like I have experienced Him to be. I'm being a hypocrite because I'm speaking to groups of women about their disillusionment with their What Is, and I'm hiding the fact that I'm still stuck in some disillusionment of my own and the God that I feel created it."

Pastor Tami, sensing my spiritual and emotional angst as I held my head in my hands, asked, "What do you *know* to be true?"

What do I know to be true? What do I know to be true?

And then it hit me! I snapped my head up and blurted out, "It's like *The Matrix*!" They all looked at me with blank stares, not quite making the connection.

"In the movie, *The Matrix*, there is Reality and then there is the Matrix. The Matrix is a made-up cyber dream world based on assumptions, expectations, and ideas that create the pseudo-physical world. But the Matrix is all a lie. The people who continue to live in it view their past, present, and future through these lies, and thereby cannot see it for what it really is or what it could be. Reality, on the other hand, is the truth. The only way to leave the Matrix and get to Reality is by choosing to take the red pill which begins a process of stripping away the dream world's blinders of all false expectations, damaging assumptions, and unfounded ideas that the person had believed before." I could see that they were starting to put it together. "I have been essentially living in a God-Matrix."

I continued to share that the God-Matrix for me had been years of assuming, consciously and subconsciously, that God was critical, unforgiving, and the great punisher of "bad girls." There was a part of me that believed in the core of His character He was spiteful and distant—basing His love for me on how perfect I could be or how much of a good girl I was. I walked through life expecting Him to be hugely disappointed in me, and so I was constantly working and striving to be better.

"Why do we believe this stuff about God?" Amanda interjected. "I mean, it goes against basic parenting instincts, doesn't it? Do you sit around and watch Savannah, to try and catch her doing something wrong? Do you give her love based on how good she is?"

"No, and it's weird, because I knew it in my head; but I just wouldn't let it sink into my heart enough to believe it. He's like us. I mean, we're like Him, in that we love our children so much that we do whatever we can to keep them from getting hurt. If Savannah kept trying to touch a hot stove, I would warn her again and again, because the last thing I want is for her to feel pain; but ultimately, if she wants to touch that stove, she's going to figure out a way to do it. When she finally does, she's going to get burned; and the pain from it isn't a punishment from me, just the natural consequences of her choice, of her not listening to my warning. It's the same with God and us. He warns us, but if we don't listen, the natural consequences can be extremely painful, not because He caused it, but because they become the "What Is" of our choices. I finally get it now!"

I looked around at a room full of smiling faces, and answered my own question: "Just like in the movie, the God-Matrix is a lie, and my only out is to choose to take the red pill of understanding how to live in His Father Heart and see His faithfulness in keeping His promises. He doesn't *want* to discipline me; He only wants to walk closely with me in the intimacy I was created for."

Goodbye, matrix. Hello, Loving Father!

It was as if all of the schooling I had ever had, all of the classes I had ever taken, all of the books I had ever read, all of the lectures that I had ever heard were inconsequential. I had over-filled my mind with thoughts and ideas *of* God, when what I needed was to be finally transformed by the grace of living *in* God. He wanted to share the parts of His heart that mine lacked and make me whole again—to *really* make it all good. I suddenly felt His desperate desire for me to see Him in full truth so that I could see myself and every "What Is" in light of it. I could feel His longing to push the bitterness out to make room for joy.

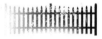

Could It Have Been Different?

I sat in my office, looking out the sliding glass door that was positioned directly across from me. The sun was bright, and the heat radiated into the room, making it almost too warm. My Bible was laid out in front of me on the desk, along with my devotional and my journal. With pen in hand, I was ready to dialogue with God some more. Over the last few weeks, He had been telling me how much He loved me and how much it broke His heart to watch me suffer all those years.

I had been looking through scripture for weeks, and I knew there had to be an explanation for all of it, I just couldn't figure out what it was. God had been clear through the conversation I had with Pastor Tami and Amanda that my "What Is" surrounding my illness wasn't a punishment. And yet, as reassuring as that was, it opened up a Pandora's Box of questions.

"How would it have been different if I had just listened?"

I heard God speak into my spirit, "It wouldn't have been different."

A little stunned, I quickly wrote it down before I asked my next question: "So would it still be the same?"

His response came back quicker this time, "Yes, but no. It would have been the same physical situation but a different spiritual response. Listening would have prepared you spiritually for what was coming."

Almost forgetting to write down what I heard Him telling me, I asked, "Could I have changed it?"

And then God posed a question right back to me, "Would you want to?"

Now, it was my turn to answer the questions, "Yes, but no. If I could have the message without the pain, but I know that I couldn't."

His next response floored me with the realization of the gravity of it. "Neither could Jesus. He chose the pain for the message."

My hand hurt from writing so fast, and I was a bit dumbfounded that we were having this crazy back and forth conversation. He was quiet for a bit, I think giving me a rest and a minute to let it sink in. He then continued, "Take up your cross and follow me."

Oh mercy.

A few minutes later, after my breathing had slowed, I continued with my questions. "But how does this all fit into the book?"

"They need to really see Me as good and as their salvation. Not their current view of Me as the One who just watches and waits for them to screw up so that I can jump on them. Sound familiar?"

So familiar, so painfully familiar.

What if without the journey that I have walked, I would never have the testimony that I have?

Suddenly, I felt a burning in my chest, a sense of anticipation, even excitement, as I began to see that I wouldn't have a story that God could use to speak to other women that would offer them healing if all of this hadn't happened.

I'm not sure I would have changed it.

The Good Girl-Matrix

"Do you realize this God-Matrix idea really changes everything? Not only how I see God, but how I see myself, my purpose, and my relationships, too?"

Feeling where I was going with this, Amanda smiled and allowed me to work it out, "How so?"

"It is impossible for me not to be changed because I am a direct reflection of Him, having been made in His image. If good girls get good things, and a lot of what I 'got' didn't seem good, then I must have been bad because I wasn't trying hard enough; hence I expected nothing less than perfection from myself, which was always unattainably disappointing. Wow! That is such a lie!"

The "aha" happening felt huge, and I took a deep breath before continuing, "The Good Girl was a façade that I maintained to protect myself from vulnerability, judgment, and condemnation. I felt like the Good Girl persona allowed my parents to be proud of me, garnered respect from my peers and trust from those that I ministered to. But *she* also forced a double life of inauthenticity, lacking any real transparency, because my value was based in what I did, and who I pretended to be, rather than who I really was as a Princess of the Most High King. *She* kept me in shame and guilt, not allowing me to truly confess, repent, and be forgiven openly for what I struggled with. I couldn't fully use my experiences and mistakes as lessons for myself and others that God could redeem because *she* had an impeccable image to uphold. *She* set me up with the expectation for absolute perfection in myself and also made it so that other people came to expect the Good Girl out of me all the time, as well."

I paused, my pulse racing, as I tried to articulate this new truth. Amanda just nodded, and waited for me to continue.

"She also set the stage for the Good Girl to be expected in other females too, especially the little one running around my house that calls me mommy. But most of all, the Good Girl did a great job of creating a barrier of lies between me and God because she convinced me that she was all a part of Him, which was nothing but a lie. I guess, for me to really move forward and walk in joy, I have to start fresh and redefine what it means to truly be a *Good Girl*, according to God, not according to my parents, family, church, or even myself. I have to see, through His eyes, that what He called me to be is so much better than the Good Girl could have ever been. Her 'goodness' was rooted in guilt and fear, but what He really wants is for my true good character to flow freely out of His love for me and the joy that He gives."

"That's beautiful, Marlia." Amanda had tears in her eyes.

"Yes, it is! I can see now that God wants to literally break the expectations of perfectionism and release the bonds of the Good Girl. He's been trying to show me that the white picket fence that I searched for didn't really exist at all!"

I had finally realized that the false expectations and lying assumptions that I used to define God's character were also used as weapons of mass destruction against my own spirit and those around me.

The "Death" of the Good Girl?

Two weeks later, I was pushing against the deadline for the book, chain-chewing gum and eating way more pretzels than necessary.

Come on, Marlia! You gotta get this done. Only a few more days! If you don't do this in time...

Four hours passed, and I was still struggling to finish the section I was working on when, obviously sensing my stress, Amanda asked, "Marlia, are you okay? What's happening?"

"I'm stuck, and I'm worried that I'm not going to make the deadline."

"What happens if you don't?"

"Then I'm not doing what I'm supposed to be doing. I'm going to disappoint my family. I'm going to feel embarrassed. I'm..." as the next words crossed my mind, I looked up at her wide-eyed, "I'm not a *good girl* if I don't get it done."

She smiled that stupid smile, like she had been waiting for me to get there.

"Amanda! I'm still operating on the 'good girls get good things' belief!"

She nodded and waited.

"Can I kill her?" I smiled, but was only half-joking. "She is ruining my life, setting me and my beautiful daughter up for stress and disillusionment because I've been modeling and teaching this to her without knowing any better. Did I tell you that she wrote a letter to Santa, and it said, 'I have been a good girl all year, so please, can I have...?' As soon as she said the words, my heart dropped and started beating fast. I continued to smile at her with encouragement, but inside, I screamed at myself. I have to get rid of this Good Girl before she destroys me and my daughter! What am I going to do?"

"Do you really want to kill her?"

"I don't know." Something didn't feel right about the idea.

"What if there is another way? What does the Good Girl in you need right now in order to relax and allow God to be the Good Father, even if it makes her have to relinquish her Good Girl title? Even if she doesn't meet her own expectations or her family's? What does she need? What did you need, Marlia, when you were trying so desperately to be the Good Girl?"

"I needed to know that I would be loved, even if I messed up." I shook my head as the truth hit me with force.

Here I was about to kill her, when God just wants to love and redeem her… God, I have no idea how to do that, but I trust You will show me.

The Restoration

> *"And I will restore to you the years that the*
> *locusts have eaten, the cankerworm, and the*
> *caterpillar, and the palmerworm…"*
> *Joel 2:25*

It had been a while since we had all been together; and as I looked at each woman, a deep feeling of gratitude for this sisterhood overwhelmed me. We had all written books or started businesses or moved away, so times like this, around a table, eating all forms of chocolate together, and laying out our souls had become rare and made me appreciate them that much more.

Each of us gave our update, followed by the questions that only seemed to be asked and answered in this safe circle. When it came to my turn, Renee looked my way with her wry smile, "So Marlia, how's that kidney of yours doing?"

I couldn't help but beam with joy as I answered, "My kidney is AMAZING!!!"

Amanda giggled as she passed the chocolate. "And boy, has it brought amazing things with it!"

Three years earlier, I received what every transplant patient prays for, waits for, lives for... THE CALL. The one that comes with such deep joy and divine hope for the life of health and freedom that this beyond-generous gift, often born out of grief, offers. We prayed all night for a family we didn't know that, while deep in grief over the loss of their daughter, chose to make the selfless and difficult decision to honor her life by giving me mine back. Two days later, my family and I received a miracle-in-kidney-form that kick-started an avalanche of things long prayed for.

In the midst of the laughter and celebrating new life, Yolanda paused and said, "That is so awesome! Do you know how Fred is doing?"

The room went quiet as a sigh caught in my throat.

Yolanda touched my hand, "'Nuff said."

We knew that I was never going to be able to have any more biological children, so while I was on dialysis and still waiting for my transplant, Josh and I had gone through the whole process and been approved as a foster/adopt family. Our hope was that once I received my kidney, we could provide a safe, loving, and stable home for children while their families worked on reunifying with them. We were even open to the possibility of adopting, but left it all up to what God saw as best.

Four months after my transplant, a little three-year-old boy named Fred* was placed with us. He came from a family who loved him very much, but neither of his parents were able to care for him. When he initially walked into the living room and sat down, he was very shy; but as Savannah positioned herself next to him and offered the toy she bought him, a sweet smile crept across his face. The social worker paused while going over the intake paperwork we had to sign. "I've been working with Fred since he came into care three months ago, and that's the first time I've ever seen him smile. I knew this would be his place!" That evening as we sat on my couch, the person who I always thought was going to be an impossibility snuggled up next to my side, and we were in love.

I wish I could say that every day was magical and perfect and everything we ever hoped and imagined, but that would be a lie. Every child who comes through the foster system has trauma, and it wasn't easy. It was downright exhausting. Fred was such a sweet boy, who also had significant responses as a result of his trauma. We knew our job wasn't to "fix" him but to love him how he needed to be loved and make sure he had every resource and opportunity to heal. As the weeks and months went on, we started to see how God, love, and great therapists began to free that child of the burdens that were never his to carry. And he bonded that much deeper to us. He chose to call us Mama and Daddy Josh, and we loved him like he was our own.

Our intention was always reunification, if possible. Even as I built a friendship with his mom during visitations, I tried to support her journey back to health as best as I could, and encouraged her to do everything the court required to get her son back. However, by month six, the social worker and judge were not seeing the necessary progress and so they approached us about adopting Fred. We were shocked but also elated and absolutely agreed! It was such a mix of bittersweet emotions of sorrow for his mom because we truly loved her too; sadness at the loss Fred would feel and relief for him because he finally had the stability wrapped in love that he needed; and joy for us because the court would make official what we already felt to the core of our beings— Fred was our son.

Three months later, everything changed when the social worker called and told us that a family member had offered to take Fred, and we would have to let him go. My mama heart was broken for Fred and for us, and though we fought hard with the court over the next three months to keep him, there was nothing we could do. Early one November morning, after our tearful last hugs and kisses, "I love you's," and prayers, those big brown eyes and my heart disappeared as they drove him to his new home.

As Yolanda squeezed my hand, I grinned and quickly wiped a tear that had trickled down my cheek, "Isn't it funny though how God knows exactly what we need, to prepare us for what we don't even realize is coming?"

Everyone chuckled as Theddee gave a whoop, "Boy, isn't that the truth!"

The pain after Fred left had been so intense that we agreed we would wait six months before we made any final decisions as to whether we were going to continue fostering, pursue adoption, or even if we needed to stop altogether. And so for months, we grieved and prayed, pouring out our sorrows and deepest desires, asking God what our next steps should be.

There's a saying, "God isn't early and he's never late, but he is ALWAYS right on time." We absolutely experienced this first hand two weeks before our self-imposed "decision deadline." YCMTSU! Just as we had started to feel kind of settled in, the thought that maybe, possibly, we were done, God happened; and life went supersonic!

Mid-June, I got a call from our social worker that there was a 10 ½ month old little boy who was waiting for his forever family, and she immediately thought of us. She gave us 24 hours to decide if we wanted to move forward with an adoption presentation, but it only took Josh and me thirty minutes of crying, laughing, and thanking God to know to the depths of us that this was our son! Our "right on time" baby, the unexpected and oh-so deeply desired blessing that God had been readying us for!

We spent the next month preparing our home and family to be his and on July 9th, I held my son for the first time and he became mine. When I looked deep into his beautiful brown eyes and then nuzzled his little neck, I took a deep inhale of his sweet babyness and the amazing promise of restoration fulfilled.

The day after I snuggled my boy, I had another "only God could do this" moment when I was also officially ordained as a Reverend within our church denomination. Though I never thought I would venture into it again, I chose to journey the long and difficult road of healing back to church ministry; because I ultimately knew it was what I was created to do… to be. I finally realized I am my most "Marlia-ness" when preaching the Word of God and serving people in His name. To not be faithful to the call placed on my life at thirteen years old felt like I was cutting out the most authentic part of myself. As I knelt down next to Josh on the church platform and the team of pastors prayed over us, I knew it was just one more way in which God was redeeming our pain and restoring back the ministry I was afraid I had lost forever.

It was Amanda's turn to wipe a tear. "Theddee, you were there. You remember the declaration that she was never going back to ministry, right?" Theddee nodded and smiled, Amanda shook her head in awe, and then I finished my story.

Now, when I said life went supersonic, what I really meant is that it went suuuuuupersonic!

The restoration of all that we had lost and the redemption of all the pain we had felt for so many years finally seemed like it was pouring out, and quickly.

Just six months into feeling like we were finally getting settled into being a family of four, I received another phone call from our social worker. "Hi Marlia." Her voice dropped off and I immediately began to panic because it felt all too familiar. Our adoption wouldn't be finalized for months, and I was terrified she was calling to tell me they were going to have to take my son back.

My voice and hands shook as I responded, "Hi Alma, is... is everything okay?"

She lightly chuckled. "Well, I think it's going to be more than okay because your son has a little brother who was just born three days ago!"

The next day, after scrubbing our hands and putting hospital gowns over our clothes, we were ushered over to an incubator that housed the tiniest baby I had ever seen. The nurse told me to sit down as she opened up the door to the bed and, before I realized what was happening, she was ever-so-gently placing my 2lb 3oz baby boy, with all his tubes and monitors, in my arms. Josh and I wept as we stared at the miracle before us. We wept with pain for what he was enduring. We wept for the loss of his biological family. We wept because God had just given our sons to each other. We wept with joy for what God was redeeming.

We visited him every day until finally, two months later, we took our son from the NICU to meet his brother and sister, who welcomed him with hugs and kisses to his forever home.

Less than a year later, with our friends and family cheering behind us, we stood in front of a judge as she declared that we were officially the Cochran family, party of five!

As Amanda passed a bar of *the best* chocolate around the table, we caught eyes and she said, "Marlia, I have witnessed your story being written for many years, through some of the greatest joys and most heart-wrenching pains. I am celebrating you for all the incredible healing work you have done and the way it is contagiously spreading to your husband, daughter, two sons, and a congregation I know you weren't anticipating!"

Tears fell down all our faces as we followed Renee's lead and cheered with our pieces of chocolate, "Amen!"

A few months later, I sat in a giant stadium watching my daughter walk across the stage of her high school graduation, in awe of the accomplishments, perseverance, and tenacity that got her there. Her eyes sparkled and a giant smile stretched across her lips as she held her diploma in our direction while we screamed her name to the heavens. As tears of pride and joy streamed down my face, I took hold of Josh's hand and quietly thanked God for her and all that He had done in her life.

It's true. Parents only want what is good for their children, and they work tirelessly to help them do the work required. And our Father has done more than we could have ever hoped for or imagined.

In that moment, my mind wandered to the rest of my life and all that it had become, and it took my breath away.

Miraculous, crazy, messy, and beautifully amazing—it's a life only God could orchestrate.

Amanda's Side of the Story

"Amanda, I am so frustrated. I want to be done with this freaking book and on the next Dare to Dream stage. How do I get this done?" Marlia's voice was taut and her eyes and body looked absolutely exasperated, slumped into one of the bean bags where we all sat in another one of the beautiful spaces at Glen Ivy.

I'd been facilitating a weekly Cocoon Day for those in the writing program. Once a week, we met early in the morning to walk the labyrinth, do some yoga, process the st*ries that were emerging, and get some writing done. Everyone loved these days, and the safe space they offered them to walk to the edges of their story and beliefs.

It had been a year since Marlia had started writing, and she'd only written two chapters before the st*ry hit the fan in her life. The sudden loss of her dad and mother-in-law had shocked her system and taken her attention away from the book; and then she'd had to say goodbye to her business and work through the possibility that she might be on dialysis for the rest of her life. Over the last year, she'd been unpacking the experiences in our little cocoon week after week. As soon as she was able to connect with the grief, chapter three [about mourning] flew out of her very quickly. But she was stuck again on chapter four and bringing her frustration to the circle.

"Marlia, this chapter is about finding the truth after letting go of and grieving the expectations. Let's talk about what truths are wanting to emerge in this chapter..." I coaxed.

"Well, what keeps coming up for me when I think about this chapter is how God had to break me with this health crisis," she started.

My heart skipped and my fist clenched out of sight, as I recognized the anger suddenly coursing through me. I'd been pretty mad about how God is often portrayed in Christendom since my university days. Taking a deep breath and renewing my commitment to handle my st*ry later, I focused on Marlia and keeping the space safe for her. The small gasps the others tried to hide around the circle told me I wasn't the only one feeling triggered.

"Tell me more about God breaking you..." I prodded, saying a silent prayer for everyone else in the space.

Marlia shared her story and perspective matter-of-factly, while I prayed for guidance. She communicated a common image and experience of a God who is simultaneously a Good Father *and* a critical, unforgiving, and the great punisher of "bad girls," basing His love for her on how perfect she could be or how much of a good girl she was.

Fortunately, Pastor Tami stepped in and asked if maybe God had been warning her because a health crisis was coming, rather than breaking her because of any disobedience.

Whew.

Pastor Tami and I co-facilitated with the careful guidance of The Master Co-Facilitator. It had to be because both Tami and I had similar st*ries around love and worthiness and disobedience and shame, and both of us were holding the tension between holding the space for love and healing in that little room and wanting to rant and rave about how terribly we'd all been conditioned to believe that our Co-Author is anything other than unconditionally loving. Over the course of our hour together, the whole room witnessed as a core belief of Marlia's st*ry matrix (and ours) dissolved right before our eyes in the safe space we'd all co-created.

Weeks passed and, each time we met, our little group of messengers held space for the unwinding of the belief system that was happening for our dear sister, Marlia. The doubts. The second-guessing. The anger and self-shaming when she saw that she'd passed this belief along to her daughter. And every time we engaged, I couldn't help but smile at how much she reminded me of myself.

It had started at her very first retreat. She'd shown up with an obedient heart and a ton of armor. In fact, the first time she shared her message and intention for the book, she'd identified the core message really clearly but insisted that this was going to be a collection of other women's stories. When I asked her if she had a story of moving from disillusionment to joy, she'd frozen for several minutes, her mind obviously searching for examples. Eventually, her eyes widened and her mouth fell open as she spoke her truth, "My whole life is full of these journeys..."

When I distilled her story and message into a message matrix, she sat with it for a few moments and then exclaimed, "Amanda!!! This is the structure of a lamentation! I just taught a series on this last month. How is that even possible?" It was her first YCMTSU moment and the moment I felt what was coming for her on this journey. Writing through a lamentation was not going to be easy.

Quickly, I'd begun to feel triggered by all of the shared religious baggage and the realization that we both had mastered the Good Girl persona with all of its over-performing and—compensating behaviors to "make sure God loved us and all would be okay." I didn't know it until much later, but this belief—despite all of my best efforts—was still quietly and insidiously taking its toll on my marriage, my business, my personal relationships, and my health. I'd certainly addressed enough layers to be able to stay in the room and support Marlia, but it would be years before I'd be able to shift this st*ry to a significant degree for myself. And truly, holding space for Marlia accelerated that shift.

Every time she moaned and groaned about the delays in her writing, I remembered my own painfully-long-when-will-it-ever-end journey through the facilitator training program. Every time she sheepishly reported that she'd cleaned her baseboards and her house from top to bottom instead of writing, I smiled and wished that cleaning had been my form of resistance rather than overeating. Every time she tried to hold in all of the tears, I remembered the first time I finally let the dam break and how healing it was. Every time she struggled to cry, I remembered the numbness and wondered when I, too, would be able to feel fully alive again. Every time she talked about throat-punching that person who wronged her, I laughed out loud, grateful that she was giving expression to some of the anger I still hadn't let myself touch. Every time she mentioned trying to kill the Good Girl, I winced with empathy. While I deeply understood the feeling, seeing someone I loved thinking about destroying a hurting part of themselves challenged me to start thinking in terms of bringing the parts of us along instead of making them collateral damage to our "healing process."

One thing I knew for sure, through this entire process, was that this woman is a force of nature and a freaking amazing writer. In fact, her natural storytelling chops are so good that when she started to try to inject a more teacher/lesson-like approach in between the scenes of her story, I had to convince her that she could communicate the lessons more powerfully through the stories. Of course, this led to a near-meltdown when she realized the length of her book was not what she imagined to be credible. More convincing ensued. Truly, this little book packed more power than many of the bigger ones I'd worked on and read because of how real and raw it was.

The night of the big Dare to Dream event, she wowed the audience with her story and moved us all to tears as she shared that the most important point of impact for her was in her own family and especially with her daughter.

It didn't take long for Marlia's spoken visions of being a speaker and advisor to shift into one that looked more like her original dreams of having more children and being a pastor. Those big dreams had inspired her to write the book that would heal her st*ry matrix enough that she could go back to her true intention and purpose and her Co-Author could restore the years the cankerworm had taken away. It's been incredible to witness this restoration unfold and this woman return to the spunky, smart-mouthed, and stunningly-powerful self that I'm certain I would find if I could travel back in time to find the two or three-year-old version of her.

Marlia is the one who made it so incredibly clear that healing through writing and community is the definition of True To Intention and what this business and I exist to offer to the world. I laughed the first time I heard her tell someone that she'd done twenty years of therapy in eighteen months; but I knew it was true, and I will always be grateful to have been part of that phase of her journey.

And I will always be grateful that she has been part of mine. After this little cohort of messengers had finished their books, the retreat space we had all called our home away from home was closed. It happened about the time that circumstances made it clear that I needed to slow down the business and deal with the st*ry that kept sabotaging my work, my finances, and my health. As I dove into the deep end of my own st*ry-healing, I knew that I couldn't and didn't want to go on this journey alone, so I asked all of these ladies to step back into my world, not as clients but as sister friends. We began meeting regularly to catch up and support each other while we indulged in our favorite savories, salties, and sweets; and the truth is, with the work I had to do over the next several years, I never could have done it without the love and support of Marlia and these women.

After more than two decades of success as a leader and mentor in MaryKay, Susan Goodson became a women's empowerment and accountability coach and founded At The Riverbank Coaching. She is the published author of *Letting Go of Shame, At The Riverbank,* and *When God Whispers,* a painter, and a leader helping women who struggle to find their voice and speak their truth.

"All I Want to Do is Write an F-ng Book!"

Susan Goodson

The words flew out of my mouth quickly and the room fell silent. I glanced at Amanda, who quickly doubled over in laughter.

I'd really never thought of doing anything other than Mary Kay, but I found myself attracted to Amanda and her work. When we shared time together, I laughed more than usual and I knew there needed to be more laughter in my life. So, when she told me about her Monetize Your Message Retreat, I'd said, "Yes," even though I didn't really understand why I was going and what I was going to be monetizing.

I didn't try to figure it out. I just showed up.

Boy, was I surprised. It was more about building a successful brand and how to make money on it.

But I have a brand and it's Pink.

Not being fully engaged and feeling more confused than ever, I found myself guarded most of the weekend. Anxious and frustrated, I couldn't imagine doing anything other than Mary Kay, and what would I offer to the mothers who would read my book?

Life coaching? Pleaaaaase! I almost barfed. *Stop encouraging me to stop and listen to that tiny voice telling me to jump into the unknown.*

I just wasn't ready.

Of course, I didn't think I wanted to write a book either back then, so...

I'd been building a Mary Kay business from the time I was twenty-four years old. Dedicated to helping women feel more beautiful and confident, I attended every networking meeting offered up in our community.

There was an event planned at the Photography museum, so with my pockets filled with business cards, I headed over there on a Thursday afternoon. It was there that my life shifted, but I wouldn't be fully aware of the impact until a couple years later.

Handing a card to a beautiful young woman named Amanda, I offered her a complimentary facial saying I would love to use her as a face model for my women's business portfolio. She smiled and politely accepted. As we continued to speak, she shared that she worked with troubled youth. That caught my attention and I leaned in to hear more about that, as I was dealing with three children struggling with addiction.

Thanks to my curiosity about how her work could impact my kids, we soon became friends.

While meeting her for a follow-up cup of coffee, she informed me she was also an editor and that our paths might be crossing because I had a book I needed to write.

"What? A book? Funny, Amanda. Did you forget I'm building a Mary Kay empire?"

The weird thing was I had been in my business for twenty-five years, and although it was a great career, something was missing. It wasn't growing the way I had hoped it would, but I was a loyalist and I was definitely not going to do anything else. PERIOD!

From that point on, each time I saw Amanda, she would say with a twinkle in her eye, "How's the book coming?"

"It's not!" was my reply as I shrugged off her suggestion and wandered off.

It wasn't too much later that I sat in a Mary Kay workshop and thought, *Okay. You want me to write a book! Fine. I'll write a book and it's going to be about shit.* (Yep. You read me right.)

I sent her a text, expecting her to hear my sarcasm and be knocked off her chair.

Instead, she responded immediately with a smile and an, "I love the idea."

Sure. She loves the idea. Seriously, is she crazy?

It was only a few weeks later that she was offering a small workshop for people thinking of writing a book and invited me to come along. I did and, in the middle of it, she asked me if I wanted to share with the group what I was thinking about writing.

I stood up proudly and said, "I'm writing a book about shit. I don't know shit. I don't give a shit. When the shit hits the fan. Up shit's creek without a paddle. You get the drift!"

Everyone laughed and thought it was a great idea.

But how can I write a book like that and honor the relationship I have with God?

So I tossed the idea out and continued to grow my Mary Kay business.

It wasn't until after my kids turned eighteen and, one at a time, moved to Washington to be near their dad and his wife that I decided to have a melt down and reconsider what Amanda had suggested all along.

It happened on a Sunday afternoon after I received a call from my daughter who happily wished me a happy Mother's Day. I loved that she called, but when she shared that everyone was together with their family, celebrating the day with her dad and stepmom, I totally lost it. My heart was ripped into pieces as I dashed into the shower and cried heavy tears knowing that although the family was all together, the only real missing piece was the mom.

Me. I am missing.

The following day, I called Amanda and conceded that there was a book I needed to write—a book about my children and the heartache I was experiencing with every choice they made and word they spoke. I told her that I'd raised three kids who had addiction problems, and I had lived overwhelmed with trying to run a business, stay married to their off-the-wall step dad, and navigate a road of total uncertainty and confusion. Lost in the mess of life, I had felt completely disconnected, isolated in the shame of having children who were acting out so inappropriately, and lonely.

"Maybe I could help other mothers facing these challenges...?" It was more of a question than a statement.

"Susan, I think it's the same book."

"The book about shit is the book about my kids!?" I gasped.

Amanda simply said, "Yes. Your book is about all the shit you have lived through raising kids who have been afflicted with the disease of addiction."

At that moment, everything fell into place and the book I was to write became a reality. I quickly signed up for her next author retreat. Throughout my journey with Amanda,

I was learning to feel safe and there would be nothing she asked that would be anything other than amazing and good for the soul.

However, when she brought out paints and brushes and instructed each attendee to illustrate some of the most defining moments of their story, I balked. I was not used to being vulnerable like this with others watching, and my perfectionist spirit reared its head and said, *"It's not safe to play in this sandbox. RUN."*

With everyone's encouragement, I chose to silence my fear and just do the best I could with what I was being asked to do. And, I took a bit of the pressure for perfection off by opting to paint with my non-dominant hand. *I mean, of course it will be imperfect!* After completing the exercise, I found myself feeling lighter and a bit more free. Not what I had expected, but I was grateful for learning new skills even if I didn't accomplish perfection.

I didn't know how the painting would play out later down the road of my life, but I knew it was time to get serious about the book.

It took over a year to turn over the rocks that held my memories in the dark.

I wanted to share my story in hopes of helping other mothers, but I was desperate not to recall all the heartache I felt as I lived the life of being their mom.

With each memory uncovered, I needed to acknowledge there was a part of me that wanted to run. To hide my tortuous past of living with and loving addicts. And I knew it was necessary to address my childhood pain of being raised by an alcoholic and abusive dad in order to find the courage to move forward and finish the task at hand.

As I wrote my story... our story... the forgiveness I experienced, not only for myself but for my parents, children, and ex-husband was beyond measure. My willingness to embrace the tedious mess of growth, and what I had thought was the heartache of abandonment, became the pivotal point of transformation.

My wounds were healing and my soul began to come alive.

As I was approaching the end of the book, Amanda was launching a production program and an opportunity to be a part of a huge launch event. She was enrolling people in August and planning to have all the books and messengers ready for a big stage in March. The program would include editing, cover design, interior formatting, and a photo shoot that would somehow get my book ready for print in time to stand on the stage in front of family and friends in March to promote what had taken so long to put together.

I was on fire with the idea of being finished and on stage. My ego was screaming, *"You have to do this. You'll never have another opportunity."* The cost didn't have to be an issue. My husband and I were right in the middle of refinancing the house, so I could just add the money necessary to be on target for the launch at the end of the first quarter of the new year.

I talked to my husband and he was on board, but there was a slight caveat I was facing and I wasn't sure what to do. You see, my husband and I were planning a three-month trip across the country in our car. It was a once-in-a-lifetime trek and I was torn on what to do. I wanted to do both.

I told Amanda that I would pray about it and that I would call her in the morning to let her know that I was ready, willing, and able to not only take this trip but to write the book while I was traveling.

I went to bed that night feeling restless; and when I woke up the next morning, I had my answer. Without discussing it with my husband, I called Amanda and told her that I would not be participating.

I think she may have been stunned and I know my husband was. I was stunned. But in my soul, I knew I couldn't take a trip with Joe and be 100% present if all I was thinking about was feeding my ego by imagining standing on stage and changing the world with my brilliance.

Writing the book had helped me to see just how many of my past decisions were based on fear of abandonment or rejection, and I just knew this was one of those. I was afraid if I didn't say "yes" to Amanda, there would never be another chance for me to stand on the stage and share my story.

Instead of doing what I had always done—choosing what was easy for my over-achieving self—I made a choice without the fear. At this moment in my life, it was far more important to pour time and love into my relationship with my spouse than to focus on being a bestselling famous author.

My husband's comment when I hung up the phone and told him what I'd decided confirmed it all: "I'm surprised you put us before you."

That spoke volumes about the decision I had just made.

In my Mary Kay business, we have an opportunity every quarter to earn a prize and about the same time I was finishing the book and getting ready to take our trip across the USA, I saw an unusual option—a paint and colored pencil set. It sparked the feeling I'd had when I'd painted at the retreat and so I'd opted to order the set as my prize and packed it in the car before we left.

When we got to our friend's farm in Great Barrington Massachusetts, I had pulled out the paint set and, with the color of fall glowing oranges and reds, I began to paint. It was a magical time in my life, and I saved each piece of art as though I was saving something more valuable than money could buy.

When I got home three months later, I set them aside while I dove back into my Mary Kay business. But every time I went into my office, I would glance at those paintings and realize they represented another part of me.

I contacted Amanda to pick up where I left off and she said that she would be happy to help and would be sending my final draft to her editing team for completion.

I knew I wasn't going to be ready for the launch in March, but I still wanted to move forward with the book. But when I heard her say that she wouldn't be helping me personally, I decided that I needed and wanted more and moved on to finding and working with a new editor.

Fear showed up again.

I was afraid to tell her my decision because I didn't want her to be upset with me and end the friendship. Fortunately, my decision didn't end our friendship and I stayed in touch with her over regular coffee chats and delicious lunches while I worked with another editor and life took me down another unexpected road.

After showing my paintings to a couple of friends and wrestling with their strong support and encouragement, I ended up having an art showing and selling some of my pieces of work.

So much was happening so quickly, and I could see now there was much more God was calling me to do. But there was no way I could have prepared myself for what was coming next.

Today I am still a director in Mary Kay. I have written two more books. I now do special order paintings. And two years ago, I chose to begin my training as a life coach for women.

Yes, exactly. That thing I was absolutely refusing to consider at the Monetize Retreat is now where my heart lives.

I never knew what "field of favor" meant until I gave myself permission to go deeper into my own personal healing and find my passion.

I believe Mary Kay was where I was meant to grow up.

It was my training ground.

It's where I learned to be brave and find my courage.

But coaching women through the grief process and helping them find their courage to speak their truth and own their stories has been magical.

As I look back, I often think about those moments when I thought, "All I wanted to do was write an f-ng book!" but God had other, much more important plans.

And now my cup runneth over with joy and gratitude.

Amanda's Side of the Story

"Amanda, I'm doing an art show... will you come?" Her voice sounded a little hesitant, or maybe concerned that I would say no.

"Of course, Susan. I wouldn't miss it. Please send me the details, so I can get it all into my calendar. See you there!"

"Thanks, Amanda. I can't wait!" she chirped happily.

Hanging up the phone, I noticed the two ways I was feeling. On the one hand, I was incredibly excited for my dear friend and her new adventure. On the other, I was still reeling from the recent shift in our relationship.

I'm sure that's what she was feeling and why she sounds concerned. I'm having a hard time sorting through all the feels, but I love this woman. I wouldn't miss her artistic debut for anything, especially after what I've witnessed in her life.

After our initial introduction and a few get-to-know-each-other coffee breaks, I knew Susan as a powerful woman; but nothing could have prepared me for the first time I saw her run a networking meeting. In just a few minutes, she had the whole group caught between laughter and tears. I'd never seen anyone tell stories, mock themselves, and empower others at the same time.

This lady is hilarious!

She also became a serious ally for me while I worked to finish my facilitator certification and empower teens with life skills. Rallying everyone on the networking team, and others she knew would love the cause, she made many important connections for me and helped me fundraise for that first workshop.

We laughed (to the point of tears usually) over coffees and lunches as she told story after amazing story of her journey, and I regularly teased her that maybe this was another reason our paths had crossed. Maybe she had a book in her? Oh my goodness, you've never seen anyone wriggle and squirm at the suggestion like she did.

The day she leaned in and said she was ready, I jumped for joy. I had just facilitated my first retreat, and it had proven to be a powerful way to get messengers started on their projects. So, I invited her to the next one.

The week before her retreat, I was a maniac trying to check all the boxes on my list. Food, drinks, snacks, paperwork, releases, games, gifts, etc. I felt a little (or a lot) in over my head already when I heard that voice say, *"Anchor."* I immediately knew that I was being inspired to "give my clients an anchor" for the work they would do—something they could take home to anchor them to the breakthroughs they had at the retreat. But what? I could not figure it out and decided to go to a crafts store and walk around for some inspiration or insight.

With only ten minutes left before I had to pick Aaron up from school, I was still trying to figure it out and feeling pretty pissed about it. Just before I reached the register, I saw an end-cap full of paint supplies. *Oh, Aaron said he's out of his paints. I'll grab those while I'm here.*

I was just getting ready to put them on the belt when I heard a familiar voice say, "Mandy Coelho? Is that you?" My heart jumped into my throat. The only folks who would call me that are from my childhood. I was right. It was a teacher from my elementary school who wanted to get all the details on my life while I was paying for items and rushing to get my kiddo from school. I did my best to hide my anxiety as I did a quick little catch-up with her, loaded the belt with my items, and found my wallet.

*Oh crap! I mixed Aaron's paints with all of the
retreat expenses!*

Then I heard the voice again, *"Nope, those are retreat
expenses. That's the anchor."*

What the hell? Okay... I finished my payment, said
goodbye to the teacher, and hustled out the door, wondering
what in the world I was supposed to do with paints!

The wondering continued for the entire week, and I
didn't get my answer until the morning of the retreat. It was
a painting exercise that would help them explore their story
introspectively and then begin to share it with the other
messengers. I wasn't sure what I was doing, but I followed
the inspiration.

Susan scrunched her nose at me while I delivered the
instructions for the assignment, and then I watched her stare
at the blank piece of paper for a few minutes while everyone
else got to work. There was obviously a war going on inside
of her. Eventually, I watched her pick up the paintbrush with
her non-dominant hand and get to work.

We laughed and cried our way through this retreat with
no huge surprises, and everyone left with their anchors and
ready to write.

Months later, Susan began to send me pictures of the art
that was flowing out of her, and I had to ask, "Susan, have
you been doing this your whole life? This is beautiful!" She
told me she hadn't—that the retreat was the first time she
had picked up a paintbrush in years. That's when I realized
the whole *"Anchor"* inspiration was not just evidence of my
reconnection with my Source and a really amazing exercise
that helped us get to the heart of the stories more quickly; it
was The Wind's way of unlocking a powerful talent, passion,
and outlet for Susan.

As Susan and I worked through the first few chapters of her book, I watched her struggle to piece together the timeline of events in her personal life. She was frustrated and unable to get into the flow of the writing until I realized what was happening. Susan's strongest memories were those of her journey as a business woman. Any time I asked her what year something happened in the business, she blurted it out quickly; yet, when I asked about her moments with her kids, she went blank. Her psyche had obviously prioritized the better-feeling, achievement-based memories and shoved the other ones to the background. So, I started playing the "get into the memory through the backdoor" game. We mapped her strong memories, and then I asked her questions like, "What happened at home right before you left for that awards ceremony?" With that approach, she remembered the key moments and was able to piece together the whole narrative.

I was thoroughly enjoying working with Susan on her book, and had just been inspired with an incredible idea for it, when she let me know that she was going to take some time away from the book and then find another book coach to help her finish.

Overwhelmed with panic *(Did I do something wrong?)* and concern *(But will they care about you and your message as much as I do?),* I didn't want to ask too many questions and make her feel like I was pushing or pressuring her to stay if she felt like she should go. So, I told her I would miss her and that I hoped she would let me know when it was done so I could support her when it launched.

The day of her art exhibition, I was still feeling torn and didn't want her to feel uncomfortable on her big day, so I arrived a few minutes late and hung back and watched her in action. When she acknowledged me during her share, that little voice that told me that "I had failed her and she was upset with me" was replaced with the truth. I knew we would be okay.

She was surrounded by people who were asking questions, so I walked around to look at all of her art on display.

Amazing. She walked around for decades with this inside her and never knew it was there?

And then I found it—the piece that she had painted for me, for us, whether she knew it or not.

A bridge disappearing into a forest.

I can't see the whole journey... just the next few steps... and I have to be able to let go of what I imagine the end will look like. Maybe I'm just the first few steps for someone. Maybe I will provide the whole bridge. Maybe we will stop working on the projects, but we can always get lost in the forest and have fun in other ways as friends and colleagues. Who am I to think I know what's best for each person anyway?

I pulled the painting off the wall and took it to Susan. "I think this one is mine," was all I said, but by the twinkly knowing smile she gave me, I knew that she knew that I knew. All was well.

And this painting would be *my anchor* and reminder of that truth for the rest of my career.

Over the last ten years, Susan and I have stayed in touch and connected regularly over coffee, lunch, and eventually zoom when I moved to Oregon. We've commiserated as caregivers and codependents. We've shown up to support each other's causes and launches. We've worked together to heal st*ries.

We've continued to laugh and cry together. In fact, we both have had a few really good belly-laughs while working on this project.

As we worked through our memories together, we were finally able to articulate the assumptions that were driving her decision to find another coach and my decision to let her go without a fight, and celebrate how far we've come since that day. We could have handled it all so much more powerfully if we hadn't been so afraid of losing each other. But hey, if we'd both been that insightful and articulate back then, maybe I would have missed out on the lesson of "letting go," and heaven knows that we've both leaned on the lessons learned through that experience.

Oh, and of course, there was the perfect story loop wrap-up when "All I wanted to do was write an f-ng book?" was replaced with "So, I am LOVING this coaching business and hosting my first retreat this year! It will be in Sedona!"

"Oh really? Did I tell you we're moving there this year? Maybe I will crash your party!"

"You're kidding me! You really can't make this st*ry up!"

"No, you can't, my friend. You really can't."

After liberating herself from an abusive relationship at a young age, Ciara Gutierrez realized that at some point in her very young life, she had started to listen more than lead. She became determined to reclaim her power and help other young girls do the same. After becoming a Certified Acne Specialist and clearing her acne for the first time in her life, Ciara founded Suit Yourself and unexpectedly opened the perfect doorway to these struggling teens' hearts. Today, she is helping young girls reclaim their power by guiding and teaching them how to first reclaim their skin. Together, she and her clients are constantly learning what it means to Suit Yourself.

A Pastor, A Mom, and A Sex Therapist Walk Into a Retreat

Ciara Gutièrrez

Slamming the front door to my childhood home, I sprinted for my car. My hands trembled as I tried to fit my key in the lock. *Fuck! What did you just do, Cici?!*

Paled with regret, I gripped the steering wheel and turned the key to start the ignition. Tears pooled in my eyes as I grappled with myself...

I never should have done that. She is never going to forgive me...

But I had to... I had to protect her...

Telling mom and dad was the only way to protect her...

I gasped as a shooting pain tightened my abdomen and folded my body in half. Collapsing onto the steering wheel, I turned off my car, surrendered to the heaves of regret, and wept.

There was only one person I could call in this moment, one person who could speak truth to the overwhelming guilt that now paralyzed me in my parents' driveway.

"Sis..." was all I could utter amongst my heaving.

"Cici, are you okay?"

"No." I shuddered.

"Okay, deep breaths. Breathe in, hold, and release. Do it with me."

My breathing finally settled and the coiled snake in my abdomen began to release its grip.

"I… messed… up, Mandy," I stuttered through my shallow breaths. "Lys is never going to talk to me again. I told Mom and Dad about the older guy she was talking to. They freaked out and they forbade her from seeing him. I feel so bad, Mandy, but I had to. What kind of sister would I be if I just stood here and let what happened to me happen to her?" Anger surfaced in my tone and then I pleaded for validation and assurance, "Please tell me I did the right thing."

"I hear you, Sis…" she paused and my anger quickly resurfaced and interrupted her.

"I wish I could just write it all down, show her how he tricked me. Show her the damage he caused. He was such a master of illusion, Mandy. Girls, not just Lys, need to know what they are in danger of."

"So, why don't you show them?" she prompted gently.

Show them? What the hell is she talking about?

"What do you mean exactly?" Curiosity eased my trembling feelings as I realized my big sis might have found a solution for me.

"Well… why don't you write your story?"

My story? My jaw clenched and my gulp was audible over the phone.

"You there?" she said quietly.

"Yes, I'm here… I just… I'm not sure what you mean exactly…" I took another four-count inhale and released.

"Well… what if…"

I rolled my eyes through the blur of my tears and dropped my head onto the steering wheel a little bit harder than I should have. *Ugh… Mandy and her "What If" questions…*

"What if… your story is the story that girl needs to hear? What if you're the person who can reach her while she is unconsciously saying yes to her *Master of Illusion?* What if your story could bring truth to that illusion and help her get out?" Her questions were posed gracefully, but they ignited a sense of urgency in me.

Yes, that's it! What if I did write it down?! What if my story could bring truth to these girls? What if they could experience how I fell in love with my captor and then they could witness firsthand how his illusions became my truths?

A sense of purpose washed over me and my mind started to wander to the even bigger what ifs. *What if I made it a teen love story like Stephanie Myer's* Twilight *series? What if I made it to Oprah's stage where I could reach millions of girls? What if publishing my story is my way of saving girls from the pain I lived through and bringing awareness around the globe?*

I fell asleep with Mandy's prompt in mind, "When you're ready to start your outline, think about the prominent scenes, the ones that will connect with your readers the most."

I woke the following morning and couldn't get my pen to the paper fast enough. Scenes from my adolescence flashed before me quicker than I could record them; and before I knew it, I'd outlined the first two chapters. After my first week of working on the outline, I proudly held seven outlined chapters and had my book's title!

◇

"No! No! No!" My body seized and I felt my husband's soft hands gently cradling my face as I came to. I noticed the taste of salt on my lips and felt the pressure of my clenched fists. "What happened?" I asked, startled.

"I don't know, Babe. You've been tossing and turning the last few nights and then, this morning, I wake up to you screaming. You were yelling for help and..." He took a deep breath and his voice almost became a whisper. "I swear you called me Jay..." His caramel skin paled with concern as his brow furrowed.

I apologized for scaring him and gave him a kiss, assuring him that I was okay. Then, in an effort to minimize the event as much as possible, I leapt out of bed to take a shower before school.

"Hey, Sis..." I called Mandy on the way home from class to tell her about the emerging night terrors.

"I don't know what is going on, Sis. I mean... it is bad. I keep waking up in puddles of sweat, screaming for help, and now I'm calling out Jay's name in the middle of the night. What am I supposed to do?" I tried not to sound frantic, but my hands trembled on the wheel and we could both hear the crack in my voice.

"So... remember that retreat I wanted you to come to?"

"Yes..."

Of course I remember the retreat. The retreat I've repeatedly told her I don't want to take three days off of work for, or leave my family for, or go dive into all my emotional baggage for.

"Well... I think if you're going to continue writing your story, you most definitely need to come to this retreat, Cici. There is something that starts to happen when we say yes to sharing our story. This retreat will not only help with clarity and insight, it will equip you with the tools to move you, and hopefully your family, through this process with more ease."

Feeling incredibly resistant to sitting in a room full of strangers, answering only God knows what kind of prompts and sharing the deepest parts of me, I exited the conversation without giving her a clear answer, "Okay, Sis. I hear you, but I'm just getting home now. Let me give you a call later?"

Always patient and full of love and support, she assured me she would keep her phone close for the next couple of days.

Wrestling with my umbrella, I struggled to get through the front door.

"Hey, what happened?" My husband questioned, surprised to see me home early from night class. "Why didn't you call me to tell me you were on your way home from school?" His demeanor was nervous and genuine.

"You know, I don't always have to call and check in with you, Alan!" I snapped, hardly recognizing my own tone as I spit back at him hastily.

"Whoa. Where's that coming from? You always call me so I can know your timing." I felt his concern shift. He was more keen to my body language and tones than anyone.

My hands started to tremble with fury. "Well! I was on the phone with my sister, so I didn't! Are you going to ground me for it?!? Sheesh." I averted his eyes and slammed my books on the table.

"Okay... I'm not sure what has gotten into you..." His tone was loving, but worry darkened his eyes.

"Maybe what has gotten into me is that I want to be treated like a free woman and not one that always has to check in with somebody!" I threw my lunch pail and stormed for the bedroom.

Ten minutes later, he opened the door gently with a glass of wine in his hand. "Hey, Babe. I'm sorry for upsetting you. Of course, you know you don't have to check in with me. It is just good to know when you're on the road in case something happens."

I apologized to him and tried to explain what Mandy told me about sharing my story. Forgiveness being his strongest suit, he cradled me in his father-like arms and assured me of his support.

I grabbed my phone and sent a text to Mandy. *Hey, Sis... You are right. I need this retreat. Count me in.*

"Good morning, Ladies! Breakfast will be ready at 9 a.m. in the lodge." Mandy's chipper voice beat my alarm clock to the punch. My swollen eyes blinked heavily as I laid in bed and reflected on yesterday's exercise.

How was that even real? I mean, how was it even possible? I shared my story for the first time—the good, the bad, and the ugly—and not one person judged me. And even more than that, each person in that room helped me, supported me, and almost facilitated in a way that helped me see parts of my story that I was completely blind to.

The assignment was to make a storyboard for your book— to craft a general outline of some of the most prominent moments and share them with the group. I'd stood there, somehow frozen and trembling at the same time as I'd pulled the post-it titled Virginity. *I cannot share this story. No one knows this story.* My hands had pulsed and a wave of nausea had washed over me.

"Where'd you go, Sis?" Mandy leaned closer to facilitate.

"Uh... I can't share this. Can we just move on?" My face paled and tears welled up in my eyes.

"Of course, you don't have to share anything you don't want to. But I do want to remind you that this is a safe space. There's no judgment here, and if this is a part of your story that you need support with, we are here. Can you tell me what you felt when you pulled that post-it?"

The tears streamed down my cheeks. "Shame. I feel so much shame."

Just as the words escaped me, one of the women heaved as tears now raced past her lips. Mandy passed her the tissue box and asked, "Pastor Tami, would you be willing to share what is happening for you right now?"

Pastor? You mean there's been a pastor listening to all this? Dear God! I'm so sorry.

Pastor Tami blotted her cheeks, stood from her chair, and stared me dead in the eye. "God wants you to know that you are, and were, a beautiful child of His when this man made these choices. He wants you to know that He is not a God of shame or guilt or fear. He is a God of love and kindness and grace; and He wants you to know that He loves you so very much and that He was holding that child who that man took advantage of, and He still is, every step of the way."

Her words broke me. *His words. He still is... holding me...*

The tissue box made its way around the circle, and then another woman raised her hand.

"Yes, Cheryl," Mandy acknowledged her gesture.

"I would like to share something with Ciara, if that is okay?" Her voice was tender but sharp.

Wiping my eyes, I nodded and met her gaze.

"Ciara, honey. I have a daughter who is just a couple years older than you." She took a deep breath. "When she was fifteen, something absolutely horrible happened; and she was coerced in a very similar manner by a man much older than her." She grabbed two tissues and held them tightly under both eyes as she let the tears loose. "Ciara, sweet girl, you have to know that this was not your fault. Not only did this man fool you by preying on your naive adolescence; but if you look at the entirety of this story board you've shown, he and his friends were working in a pact of silence. They knew what they were doing when they lured you young girls in and they took complete advantage, knowing they had each other as a source of backup. You have nothing to be ashamed of, sweet child, and you need to know that."

I had never thought of that. His friends WERE doing this with my friends. I always thought I was special. Special to him. But no, they were all trying to pass us around, and in doing so, created their own circle of silence and conduct.

Another wave of nausea flushed from my stomach to my chest, and I started to sway in my stance. Mandy caught me and guided me safely down to the couch. I took a minute to gather my balance and then felt myself lunge towards the restroom where I heaved and retched up my dinner.

I gulped as I reflected on my night's end cap and then heard Maggie, my bunkmate, ask, "How are you, Cici? Are you planning to come to breakfast? If not, I can bring you a plate…"

"Thank you so much, Maggie. I'm okay. I don't really have an appetite."

"Okay, Sweetie. Also, I didn't feel like last night was the right time to mention it, but I want you to know that I would be happy to support you professionally in any capacity that I can. You are not alone in this, and your body can certainly heal from this."

What are the chances? A pastor, a mom of an abused teen, and a sex therapist—all at this retreat? All here in what felt like a perfect design for me to embark on this next chapter in my journey. And the sex therapist just happened to be my roommate? YCMTSU.

Needless to say, I left the retreat feeling more divinely supported than any other time in my life. Fully committed to sharing my story with the world, I signed up for Mandy's Cocoon Writing Group.

◇

It was Tuesday, the day to meet with the sisterhood and get some writing done. Fully equipped with water and French fries, we all sat down with our headphones and started working on our chapters.

"Ugh!" I chucked my pen, almost cracking my monitor.

"What's up for you right now, Sis?"

"I can't get past this scene, Mandy!" My eyes reddened as they swelled with tears. "It's so frustrating! How could he have done this to me? I thought he loved me! It just doesn't make any sense. He ruined me."

Just then, I heard a still voice inside. It almost sounded like my voice, but it definitely was not me.

"My heart bleeds for him... more than it does for you."

Rage caught in my throat. *WHAT! Did I just hear that?!*

Mandy rested her gaze on me and pushed her pointer finger gently against the tip of her nose, a tall-tale sign of her seeing something the normal eye cannot see.

I met her gaze and could feel the rage gathering in my chest. Unable to speak, I grabbed a small post-it and wrote down the words that my spirit just heard so clearly. I handed it to Mandy.

Her eyes widened, "What do you think it means?" she asked as she handed it back to me.

"I have no fucking idea! But I'm pissed at it!"

"Why don't you try taking a walk in the labyrinth and ask what it means," she said, gently encouraging me to get some fresh air.

I walked the trail of stones in their circle of mazes and silently prayed, "God... please tell me that was not You I just heard."

"It was me, Isabel." The voice was still and confident.

Ever since I was a child, I always heard the Lord address me by my middle name. It was almost like it was His secret code, His way of saying, "Yes, it's Me."

"No. How? How could that have been You? How could Your heart break more for him than for me?!" My rage became venomous and I felt myself losing control. "He hurt me! Broke me! Stole from me! Stole from my body, my innocence! I am so fucked up because of everything he did to me! Your child! And you're gonna tell me that Your heart hurts more for him!?!"

"Yes, Isabel. My heart breaks more for him because he does not know Me. He follows suit only to what he knows... what he has learned. And he knows no road back to Me. He will never experience my healing the way you can."

I stopped and pondered His words. *He only does what he knows... what he has learned...*

What exactly is that supposed to mean?

I made my way back to the writing circle and told Mandy I was done for the day. On the drive home, my youngest sister called me.

"Cici! Dude! You're never going to guess who I just talked to! I'll just tell you. Luke! Jordan's brother! He was saying the craziest shit, man."

Luke? She talked to Luke? We haven't heard from him in years.

"We ran into each other in the library, and he asked me to tell you something. He asked me to tell you, "Sorry.""

"Sorry?!" I spit out, still spinning with anger from the writing group.

He said that he always knew what Jordan was doing to you and that he should have stood up for you. He said that Jordan's step dad abused all of them since they were kids; and even though nothing makes it right, he believes Jordan's actions were just a product of the abuse."

Her words stole the air from my windpipes, and I felt my throat begin to close. Gasping for air, I rolled down my windows and pulled to the side of the road. Quickly, I pushed my door open and collapsed in half as I felt my stomach begin to heave.

What? How? Wait? His heart bleeds more for him than me...

"Hello??? You there? Cici! Are you okay?!" My little sister's voice became frantic, and I could hear the instant regret in her plea.

Closing my eyes, I took a deep breath, "Yea, I'm here. I'm going to need to call you back."

Suddenly, the words that had just caused me so much rage were now unshackling all my beliefs, all my guilt, and all my shame.

So... does that mean it wasn't really even about me? It wasn't about me being smart enough, clever enough, or brave enough to see it or leave? I was just a victim, a victim of his circumstances?

"He follows suit only to what he knows... what he has learned."

And I... I was following suit to him... but what about before him?

His words played with me, taunted me. And then, I saw it. All at once, scenes from my childhood cascaded before me.

Memories of my mother dropping her chin in defeat against my best arguments.

Echoes of my father's tongue, "You know how she is, Jude, all hell will break loose..."

My stomach sank as I flashed to the backseat of my mother's car at twelve years old. Defeat in her tone and tears in her eyes, "Why do you always make things so hard for me, Cici? It's never easy with you."

And then my dad again, "Just let her be... let her cool down."

A sudden pain stung my cheek and a fire ignited my nervous system. I was six, screaming back at my mom because I wanted to stay the night with a friend. Burning with fuel, I knew I could get her to say yes if I just screamed loud enough. SMACK. Her hand crashed against my skin before I could even register what had happened. I ran away from home that night, and to my six-year-old knowledge, they had not even come looking for me.

I was always too much. Too much of a fighter, too loud of a screamer, too argumentative, too strong willed.

These were the titles I came to identify with. They became my truth. And with them, came my shackles.

You see, under that girl that was too much, too loud, or too argumentative, was a little girl that just wanted everyone to see what she had inside her. She had questions. She had answers. And she had power. But then, something happened. Their words became more powerful and that sweet little girl realized, or so she thought, that her power exhausted those around her.

It was better if she just complied. Wasn't too loud or too argumentative. And so... she began to follow suit.

It's almost as if I was served on a platter for someone else's brokenness. A man, abused as a child, who only learned power through control. I was the perfect prey. Compliant, stripped of power, and eager to please.

I took a large piece of my power back when I left my abuser at nineteen, and since, life has continued to present opportunities for me to reclaim more of that six-year-old child who lost her voice. As a wife, a mom, a daughter, and a professional.

It really wasn't even about me. It wasn't about me being smart enough, clever enough, or brave enough to see it or leave. I was just a victim, a victim of his circumstances. A victim of abuse.

But if I became a victim of abuse because he was a victim of abuse... how does this cycle begin and, more importantly, how does it end?

◇

This unshackling launched me into a tornado of what Amanda calls the upside-down; and after a few long months of counseling, acupuncture, and heavy supplementation, an opportunity to share my story on a grander scale came across my path. The director of Cal State University Fullerton's Tusk Magazine asked me to share my story as a centerfold piece.

"Liberated" was the first bold piece of me that I shared with the world. A story of resilience and heartbreak, of failure and triumph, and of truth and hope. When it was finally published, the feedback was overwhelming. Women *and* men wrote to me and thanked me for my boldness, for my transparency, and for lifting a veil that many of them didn't even realize hung in their lives.

After witnessing the impact that small part of my story made, I became determined to not only lift the veil of abuse for victims, but to make sure my own step-daughter and her friends never fell prey to it.

So... I stepped back into the work. With a trembling hand and determined heart, I reopened my laptop and started where I had left off. I created all the structures Amanda recommended. I set time aside, away from home, to work on the book. I created my writing entry ritual and closing ritual, and I was making progress. And then... life presented me with another catastrophic turn.

My husband and I lost our first pregnancy.

If the baby was all I lost during this time, I might have recovered sooner, but it wasn't.

I lost my faith... my God.

My entire belief system shattered and seeped into our blood-stained carpet that night. I really thought that I had known the height of my rage the first time I was deceived... when my abuser became a master of illusion and robbed me of so much innocence; but here I was again, feeling completely deceived and robbed.

However, this time, I was not deceived by a fractured man who was following suit to a cycle of abuse. This was my creator. My great protector. My God. This was everything that I had ever known. The heavenly father in the sky who I had been taught... trained... to love and trust with everything since the time I could open my first children's bible or hum my first worship song.

I began to question everything. . .

Why did I ever believe there was someone in the sky who was looking out for my highest good? Why did I ever think that was real?

The questions spiraled, and I became venomous with myself.

You're an idiot, Ciara! How could you? How stupid are you? You really thought...

I pulled away from pretty much everyone. I found myself not just angry at this Being in the sky, but at everyone. Angry at my husband for having no way to feel the emptiness and pain in my womb. Angry at my friends for constantly saying the wrong thing to "comfort" me. Angry at my family because they perpetuated the biggest lie of all—God. I was a walking grenade just waiting for someone to pull the pin.

After my body recovered, I returned to work. I hated feeling like everyone's eyes were on me. I hated every warm palm that met my shoulder in an attempt to comfort me. I hated every happy mother holding their beautiful newborn. I hated it all. All I wanted was to get through one shift without exploding; and then, inevitably, someone pulled the pin.

Towards the end of my first shift back, I overheard a co-worker make a joke about her friend pushing her down some stairs because she just found out she was pregnant.

Talk about launching a grenade.

That poor girl. She had no idea who was standing next to her. After being politely dismissed by my very supportive manager, I found myself heaved over my steering wheel, unable to go back inside my home. I called the only person who I trusted to not pour gas on my fire.

"Mandy, I feel so broken right now."

"I can only imagine. You're going through some awful shit, Ciara."

"This girl... this terrible girl at work. She said the most horrible thing about aborting her baby, and I just cannot understand how God would give *her* a baby and take mine. How could He? Why would He? I have always been faithful to

Him. I thought He loved me, Mandy. Why would He do this?"
My voice cracked and the pain ripped deeper and deeper
with every breath.

"Sis, I am so sorry. I can't even begin to imagine losing
a child. But..." She took a deep breath, as if asking herself
if it were even a good idea to say what she was thinking.
"But what if... God doesn't *give* babies to us? What if He
doesn't take them away? What if... He has given us the gift of
conceiving life and losing it when it's not developing the way
it should?"

I wiped a tear away. "But I've always believed that God
gives and takes life?"

"Yeah, I know. But..." Again, another deep breath. "Just
because it's what you were taught and what you have
believed... doesn't make it true. If it were true, wouldn't that
make God so awful?"

Her words paralyzed me.

*Fuck. I've been following suit my whole damn life. One thing
after another. Since the beginning of my time, believing and
internalizing everyone else's truths as my own.*

The next year was full of ups and downs as I searched
for what my truths were and created a new understanding
of who God really was to me. I was just starting to stabilize
when the next tragedy hit—the sudden loss of my father.

I remember looking in the mirror a few months after his
passing. My eyes were empty, hollow, and encircled with
darkness. My acne was raging worse than ever before and
I found myself face-to-face with one of the most dangerous
masters of illusion yet—substance. Grief is a tiresome
thing, and I had found it so much easier to just disappear.
Like a thief in the night, cannabis and alcohol became my
new shackles.

During that year of self-medication, I also had one of the scariest moments of my life—the threat of skin cancer. Furious that no one had taught me that my love for sunshine could jeopardize my health, I decided to get my skincare license and try to learn how to reverse the damage I had unknowingly caused and maybe even clear my acne.

When I stepped into skincare and started my education to become a Certified Acne Specialist, another layer of my conditioning was unveiled.

"Acne is a bacterial problem, so take antibiotics."

"Acne needs to be dried out, so strip it with harsh acids."

"Acne is completely inherited; so if you have it, you have it for life."

None of this was true. The truth was that my acne was an exasperated condition of how poorly I was treating my insides.

The truth was that my acne was raging out of control because I was spiking my testosterone levels with cannabis and feeding the acne-causing bacteria with the high sugar content of alcohol.

The truth was that my self-medication and lack of acknowledgment for what was truly happening within my heart was the root cause of my chronic condition.

There are so many lies we are taught to believe; and beyond that, so many truths that are rarely shared with us in regards to how to properly care for our skin. I found myself, again, pissed.

How could "they" rob us of this essential knowledge? Even worse, how have these acne-clearing companies created such an illusion to what proper acne care looks like?! It should be criminal!

I quickly recognized the feelings of deception and anger as I spotted my new master of illusion. However, this time I was educated; and with this education, I found my power. I cleared my chronic acne in four months after becoming a Specialist. Once I cleared my acne and shared my journey online, a large number of women started to reach out for support.

Then, I noticed that many of my step daughter's teen friends who were struggling with acne, saw my transformation and started to feel safe enough to ask questions. I began working with a large number of girls and women. One after another, I watched them all take back power over their skin; but the most beautiful part of our work together was that it wasn't just their skin that left transformed. They left my space a completely different person than when they walked in. They left empowered.

Sitting in front of someone, asking for help with something that you've felt powerless to for the greater part of your life, is probably one of the most vulnerable places one can find themselves. I noticed that during my time with these women, the journey became about more than just skincare— it became about selfcare. My room became a haven, just like I had always dreamed. I never would have imagined that it would start with an acne journey; but that point of connection, trust, and safety created the space that I always wanted to create for women. A place where they could be transparent and honest and fall apart if needed. A place where they felt supported, cared for, and free of judgment. A place of self-reflection where they could find their own way, their own root causes and then discover the power they needed to overcome it.

When the pandemic of 2020 started, many of my friends in health care started to reach out in desperation because of what was happening under their masks. Unfortunately, my room was shut down; and due to the quarantine, I was legally disempowered to help them with treatments. Another master... nope, not this time. After one day of allowing myself to feel completely disheartened and disempowered while locked in my home, I got busy. I called a close friend of mine and asked her what she thought about buying products at wholesale cost and then making small kits to drop off to these heroes who were putting their skin, and everything else, on the line. She jumped on board, but upleveled my strategy by suggesting that we ask for donations.

Within two weeks, we raised over $8,000 dollars in professional, medical grade skincare. The idea of creating a couple kits divinely toppled into a movement. Before I could blink my eyes, all the angels were showing up. Just like at Mandy's retreat—everyone I needed, just when I needed them. It felt like it happened overnight. We suddenly had twelve donors, a website, social media accounts, and news outlets asking to tell our story. We ended up curating over 2,000 skincare kits and donating them to every COVID unit in our county. If magic was tangible, this was it. But, it wasn't enough. Our heroes needed more.

We started getting mass amounts of emails and calls asking how to get more of these products. So... what do you know... more angels showed up; and before I knew it, I had a full website and online store that made it possible for me to offer complimentary virtual consultations. Another angel, Face Reality Skincare, saved the day; and beyond donating $70,000 in skincare, created a drop ship program that allowed me to send products to heroes with a hero discount to thank them for all they were doing for us. Then, as if it couldn't get better, I suddenly had relationships all around the United States and was doing what I love while working online... at home.

Working with the heroes was one of the most gratifying experiences I have ever had; but even more importantly, it reaffirmed all of the truths I had just discovered about acne. Acne is treatable, and acne is an inside job. Once I was able to coach these heroes on acne-induced diets, educate them on the dangers of self-medicating their stress, and get them proper products, it was game over. Even without me ever putting a hand on their acne-ridden skin, their facial and bodily acne was coming under control within the same 3–4-month period.

Another YCMTSU divine blessing—my safe haven wasn't confined by the four walls of my treatment room. I could empower, educate, and make a difference from behind my computer and there weren't any limits of distance or shutdowns.

I am now two years into being an Acne Specialist and, as I'm finishing this chapter and thinking about finishing my book, I'm thinking about how many more people will be excited to support it because of the work I've been doing to help people find what suits them. I'm thinking about all of the teens and women and heroes I now have relationships with. Teens, women, and heroes that trust me and feel safe to be open and honest. Teens, women, and heroes that are now empowered, confident, and ready to stop following suit.

It is nothing short of a divine plan and a YCMTSU scenario that life put my book on hold while I journeyed to find my power and learn how to suit myself when it comes to my faith, my relationships, my skin, and so much more. Now, I don't just have a grasp of my power and what I am capable of, I have the business, the education, and the life-long connections. I have the testimonies, the experience, and the gateways. But most importantly, I have the knowing that as I continue to discover all the ways in which I (and we) have been conditioned to follow suit, the angels do and will always show up. Whether that is in the form of an unlikely trio like the pastor, the mom, and the sex therapist, or in the form of graphic design artists, strategy specialists, and generous skincare companies. They always show up.

Amanda's Side of the Story

My facilitator senses noticed the big gulp and the beads of sweat when she realized the next part of the story she'd mapped to tell was the one captured by the word "Virginity." There was a long, pregnant pause as the room full of all the right people held her in a loving gaze, waiting for her to proceed.

I'd been facilitating retreats for about sixteen months by the time we landed in this moment together. I'd witnessed brave souls share extreme tragedies. So much abuse and abandonment. Death, loss, and grief. Ruptured relationships. Epic comebacks. I'd seen the various forms of resistance: procrastination, distraction, taking calls and getting lost in emails, over-eating, etc. I'd watched eyes lowered to the floor and dimmed by shame begin to glow with the experience of compassion. I knew the power of a few intentional souls holding space for someone's story, and I said a silent prayer that my sister would find the courage to let these women hold her as she shared a story she had long buried and left behind.

While I hated watching her wrestle, I was grateful for the moment to address what was happening in my own mind and body. Just behind the calm exterior of the mindful, experienced facilitator, were huge big sister realities.

How did you not see what was happening to her?

My mind served up at least half a dozen memories of calls I'd received from her, emphasizing the words and phrases... clues... that I missed: "So, my friend is... what would you tell her in this situation?"

Ugh. My face flushed with shame and I looked at the floor and took my own deep breath as quietly as I could.

You saw this coming. You saw how she was being conditioned. You called him on it. And yet you didn't see when it started? Where were you all this time, Amanda?

Regret squeezed my heart as I looked up at the young woman in front of me, who was still questioning her courage and strength, even after leaving an abusive relationship.

Looking around the room, I realized that the pastor, the mom, and the sex therapist had shown up for Ciara, but they had also shown up for me.

The pastor was Tami—the woman The Wind had dropped into my first retreat to show me that True To Intention was more about helping people heal so they could become who they were always meant to be than it was about keeping their messages on track and engaging. For more than a year, this woman had shown up at every retreat, served the room with her story, and upped my game as a facilitator with all of her questions and insights.

She's here to remind Ciara of the Truth—to dispel the shame that never should have been hers to begin with and replace it with the reality of Unconditional Love and Grace.

The mom was Cheryl—a powerful facilitator with whom I'd shared many transformational rooms. We had met out of a common desire to support youth and witnessed each other dig ourselves out of old stories and wounds for four years, but I was very clear (and grateful) that she had at least two decades in personal development and healing on me.

She's here to reflect the Mother's Heart to Ciara—to show her the ferocity of the maternal instinct to fight to protect and nurture their young with her own story of standing next to her daughter through a similar situation.

The sex therapist was Maggie—a new client whose focus was on developing and rekindling intimacy.

She's here to hold the space for healing and restoration of this essential part of Ciara's humanity and help her navigate this with her man.

Just then, Ciara found her voice and shared the rest of the story while I slipped Tami a note to say I'd need to process this experience later, set my big sister feelings aside, and focused on the healing opportunity here for my little sister.

Once the stories were shared, it was time to discuss branding and structure and we had a blast brainstorming and giggling into the wee hours of the morning, thanks to Maggie's playful approach to intimacy. The next day, I stole some time with Tami to process all the tough shit that had come up for me during Ciara's share and I thanked Cheryl for respectfully stepping in during the moments where she noticed it was tough for me to stay neutral as a facilitator.

What would I have done without these ladies at the retreat? I'm really glad I never had to find out. The perfect team always shows up to help move the individual and collective stories forward. YCMTSU!

Like so many messengers I'd witnessed by this point, I watched the real work roll out red-carpet style at Ciara's feet. Once she realized she would have to make the reader fall in love with her abuser the way she had, in order for them to see just how easy it is to get lost in a relationship, the work intensified and the writing became a lot more difficult. Eventually, The Wind nudged her out of the writing and onto another path of healing. Marriage, stepmotherhood, and career came with many opportunities for her to face the old st*ries that would need to be healed before she would be able to complete and publish the book.

We celebrated when her story was published and the incredible feedback affirmed the need for stories like hers to be told, and she developed the outline and content when inspired over the next several years. Every time she'd move it forward, life would serve up another opportunity to face a bully, a challenge, or a wound. Though she would go upside-down, she never ran away from the hard work in front of her, even when it meant facing the origins of the story that she discovered in her earliest childhood memories. It was hard to watch her be so hard on herself about not getting to the writing, but I understood. I'd had to battle with the same voice for six years while I healed before I was able to make good on my intention to write a book. I just kept praying that someday she would also be able to look back and see exactly how all of the apparent distractions, detours, and delays were actually divinely orchestrated for her highest and best... and for the highest and best of all of those whose lives she would eventually touch with her message.

One thing I knew for certain since I met her: This one is here to change the world.

Eventually, when she stepped into the skin care industry, I watched her wrestle despite her excitement: "Mandy, what is this going to do to my plans for the book? How can I possibly...?"

As I listened to her share about her passion for helping others, especially teens, learn how to take better care of their skin, I heard it... the connection.

"Ciara, the righteous indignation I'm hearing from you about the lack of education around skin, and how it affected you and your own body, reminds me of your message."

"What?!?" she asked incredulously.

"Well, you're upset because the young and old have been DISEMPOWERED. They are literally unconsciously following suit—the conditioning they've experienced—eating poorly, mis-managing stress, etc. What if this is all part of the bigger work you're here to do? I mean... you've been telling me about these powerful moments with women and girls on your table, where they share some of their biggest insecurities and struggles and you meet them with love and empowerment. Isn't this the same thing? What if you called it 'Suit Yourself Skincare' since the goal is to empower them to pay attention to what works for them and what doesn't. Your visual branding could look like a game card, but have your own..." I paused, searching for the right visual. "Fire... yeah, that makes sense, doesn't it?"

"Ohhhhhhhhhh shiiiiiitttt. You're right!" she exclaimed right and we quickly enlisted the support of Alyssa, our brilliant graphic designer sister, for her visual branding.

I've loved every minute of witnessing this powerful young woman reclaim the fiery power she brought with her to the planet. From the time she was little, it was clear that she was going one of two ways: 1) She was going to turn the world on its ear for the good, or 2) She was going to end up in prison or worse. It was excruciating to watch her fire be smothered by well-intentioned people who simply didn't know how to interact with such big power and emotion in her childhood, and it was infuriating to see the impact of it throughout her teens and early twenties. Little did I know at the time that my own fire had been nearly squelched at an early age... that I'd ever had one... that, when I finally woke up to this fact, *she* would be one of my biggest inspirations and models for reclaiming it. But *she* never lost it. She never let it go out all the way. She set goals, worked her ass off to achieve them, and surprised herself with successes. And she surrounded herself with people who would fan her flames when she became weary from all the internal work required, because this message of Suit Yourself is going to invite her to reclaim more and more of her wounded parts and more of her potential at every turn. In fact, as we work on this book, I'm watching her stand up to narcissists and an unethical workplace with fierce determination, integrity, and the fiery strength she brought with her to this world. Today, with all of those folks in her corner, there's nothing she can't do.

Of course, her book will change lives one day; but in the meantime, she is igniting the fire of insight and empowerment in her family, friends, clients, and all of those who watch from afar and wonder, "How does she do it?"

She doesn't do it; she IS it.

Cheryl Herrick is a serial entrepreneur who enjoys working on projects that approach common industries (i.e. medical devices, the automotive industry, and home-building) in an unconventional way—through innovation and, most importantly, the business philosophy of Dr. W. Edwards Deming. Her current project is working as a partner in Global 1 Habitats, which builds unconventional houses, at a rate of 1 per day, to help with the affordable housing crisis. Her passion project, Racing for Warriors, uses auto racing to give back to military service members with PTSD and other wounds of war. Who says healing can't be fun?!

Racing Toward Freedom

Cheryl Herrick

It was a race day like any other race day. I pulled my Novacaine into the pits in Del Mar, CA, the warmth of the sun burning off the ocean haze with a mixture of salty air, fuel, and exhaust from all the old muscle cars pulling into the venue. I did not realize I was about to be gifted with something that a business would later be built around. I was simply showing up to race my car with a bunch of other friends who are well-known in our car world: busy, successful entrepreneurs that love to race and make the components used in the cars we race.

I unloaded everything out of my car. (Yes, I race her, but she is also a pack mule with a trunk big enough to hide five dead bodies!) While I was in the pit area, my friend, Rob, approached me about a fundraiser for a charity that helps wounded military Veterans and asked if I would like to give folks rides in my car in exchange for donations. I agreed happily, as many in my family have served; and I have a very deep and abiding respect for our armed forces.

That day, I was racing not only my 67 Nova, but also a pink-ish 65 nova surf wagon. The reason I mention this will become obvious shortly, but get that visual into your head now: pink-ish surf wagon with a white top and surfboard rack on top. Got it? Good. Back to the story.

I offered to give rides not only in my Novacaine which can take one passenger, but in the Nova surf wagon which can take three passengers. As the weekend unfolded, we were getting more and more folks that wanted to ride.

Eventually, a line started forming near both my cars. People were signing up to ride with "the ponytail" three at a time in that pink nova wagon. (Because we didn't have to wear a helmet at these low-speed events, I was wearing my hair in a ponytail and it was flying behind me in the breeze.) And because I could take several passengers, I ended up with groups of Veterans and active-duty Military folks in the wagon with me. Quickly, I noticed that many of these brave men started to have emotional reactions to the ride—either joy, enthusiasm, or tears. Whatever their response, it was more dramatic than the lay people I had taken for rides. I was very curious about what was coming up for them but also didn't want to pry. However, after about a day and a half of this reaction, I finally screwed up my courage to ask one of the gents who I had been chatting with and learned was a Vietnam Veteran.

When we pulled into the pits and parked, I looked over at him in the passenger seat, while his two friends chatted in the back seat, and noticed tears running down his face and a somewhat distant look in his eyes.

"Are you okay?" I asked.

"Yes," he answered.

"Would you mind my asking what the tears mean?"

"Those were the best thirty seconds of my life. I have not felt that good since before I went to war." He looked directly at me and said, "You changed my life."

Then we were both crying, and a seed was planted.

Thirty seconds. One ride. To change a life. I like those stats...

And it wasn't just him. That same reaction happened over and over across the weekends we were hosting those fundraisers.

Race cars and change lives at the same time? Who woulda thunk it? I wondered as I left that event determined to continue to help with these fundraisers in whatever time I could spare from my very busy job at the car parts company I was helping my dad rebuild.

PonytailRacing.com

About six months to a year before this life-changing day at the track, I had attended a retreat with my good pal, Amanda, in an effort to find my own way to change the world. For fifteen years, I had done self-development programs for teens, facilitated creativity programs and retreats, led business system development seminars, and had done some speaking. I walked into that retreat assuming I'd do more of that in a conference room, talky talky type program; but frankly, some of those talk, talk, talk events were starting to feel old to me and the idea of finding a way to make it FUN kept yammering in the back of my mind. As I searched for ways to lighten it up, I thought maybe I would facilitate programs with my kids, which always brings out the silly, fun side of me; but I still didn't feel like I had gotten to the heart of what I TRULY wanted to do.

All I knew was that I was beginning to feel alive again and wanted to help others feel that way, too. After seven years of feeling disconnected from my fun, alive self, I had reconnected with an old flame—truly one of the great loves of my life. Our relationship wasn't always easy; but it was a place where, for whatever reason, I received some of my great life lessons. During this last go-around with him, he had catalyzed an aliveness in my life that I had been missing, and facilitated what I now understand was an inner revolution for me emotionally, spiritually, and most assuredly in the bedroom. There had always been an agreement of "no judgment" between us, which created a space for us to share the hard details about ourselves with each other—the places where we felt fragile, uncertain, and at times fearful. Those were things we could safely talk to each other about. Through both the conversations and our physical connection, parts of me were being rewired in a very healing way, parts that had been squashed out and/or disconnected from each other in previous years.

Losing parts of ourselves is hard to notice at the time it's happening. It isn't like a lightning bolt that strikes loud and hard on a particular day; it's like a fog that slides under the door, slowly dimming the light in the room until you realize you can't see your hand in front of your face. And that was the state I was in when Steve came back into my life.

The combination of the rewiring I had gone through with Steve and then, at the tail end of that breakup and just before Amanda's retreat, my first foray into skydiving, immediately followed by my re-entry into car racing, started to breathe back into me the wonder of the little girl who had been racing motorcycles at seven years old and being silly and goofy with her friends at the race track.

All the while, there was still this "thing" I wanted to do that I could not quite put my fingers on.

After the retreat, in an attempt to gain more clarity, I did some work with another friend, Ronda, trying to come at it from a different angle in the hopes the answer would come.

Working with her definitely helped. It gave me a name for what I thought was a program but what ultimately became the name of my first LLC, Spark of Ignition. I used that name for quite some time because the clarity I'd realized was that I am all about creating a spark for transformation to happen for people.

But I still wasn't over the finish line yet. I now had the idea *of what my aim was, but* I had no idea how I was going to do it or who I would serve. None of those other details were clear. So I went back into what I call incubation mode. I knew enough to know that I didn't know. I wanted to know. I was impatient to know, but I just didn't have it figured out yet.

Time continued to pass and I still hadn't made what I considered "enough progress." (To be fair, NO ONE would have considered what I was doing as progress. LOL!) Knowing you have something inside that you could give yet not knowing entirely what the "thing" is can be an exasperating experience. It certainly has been for me. My dad and I have a saying: We have a lot of patience; we just use it up real fast! So, while I was impatiently attempting to be patient, I re-engaged my friend Amanda for a private one-on-one retreat.

As part of the pre-work, I had written a bunch of things down and taken a ton of racing terms, I mean a ton, and correlated them to lessons and exercises and meanings. Imagine sheets of chart paper full of columns of terms, meanings, and exercises. I think I had about five pages of those suckers. (I have a photo of the madness.) Even after doing all that work, I still didn't feel like I 1) had enough to share, teach, or give to anyone, and 2) it still didn't feel FUN! I know, I know why all this damn insistence on FUN?! You'll see...

I showed up at my private retreat armed with all this prework I had done. The amount of it was significant because of the years of work and life experience I had. I was struggling to decide which *market* to serve and which *parts of my background and life experience* to bring to the forefront. I felt so strongly that W. Edwards Deming's System of Profound Knowledge—the business philosophy that has been seminal to my entire life, to child raising, to interactions with everything—needed to be incorporated into what I was doing somehow; yet I was not really sure how.

"Amanda, I am not sure how I will bring my love of racing, Deming's philosophy, my sense of humor, and my penchant for fun all into one program." I had spent all this time thinking I had to figure out a way to bring each part of myself to its own individual program or offering. I mean, how would I blend my creative programs with racing, for heaven's sake?

"Why would you NOT bring all of that to the program? Why would you NOT share all the parts of yourself and your passions and experience? Imagine the amount of energy you'd have all in one place."

She rightly suggested that the powerful thing would be to bring all of myself to the party. I know, what an idea, right?! (Some of us are quicker learners than others.)

Amanda and I spent a day and a half (I think. I've slept since then, so the timing could be different.) working on a program for me to offer and I finally felt like we were getting closer. I was beginning to see some of the pieces coming together on a map I had drawn of a fictional race track (that had its roots in the Full Course at VIR, one of my favorites!), and then laid Dr. Deming's systems diagram on top of it to demonstrate his system by way of racing.

NOW, we were really getting somewhere...

We had gotten a lot more integration in bringing all my experience and expertise into an offering, and we had discussed the possibility that my target market was entrepreneurs who loved racing. Heaven knows there were a lot of them, and they would learn the business philosophy fast if it were laid out in racing terms. The only piece we got a little stuck on was *how* I would market to them.

"Maybe if we get out to the track together, have a little fun, and blow off some steam, the ideas will flow," I offered as we finished our long day of strategizing. There was a race I was registered to participate in at Autoclub Speedway in CA, and I had invited Amanda to join me so she could get firsthand experience of the community, the people, and the FUN!

When we arrived, I noticed I was the only OLD muscle car out there. We pulled into the track, unloaded everything, and I set about looking up my setup parameters for that track with the car. People walked by and looked at the car and us. There was a lot of interest but not much engagement. After I got the car sorted, I went track-side and watched other people race for about thirty minutes to learn the track configuration. (Racer's tip here: If you wait and watch, you will get to see where everyone else is having trouble, why, and what to do instead. For example, I saw I needed to go slow into corners and fast out of them. Most were going fast in, which meant they were slow coming out rather than accelerating and finding time. Life can be like that, too, sometimes. A moment of pause or reflection gets us further ahead than racing in {pun intended}.) So, I watched in order to avoid others' mistakes.

As I was heading back to the car, a guy came up to me and asked just snidely enough, "Are you ever going to run on track or are you just here to poke around?"

I smiled. "Oh yeah, I'm gonna run."

His opinion was fine with me. I learned a long time ago that when I come into a new arena, I don't run my mouth; because I have no idea who is there or where I will land in the lineup. I've raced at amateur events with Al Unser (multi-time Indy 500 champ) and beat him, but I'd rather watch, learn, and let my driving do the talking, good or bad as it may be on any day.

I got in the car, took my first lap at about 50% speed to feel out the car, the track, etc. and make any corrections. The next lap, I went for it—"full send" as we racers call it—and it was a good run. Fairly fast, I was later to find out. After I took a few more runs, getting faster with each one, my car became the talk of the track. Amanda and I were pretty busy most of the rest of the day talking to people who were interested in the car, her engine, how she could handle so well for an old car, who the heck I was, and how I came to race at all.

As the afternoon passed by, Amanda looked at all of the guys surrounding my car and me and said, "Okay, we will have no problem marketing your stuff. All you have to do is pull up somewhere in this sexy beast and race it, and everyone will want to know what you are up to." We had a good laugh and agreed that was very likely true.

Even though we had a great weekend, I still felt like I was missing a piece of the puzzle. So back into incubation mode I went as I continued at my demanding day job and devoted my extra time to my kids and the veteran fundraisers. Unfortunately, a storm was brewing inside the business I was working in, and that was not something I expected or anticipated. As it was happening, I started to see that it would have a dramatic effect on my life, my racing, and my income. As the changes in my day job continued to unfold, I moved from one coast to the other and began doing some business consulting with the full knowledge of the owners at said day job. They supported me actually, likely a sign they knew what was coming. The consulting work had me in and out of Canada, and I was simultaneously doing a bit of work in the USA, as well, and marketing to drum up more business stateside.

While all this was taking place, two other things were happening: 1) I was volunteering at Camp Pendleton Marine Corp base, and 2) I had started a mastermind group based on the book, *The Science of Getting Rich,* by Wallace Wattles (I HIGHLY recommend that book to anyone and everyone!) and invited Amanda to join in the fun. It was part of my strategy to get my mindset straight.

It was during one of these meetings that it occurred to me: "Oh! The programs I have been wanting to put together should be for military folks! That is the primary market I am meant to serve!" No sooner did I say it when I notice that the vision board on my wall had a picture of a military guy on it. "Oh my heavens, ladies! You won't believe this! There is a military guy on my damn vision board! How did I not put this together before?" As the ladies fell out laughing, I marveled at the realization. I still didn't know all the details of how it was going to come to pass, but I knew with certainty that they were my primary market to serve.

That's how this transformational journey has worked for me. The more I push, the less the answers come; the more I take action in my life in general, the more what I am intended to do notifies me. I may have a basic idea, but what I think

will happen in the beginning is never what it ends up being.
I do however have to take action, so I can get feedback and
know what the next action is.

As I continued to fly in and out of Canada and work to
drum up more consulting work, an opportunity to buy a
house back in NC came up, and it was too good to ignore.
The timing could not have been worse, financially speaking,
but the deal couldn't be passed up. So, I screwed up ALL MY
COURAGE (and that of a few other people), and said yes to
the house. It freaked me out but also excited me. Immediately
following the signing of the contract for the lease to purchase
the house, my consulting gig in Canada abruptly ended. Now
I was in scramble mode... major scramble mode. As a single
person, there is no partner to catch me when things happen,
but that doesn't mean people don't. I have had more unseen
hands step in and help to get me from place to place, and I
am grateful for it. As the helping hands were extended to me,
I was kept afloat. Part of that gig was helping my dad move a
bunch of stuff from a shop building into storage with him, my
brother, and me as the workforce.

Little did I know that there was an important lesson
waiting for me.

Picture this. It was cold and dark at about 8pm on one of
the last couple days of December in North Carolina. We were
moving a big piece of machinery out of a shipping container,
and I heard a quiet voice inside of me say, "It's late. It's cold.
You're overtired. You really should go home and rest." But,
in the interest of helping my dad and showing solidarity with
my brother who had been working like a fiend, I pushed it
aside and kept working. I stepped back to guide my brother
out of the container as he drove the commercial size forklift
(telehandler). Tripping over something that had been set on

the ground behind me, my feet went out from under me and I fell hard. Really hard. I knew instantly that I had broken my wrist—not a small break, but a BAD break. I was right. It was so broken that it took a surgical procedure, a titanium plate, and eleven pins to put this humpty dumpty back together again. All because I ignored that voice and didn't take care of my own needs first.

Two days after surgery, I had an allergic reaction to the pain meds and had to be taken back to the hospital for help. My mom was in town at this time. She, by her own description, is more of a tough love mom than a warm and touchy-feely mom. Upon arriving at the hospital, we were told to take a seat in the waiting room and they would get to us. I'd like to point out here that I have a pretty high tolerance for pain and illness, as does my mom who was a nurse in a previous life; but on this occasion, my mom did not think I was okay; because I wasn't. She had a confab with the intake person and told her if anything happened to me as a result of being left sitting so long in the waiting room, they would all regret it. Sometimes a tough love mom is such a blessing! It took several IVs to flush out my system and restore me to health, but we got there.

Once we were back home, she decided I needed living room furniture immediately, not later after I had saved up for it. So, she and my rockstar daughter, who had helped me with every last thing the whole time my wrist was jacked up, went shopping to find a living room set up for me. More helping hands showed up and gave a million percent more than I would have ever asked for or expected. Just like the house itself, my job was to say yes to the support, even when it was uncomfortable to have others showing up for me.

You gotta love that The Universe was serving up two lessons at the same time: 1) Say NO to compromising my own needs, and 2) Say YES to receiving support. And, you know, the weeks of being able to do very little other than sit with my arm in the air and think really helped me to take these to heart.

Interwoven through all of this were convos with my friend, Amanda, getting support and encouragement in ways big and small. You know how sometimes it is hard to put into words the ways in which you are helped by someone— it's more of an overall sense that they have your back, they care, and you can rely on them? That's how I feel with her. During one of our *Science of Getting Rich* mastermind calls, I mentioned that the titanium that I now have in my wrist is a reminder to listen to my intuition and not get pulled off-course by the needs of others to the point that I end up compromised. We joked that my titanium plates were going to serve like Wonder Woman's magical cuffs, deflecting anything coming my way that would invite me to compromise myself.

With these lessons integrating in so many ways, I was finally ready to put all of the pieces together for my message and mission. The Universe had impeccable timing. I am convinced it goes ahead of us in time and space and plans in love, knowing when and what we will need so it can deliver it to us.

A prearranged visit was about to happen with one of my other nearest and dearest friends, Deidre, who was able to give Darling Daughter a break from my care. She also brought laughter, as always. As I told her about the daydreams unfolding while waiting for my wrist to heal, I relayed to her that I could not figure out all that I wanted to do for Military folks, but I knew I wanted to take them racing like I had for the fundraiser events. In particular, I wanted to take vets with PTSD. I mentioned I wasn't sure what other kind of programming to offer to serve them in conjunction with the racing but that maybe she could help me figure it out. She said the magical statement that was the final piece in figuring it out: "Don't complicate it. Just take them racing. Once you do, they will tell you what else, if anything, they need." And there it was. All along, I had been overcomplicating it. Me, the FUN-haver, was making it NOT fun by trying to make it be too much (and not in a good way).

Immediately, I realized, "You can't make this shit up." I had been 100% prepared for this mission. Part of my job at that company that I had raced for and represented was to organize and put on races and racing schools. So, the very program that I was about to embark on was something I already had expertise in from a previous position... and I was good at it. Really good at it. I had decades of practice implementing the Deming philosophy to set these massive events up in ways that were streamlined and easy for anyone to step into and support. Plus, I was still friends with all of the racers who had cars, who I was pretty sure would be up for supporting veterans. You really can't make this up.

Next and immediately came the question, "How will I come up with the money to do my first event?" Again, Deidre reminded me to keep it simple. She asked what was the minimum sum of money I would need to put on a "no frills" event. Without all the added niceties like swag bags, lunch, etc., what would it take to host it? I told her the number and as soon as I said it out loud, I knew the first event was already a reality. I just knew it.

A few weeks later, I got a call from my friend, Mari Sparkjoy, who I had met only twice via her husband Keith who I'd met at a Deming Conference towards the end of my tenure at the very busy day job previously mentioned. When we'd met, she had offered me an all-expenses-paid, ten-day trip to Alaska that she and Keith were unable to enjoy. Seems like a no-brainer, right? Well, sure, unless you're still feeling a little challenged when it comes to receiving. After being talked off the ledge about this generous gift by Amanda and a few friends, I decided to accept it and go. (Amanda, or little buddha as I think of her, knows just the right way to ask things to help us arrive at our own answers without putting any judgment or opinion on it.) That trip was the beginning of a beautiful and fun friendship with Mari. Emphasis on *fun*. She is definitely all about the fun!

So, when Mari called to check in on me after my wrist break, we somehow got onto the subject of this inspiration to help Veterans with PTSD via racing. Mari, a true possibility thinker, was very supportive of the idea and very positive that I should go out and do it. This all added fuel to the fire of wanting to do it and figure it out.

About a week later, I got another call from Mari. She explained that the Sparkjoy Foundation, their family foundation, would like to sponsor the first event in total. The whole day. Well, you could have knocked me over with a feather. I didn't even know what to do at first, other than the obvious of saying THANK YOU! (Have you noticed the YCMTSU part of this yet? The Sparkjoy Foundation sponsored the first event for an LLC that I'd created and named Spark of Ignition five years earlier, and is now Ponytail Racing LLC. Come on. You can't make it up!) That one event would turn into a series for which the Sparkjoy Foundation has been the primary financial backer for years now. They became a dream partner in this Racing for Warriors (RFW) initiative to reduce PTSD-related suicides by having fun in cars on racetracks.

As the leadup to the first event happened, there was a crew of other people who rallied to support what we were endeavoring to do: my brother and my dad, my friends (Brian Peacoe, Bret Voekel, Kyle Tucker, Ken Jarvis, and Nate Megginson), my sister-in-law Deb, and my darling daughter Andie.

As all the excitement and planning was happening for this first event, I had an appointment to go see the surgeon about my wrist. He had yet to see me since I had been doing rehab at his physical therapy clinic, and I got troubling news. Seeing very little movement in my wrist or fingers, he explained that I may be one of the "one in one million" who never regains use of the functioning fingers and hand movement. Grief, fear, and rage flowed through my veins as I wondered about the impact of all of this on my plan to give back to Veterans via racing my car.

When I left the appointment, I called Amanda, who reminded me that it was okay to feel whatever I was feeling and that I was the one who got to decide what happened next for me.

Over the next ninety days, I channeled all that rage into physical therapy and getting better. *No one* was going to tell me my hand would never work again. *No one.* I was lucky to have a physical therapist who agreed with me and pushed me hard and helped me regain 100% use of my fingers, hand, and wrist so that I could be in tip top shape for these veterans at our first event.

As the big day approached, I was thrilled with how the pieces were coming together, and I was giving regular updates to the Sparkjoys about how it was unfolding. The stories I was hearing from charities, military folks, and veterans' families and friends about the need for support were both touching and motivating. One day out of the blue, I received a text from Mari that asked if I thought I could do one event a month for the next year. I responded that I thought twelve was possible, but ten was definitely doable. A couple weeks later, she called and told me not only did The Sparkjoy Foundation want to fund the first event, they wanted to fund the first year of events!

Yeah, The Universe is amazing like that. In one instant, everything can change.

I was excited, inspired, and exceptionally grateful that they had caught the bug with me. As the planning continued, I reached out to Tarheels Sports Car Club; and they donated their time and course setup, equipment use, and, above all, their friendship and commitment to the Veterans. To this day, I get choked up thinking about all the people who joined this movement *before one race car hit the track.*

The first event was a beautiful crazy day. We had a great turn out of Veterans, volunteers, and racers. There were bumps along the way as well. The thing about events is people only know what they got; they don't know what we intended to give, so bumps will happen and our job is to keep rolling. There was so much connection and joy in the eyes of everyone at the event, the laughter was amazing, and the teasing and joking was terrific. By the end of the day, I realized we had formed a family of sorts.

Many spouses searched me out before they left to thank me for creating an event that their partner wanted to leave the house to attend—that many had not stayed at any event more than thirty minutes and yet lasted all day at ours. I let the tears fall as the gratitude passed between us.

The tears I did not expect were those of the racers who thanked me for letting them be involved and told me they wanted to come back regularly. Even the workers we hired from the track thanked me and specifically asked us to request them for future events. Many set their schedule around our events.

And now, two years in, most of those same people help us with every event, so it makes for a fun day. Everyone knows their tasks and, most importantly, the spirit of the event. Anyone that comes to support our events MUST have an attitude to serve and make it about the Veterans, not themselves. We are creating a love bubble and anyone who can't do that, can't come back to help. Essentially the idea is "don't be an asshote." LOL!

My racing friends come from near and far to serve the heroic people who have served all of us, who have sacrificed and put their lives on the line. At every event, we hear stories from the Veterans. We don't ask them about it because we don't want to pry and we are ALL ABOUT THE FUN! But at every event, they tell us about the ways in which they have coped, the scars they carry, the losses they've suffered, and the people they miss. It's our great honor to listen. In the interest of protecting those sharings, I won't go into detail about them because it's not my place to do so... but just know that many people have suffered, that we may all be free in our country of birth or migration, and that the honor and dignity that many of these bear their heavy burdens is remarkable. The one piece of information I do feel I can say is that PTSD takes lives and we endeavor to be a buffer between life and death and we do it simply by showing up, caring, and mixing it with a little octane and laughter. We are many, many events in, and this racing series is still teaching me how it helps with suicide, depressions, sex trauma, anxiety, fear, and many other things. That's how I know it's not mine; it was meant to be created, and the Sparkjoys and I happen to be the people blessed to bring our brand of motorsports therapy to the brave and weary souls who need it.

It's funny, right? The whole time I was incubating this idea, the program itself was the easy part and existed on day one. But it was delayed because I had to get myself ready to honor my own needs, let go of everything I thought it *had* to be and do, let it be the simple thing it is, and receive support before it could all come together outside of me. It really wasn't difficult to create the program, but none of it would have happened without the love and support of my family and friends for many years as I rewired myself as a person… with the help of many. No journey of creation or transformation happens without taking some lumps, having some hard times, and surviving some failures.

Here we are a couple years into the program and it is the same simple FUN racing event that was hatched while I was rehabbing from a broken wrist, but that had been seeded years before when I gave rides in exchange for donations. That weekend in 2013, the name Ponytail Racing, the market I was to serve, and the method of service were all given to me, but *I wasn't ready to see it.* I personally had to go racing for several years and rewire my own brain, heart, and soul from the significant trauma I suffered as a young child— and the disassociation that had helped me survive but also separated me from my passions and prevented me from including them in all of the work I did in the world until now—so that I could do it for others. Essentially, I had to use racing to heal myself before I could use it to serve others. How much more lucky could I be?

And since creators need to be involved in new things, I am adding to the way I can serve Veterans and others. Let me start by saying when working with friends and family, boundaries are key to being able to do it. We have to be able to speak for ourselves and also to find a way to stay grounded when the storms come, and they WILL come. I find writing in the morning, meditation and getting physical activity is key for managing things. Back to the product we are working on now... What would you say If I told you we have created a company that could build a house with no wood (other than kitchen cabinets), no nails (not 3D printed), and we could complete one house every eight-hour shift that is elegant, energy efficient, environmentally responsible, and also economical for developers to get at high volume to serve Veterans and other underserved markets? Would you say I am lucky to be involved?

It's funny how it came to be and how the lessons I learned from the journey to Racing for Warriors made this process a bit easier. We have a friend in the racing community who regularly calls to chat and talk racing and business. One day, he told me about this guy who is making weird houses and wondered if we wanted to learn about it. I suggested he call my dad and the craziest thing happened. Through the course of the conversation, my dad realized that it is his (OUR) cousin Larry that is the inventor. He hadn't seen him in about sixty years. SIXTY! So, my dad and Larry caught up on all the years of family info and then talked about the houses. Inspired, my dad called me and said, "Let's see if we can give a little help and support to get him launched." We had no intention of getting involved—only in helping him. As we began to help him, it became obvious that it would be fun and good to all work together—that his innovation could benefit from our expertise in manufacturing and production and vice versa. Can you imagine a sixty-year separation, at the end of which everyone's life experience comes together to offer a solution to a national crisis of workforce housing? I mean, you really cannot make this stuff up.

Amanda's Side of the Story

I shook my head in awe as I reviewed all of the posters and post-it grids that hung on the walls of the apartment Cheryl had rented for this retreat. Business growth. Systems development. Transformation. Recovery.

This woman is such a badass. So much to offer. And these grids don't even capture her own story or the skills she brings to these offerings.

I'd met Cheryl in a facilitator training for a teen life skills program almost a decade before this retreat; and I'd marveled at how quickly she'd succeeded, especially when it came to the business side of it. Every time I volunteered for one of her workshops, I watched her surprise our master facilitators with her amazing instincts and powerful communication in the room. I'll never forget watching her lovingly support (read: reprimand) the adults in the room who were obviously the ones creating lack of safety for the youth.

As we developed a friendship, I realized what a deep well of experience and wisdom this woman is. Beyond her business prowess and her facilitator chops, she is a true seeker, a faithful friend, and a devoted daughter. She is also an incredible mother who has protected, defended, and walked alongside her children through some excruciating traumas and transitions.

There was no coincidence that she was in the same retreat as my sister. Not only did her personal experience help Ciara to see what I couldn't have, but I rested knowing that she could and would (and did) easily help when my big sister feelings became too much to manage as a facilitator. When she showed up for my first 3-day Dare to Yes event and offered to support with logistics, it was easy for me to let go of all of those details and focus on facilitating.

This woman knows how to design, plan, execute, and facilitate an experience like no one else I know. I would LOVE to see her in action with CEOs! I thought as I took in the details on the business development grid. *There's got to be a way to pull all of this together and make it fun.*

"Cheryl, what do you think about laying these business principles and transformation alongside your love of racing? Like a race track..." Sometimes what comes out of my mouth surprises even me. Her eyes glistened with curiosity and she leaned in. "I mean, do you see any obvious parallels between the mindset, systems, processes, and experience of a racer and a CEO?"

That was it. I spent the next several hours belly laughing and crying as Cheryl told me story after story of "lessons learned on the race track." The glove compartment. The car catching on fire. The spin-out through the turn. Even with a little enterprise, I could relate experiences in my business growth to the emotionally-charged and fun stories she was sharing.

The race track laid out pretty quickly, and we talked about the possibility of her focusing on CEOs who loved racing. Of course, that was confirmed the day we took her sexy ride to the track and watched everyone's heads explode a little as they witnessed Cheryl's knowledge and ability on and off the track.

Yes, the racing is definitely where this is at for her. It lights her up and magnetizes people to her.

I was surprised when that level of integration didn't quickly propel her message and work forward, but we stayed in conversation about all of it in our *Science of Getting Rich* masterminds. I'll never forget the moment we both realized that the veterans were not only the missing piece of the message puzzle, but that she had given herself the answer years before by putting one on her vision board. You cannot make this shit up.

After that, it was all magic. The sponsor with the name so similar to the LLC she'd created. The resources and donations. The other drivers who offered their time and talent. The veterans.

When she called me after the first event, we both cried.

If I could only choose one lesson I've learned over and over again since the beginning of this journey, it's that transformation, healing, and integration do not happen as a result of what we *do*. It is the result of our *being*—our embodiment of the principles and lessons we seek to share with the world. When we *become* a safe place for others, their bodies, minds, and souls can do what they already know how to do... heal, integrate, and savor life again. So, instead of facilitating rooms full of individuals and showing them how to build epic enterprises, she's building the epic enterprises that are meeting needs and creating physical and emotional spaces where people can heal and thrive. And when a CEO wants to learn from her, they get to learn through the experience she's created. It's the same recipe: break frame from the routine, experience a safe space with people who care, answer the questions that come, and add a little fun.

That's what Racing for Warriors has proven to the two of us, beyond a shadow of a doubt; and I believe that is the direct result of all the work Cheryl has done to *become* a safe place for others with the empathy, compassion, and incredible sense of humor that helps others lighten their heavy loads.

My Co-author wrote Cheryl—her message, her expertise, and her friendship—into my life so that I could learn how to be a mother, friend, facilitator, and business woman.

Now, for that book writing retreat in Bali!

Dr. Rev. Ahmondra McClendon is an Ordained Progressive Christian and Interfaith and minister. Through her Multi-faith Diversity Educational program, she empowers individuals to reach across the table and engage in constructive dialogues. Rev. Ahmondra is a demonstration of "Passionate Living" in action, and she motivates others to contemplate the deeper issues of life and get into action. She believes every woman can live a life she loves and love the life she lives. Embracing her dream of creating healthy living environments for women, she developed *The Butterfly Way,* a program that teaches women to transform pain and suffering into life-affirming transitions.

"That's So Sad!"

Ahmondra McClendon

When I saw a friend at the grocery store who I hadn't seen in a while, she asked how I'd been and what I'd been up to. Twenty minutes later, my sweet friend pulled her jaw off the ground and exclaimed in the middle of the produce department, "Dang, Girl! Your life sounds like a country western song! Where the singer lost his job, his home, his woman, his truck, and his dog all in a week."

I stared at her in disbelief. *She isn't going to tell me how sad my story is?* But then a realization hit me, and I burst out laughing. *She is right. The past year of events does sound like the lyrics to a country-western song.*

We finished our conversation and I finished up my shopping trip, shaking my head and murmuring to myself about everything that had happened since I'd taken on this project.

I'd had the bright idea to write a book and create a program called *The Gift of Transitions*, teaching women techniques for managing difficult transitions along life's journey. I wanted to show them they had the power to face anything and still create whatever they wanted in life. Just because stuff happened doesn't mean we have to stop realizing our dreams. It is possible to have it all. After all, we can create a whole human being as we go about living our life!!

I was confident in teaching this lesson because I had successfully managed difficult transitions. It was possible to move forward, even in the face of no agreement. I had "life" proof that the impossible was indeed possible. I wanted to share this message with my Sisters. I was an expert in this area and had experienced the transitions to prove it.

By the time I arrived at Amanda's big event to launch the book, I was an Ordained Interfaith Minister who had spent the last year using my gift to help others through terrible transitions. I wanted to share with the audience how important it was to have the awareness and tools to navigate through life's transitions, especially after the year I'd just had.

I stood in the back of a packed room, listening to the speaker on stage, trying to figure out how to share my experiences with transitions in five minutes. *Seriously! Five minutes? Who came up with that crazy time restriction?* I heard my music and realized it was showtime.

I stepped onto the stage.

"Good evening, everybody. I'm Reverend Ahmondra, and I need your support tonight. I'm going to share a story about transitions, and when I point to you, please respond with this phrase: 'That's So Sad.' Let's practice on the count of three, say, 'That's So Sad.'"

The audience responded and I started my story.

"In 2012, I was living my best life. I was writing a book, enrolled in One Spirit seminary, delivering transformational workshops to women and teens, and I could see the pacific ocean from my living room. That all changed with one phone call. My niece in Bermuda called to inform me her sister, who was studying in England, had taken sick and was dying.

"OH, THAT'S SO SAD!" The audience responded to my pointing at them.

"I immediately booked a flight to England, and upon arrival, took a three-hour bus ride to the hospital. I took one look at my niece and knew I needed to get her home so she could make her transition surrounded by family and friends."

"OH. THAT'S SO SAD!" Their voices were full of empathy.

"For the next three weeks, I did my seminary work and helped her get strong enough to leave the hospital. She returned to Bermuda, and I flew back to California, knowing I might not see her again in this life."

"THAT'S SO SAD!" The voices softened even more.

"When I arrived in California, I breathed a sigh of relief, but the phone rang, and it was my aunt in Bermuda saying my Uncle was in the hospital and dying."

"OH, THAT'S SO SAD!" Now, audience members looked at each other in astonishment.

"I hopped a plane to Bermuda. I found my dying niece on one wing of the hospital, and my dying Uncle on the other wing."

"OH, THAT'S SO SAD!" The looks on their faces told me they were wondering if they should still be saying this... like these words didn't quite capture the gravity of the story I was sharing.

"I stayed until they made their transitions and then flew back to California. Before I could even unpack, my stepmother called to say my father had died and, if I wanted to attend the funeral, I had three days to get to New Orleans. (This was Thanksgiving week.)"

"OH, THAT'S SO SAD!" Their voices fell to an almost-whisper, full of disbelief.

"I flew to New Orleans and arrived just in time to attend my father's funeral. I arrived back in California on Thanksgiving eve. I remember walking out of the airport, seeing people hugging, and being so happy because relatives were coming for a holiday. I stood on the curb feeling completely alone."

"OH, THAT'S SO SAD!" Now, it was a whisper.

"When I arrived home, there was a letter on my door from the landlord saying they were moving to Oklahoma, and I had thirty days to vacate my apartment."

"OH, THAT'S SO SAD!" Now, there was a tinge of indignance in the unified voice.

"That Sunday, I went to church, my place of refuge. The minister announced she was closing the church and moving out of the state."

"OH, THAT'S SO SAD!" And then someone added, "NO, that SUCKS!!"

"Oh, and my boyfriend of ten years also left me, but that was a GOOD THING!"

The audience laughed with me.

I know it seems hard to imagine that I could survive a year of such intense transitions, but Spirit had prepared me with a whole lifetime of "You Can't Make This Up" moments of transition and helped me develop an approach to creating a "Flight Plan for Life" that I was ready to share with others. With every dream, disappointment, and detour, I had the opportunity to reconnect with Spirit and reclaim parts of myself that had been diminished, devalued, and derailed throughout my tumultuous childhood and young adulthood.

In 1980, I opened the Top Drop infant care center after two years of dreaming about an infant in-home childcare facility.

I'd held my vision and, at every turn, faced opposition; but I moved through those oppositions.

At the time, I was married, childless, and had a great job making a fairly decent wage. Our home was big enough, and my passion was big enough. Every day at work, I would design my childcare center—what it looked like and who was there—and research what I needed to do. Paperwork. Home modifications. TB tests. Applications. The in-home inspection and interview.

I was at work when I got the call and the answer I didn't expect, "You have met all of the qualifications; however, I don't believe that you're going to run this childcare center. I don't believe a young woman with a good job will leave and run a childcare center. I think that you are going to have somebody else run this childcare center while you keep your job, and therefore I am not going to give you a license."

With one personal opinion and one stroke of a pen, this woman had utterly crushed my dream. I didn't know what to do. I didn't appeal it because I didn't know that I could, but I didn't let my dream go. I held onto it deep within my heart until the day a coworker showed me an article about a new program that was starting to help people get licensed to start businesses to take care of children. The program was perfect. It was comprehensive and provided everything needed to open and run a successful childcare business; however, it required six-month full-time attendance. You could not hold a job and attend the program that only offered a small stipend.

I had a decision to make. I had to leave my job to attend this six-month training course. I had no idea how I would do this, but I was determined that I could.

I answered every objection from my husband and assured him I could make it work and my work granted me a year's leave, but the financial pressures began immediately.

But I had faith and prayed... a lot. There were days when I didn't have gas in my car. I would say a prayer, and in the mailbox, I would find a check for five dollars—just enough money to get gas to attend the class for a few days. Friends helped when I didn't have enough money for food.

Every single day I walked in F.A.I.T.H. (forging ahead into the hinterlands, a place of unknown origins). Walking in F.A.I.T.H. (finding answers in the heart) meant going within for guidance and motivation. Those closest to me didn't offer support. My father said my business wasn't going to be lucrative and my husband discouraged me and pushed me to return to work, even though I kept up my end of our agreement.

I remained steadfast and refused to release my dream, managing whatever opposition came my way. At the end of six months, I transitioned from being an employee to being the owner of a licensed family daycare business. From day one, my business thrived, but three years after opening my infant care center, my marriage fell apart.

The night I watched my husband of ten years walk down the steps and out of my life forever, I was relieved and overcome with sadness all at the same time. I sat at the top of the steps with my head in my hands, crying. I cried because I had married as a way to escape the debilitating grief I felt after an unidentified assailant murdered my best friend. A grief that had distorted my reasoning, causing me to marry a man I didn't love.

I cried because I was an abused woman and didn't even realize it. I cried for the three babies I had lost. I cried for the demise of the secure, positive, motivated woman who had given up her hopes and dreams. I cried for the loss of my voice and the twinkle in my eye. I cried for the adultery I had committed to prove to myself I was a desirable woman. I cried for those who would be horrified to hear that we were not the perfect couple after all. I cried for the years I'd lost living in an unhappy marriage. I sobbed uncontrollably because I didn't know what I was going to do. I had no idea how I would accomplish what I thought was impossible— building a new life as a free single woman.

With each tear that fell, so did one of the invisible bars that held me captive in my invisible prison. My tears watered the soil of my new garden of life. It was time to dismantle the foundation of the pain of my current life. The desire for change ignited my transition from imprisoned woman to free woman.

When I found myself a divorcee after ten years of marriage, I was terrified. This was new territory, and if I was going to make it, I needed to return to college and earn my degree. I had walked around in life for ten years feeling like a failure because I dropped out of college after three years. Without the money to complete college, I had just walked away.

It wasn't easy to come back and complete this dream, and I was confronted with the monumental task of facing the consequences of how I had left college in my twenties. Because I didn't withdraw from any classes, or discuss it with anybody, all of the classes I had walked out of had converted into Fs. I had to find those professors that had given me those F's and see if I could get them changed to incompletes. It didn't seem possible, but by the grace of God, I found all the help I needed and was able to enroll with a clean slate.

Then, I cleared the next barrier of getting my junior college classes accepted.

After clearing my record and getting old classes converted, I was looking to complete three years of college. And so I buckled down and went to work. I was the most senior student in all my classes, which bothered me at first as I listened to the internal voice that said, "I can't do this. I am too old, and they are younger than me and brighter than me." Then, one day, I looked at myself in the mirror and said, "If you keep saying you can't do this, you won't do this. Now you can do this, and you will do this."

After creating that new affirmation and stepping 100% totally into this New World, I not only excelled, but I earned a scholarship from my department of Consumer Family Studies Dietetics and graduated Summa cum laude. The day I graduated and walked across the stage was the day I transitioned from being a college dropout to a college graduate.

Although I was transitioning into a new life, I still faced a transition I didn't even realize I needed to make.

I felt incomplete, even after reaching my lifelong dream of graduating from college. That major accomplishment didn't even touch the empty feeling I had within. I had no idea that I was experiencing a lack of connection to my God-self.

Unbeknownst to me, that connection was hidden under my drug addiction. One night in sheer desperation and depression, I asked God to take control of my life and use it in service to children. I also apologized to God, saying, "Lord, I'm sorry, I am going to keep using drugs because I don't know how to stop." I had tried to stop using drugs and alcohol (daily) many times but couldn't. I was what you call a functioning drug addict /alcoholic. I could function in the world, which kept me from believing I had a problem.

On the outside, my life looked amazing. I was a college graduate, single, and had a great job as the head teacher in a sizable day-care facility. I was financially stable and had just been accepted into the Master of Social Work program at San Francisco State University. I didn't know it, but the prayer I uttered that night was really a plea to God to help me transition from active addiction to recovery.

They say God has a sense of humor, and that is absolutely correct. I heard about a fantastic program that trained volunteers to provide drug/alcohol prevention classes to elementary school children. I signed into the program and completed over 50 hours of drug and alcohol training. (You would think after all that education, I'd get a clue about my addiction, NOT!) My addiction would do anything to stay active, and so it prevented me from seeing the truth: I had a problem. And so, I started volunteering in elementary schools, teaching children about drugs and alcohol.

When I didn't get the lesson out of that training, God had a contingency plan and upped the ante. I was hired as the director of alcohol prevention for elementary schools in the city and County of San Francisco.

As the director of this citywide program, I was deeply involved in meetings about drug and alcohol prevention programs in the city. One evening while attending a community meeting, I heard the Priest at a local Catholic Church announce they held narcotics anonymous meetings every Friday night and that anyone who had a drug addiction or knew of anyone with a drug addiction could attend. I made a mental note to attend that meeting to find out what resources were available for drug addicts... just in case I came across someone with a problem!!

The following Friday night, I attended that Narcotics Anonymous meeting. In an hour, the veil of addiction was pushed aside, and I found myself up close and personal with my addiction.

To my astonishment, I heard words that identified precisely how I felt and what was going on with me. I was a woman whose life was controlled by drugs and alcohol. I was suffering from the disease of addiction. Although there was no known cure for this disease, it could be arrested. Those suffering could go into recovery, get relief from active addiction, and live a life free of drugs and alcohol.

I wish I could say that I was totally and utterly elated because I finally had discovered what was wrong with me. I now knew why I had to use a substance every single day to feel normal. I had been using drugs and alcohol daily for twenty-two years, and I couldn't say when my usage had crossed that invisible line from social use to addiction. All I knew is that to cope with life, I put something in my body every day. I didn't use to get high; I used drugs to function.

This new knowledge devastated me. I had held the same beliefs about drug addicts and alcoholics that many people did. They were weak-minded people and losers. I was so ashamed that I was one of those people. I hung my head as I introduced myself as a drug addict/ alcoholic. To my astonishment, those six people sitting around the table applauded me, smiled at me, and welcomed me. At that moment, my transition from active addiction to recovery started. I saw a pathway back to normalcy for the first time in my adult life,

In 1994, I found myself feeling disheartened and depressed. I'd accomplished much in life. I'd ended an abusive marriage, returned to college, and earned a bachelor's and master's degree while recovering from a drug addiction. I had my dream job of working with children and families at the department of social services in San Francisco. I lived in a beautiful loft apartment, had a new car, traveled, and had many friends who loved me.

Yet, I found myself asking, "Is this all there is to life?" Something was missing, and I didn't know what. After sharing my situation with a good friend, he invited me to a meeting at Landmark Education. I walked into a large room with about 100 smiling individuals and was immediately suspicious because 95% of these individuals were white. A room full of smiling white people made me nervous. Why did they look so happy, and what did they want from me?

The moderator for the smaller group of new people started talking about living life in a new way. It appeared that this group of people was engaged in a program that helped them step out of their comfort zone into a bigger world. They lived life not from what they knew but from possibility. I was so impressed I signed up for something called the Landmark Forum, and in three days, I took an in-depth look at my life. I discovered my life was limitless. I had made up stories which placed limits on my options. I learned I had the power to create a new life story that had no limits attached. I could see a possibility and then step into that possibility and have it happen.

After the Landmark Forum, I registered for a free eight-week seminar. One night, a gentleman stood up and announced a group was traveling to Washington, D.C. to see President Nelson Mandela receive the yearly Hunger Project

Award. Without thinking, my hand immediately shot up, and I heard myself saying, "I want to go." I saw a possibility. Although the voice in my head was screaming, "You can't go to an event like that."

Two weeks later, I'd acquired $500 in gifts from friends who were simply responding to my excitement, gotten time off from work, secured lodging in D.C and was sitting in a room with Nelson Mandela. Determined to live my new story of unlimited possibilities, I set my intention to shake this man's hand; and I did. When I shook the hand of my hero, I realized nothing was impossible in life; it was all about living from Possibility.

After working for ten years as a child welfare worker, I saw a new possibility for myself. I decided I wanted to be a professional speaker. I was blessed with the gift of gab and felt very comfortable speaking in large groups. I would tell people all the time, "I am going to travel the world and run my mouth."

That idea turned into an intention—one I was going to manifest. I researched and discovered I could take early retirement from my position and maintain my health coverage for life. It didn't matter that I wouldn't receive full retirement benefits because I would make money as a professional speaker.

As I made preparations to retire, I refused to listen to the naysayers who said this was a terrible idea and composed my retirement letter. I took the letter and put it in my desk drawer. Each day, I agonized over whether to submit the letter to Human Resources. I would go home with the letter still sitting in my desk drawer. What was I afraid of?

On one particular day, I found myself staring at the closed desk drawer, knowing what was inside. In frustration,

I blurted out a prayer for help. "Lord, send me a sign that this is the right thing to do because I am too afraid to move forward." All of a sudden, I looked up, and a coworker was standing right at my desk. I was so intently staring down that I didn't see her walk up to me. This particular coworker was a woman of God. We called her The Prayer Warrior.

After she listened to me share about my desire to travel and speak and help people find their path in life, she said to me, "No one can take your blessings from you, but you can give them away. If God has directed you to retire from this job, you need to go ahead and do that. He already has a door ready to open for you to step through, so go ahead and move forward in faith. Let your heart be your guide."

The next day, I took that retirement letter and turned it in. After leaving human resources, I checked my voicemails and discovered a message from a good friend saying, "I am working for the organization monster.com, and they are organizing a county-wide speaking tour for college students. They are looking for motivational speakers, and I submitted your name. I remember you saying you wanted to be a professional speaker. Give me a call because the tour is going to start in three months."

It was no coincidence that my official end date was in three months. I just smiled and shook my head and said, "Okay, God, I got it."

In three months, I found myself standing on stage with seasoned professional motivational speakers. In eight weeks, I traveled to five states and spoke to over 3500 students. I had transitioned from a professional social worker to a professional motivational speaker. I did it all by standing in a possibility!

My life was running smoothly until my mother was diagnosed with cancer and given less than a year to live. I was facilitating transformation courses with a company based in the United States but did work in Asia, and I'd been traveling back-and-forth steadily to Singapore and Malaysia for three years. It was my dream position because I was traveling and running my mouth, but it had also started to take a toll on my physical body. I was making that seventeen-hour flight once a month, and it was time to do something else. I wanted to write, but I had no idea of how to become a published author and sustain myself at the same time. I didn't even know how to create the space or the time I needed to write.

After my mom's diagnosis, I did the only natural thing I knew to do: I packed up her house, moved her in with me, and terminated my contract with the company. All of a sudden, I had the time to write and be with my mom. To me, that was a blessing, but then an even bigger blessing showed up.

I received an email from a professional women's network asking for manuscripts. They were looking for women to write chapters in the collaborative book series they were getting ready to publish. I signed up, and over the next year, I authored chapters in six books. When my mom made her transition, I also made a transition. I went from traveling and running my mouth, to staying in place and running my fingers over a keyboard. I transitioned from a professional motivational speaker to a published author, with stories in *Chicken Soup for the African American Soul.*

Excited to experience more of the "Wow, your story changed my life!" feedback, I was thrilled when Spirit inspired me to write *Baby Snatchers,* a fictionalized retelling of my experience as a social worker to expose the underbelly of a system intended to help children. I laughed and cried as I wrote the book, realizing that it was helping me heal my internalized pain and rejuvenate my energy. Eventually, I met a young woman in a transformational community named Amanda and when she told me she was an editor, I reached out for help to get the book ready for publication. She helped me refine and expand characters and plot lines to achieve my true intention, and then I told Spirit I was ready for a publisher.

Spirit had other plans. The publication of the book wasn't the end goal; the writing of it was. When the time is right, I know *Baby Snatchers* will be released into the world.

It was just a few years later that a friend of mine and I started to talk about working together to support women through transformation and the inspiration for *The Gifts of Transitions* sparked.

I really thought I knew what life was going to look like when I finished this incredible book on transitions; and yet when it was done, I looked up and realized life had taken an unexpected turn. Even though we may have a clear view of where we are heading, it's not uncommon to encounter changes along the way.

When pilots begin a flight, they file detailed flight plans. They know exactly when to take off, what altitude they must reach, what turns to make, and the direction to fly in. But sometimes they may need to make adjustments during the flight. Depending on the circumstances, a layover may be added before reaching their final destination. They may need to refuel the plane, drop off or pick up new passengers, make a repair, or wait out a major weather change. The pilot will reach the final destination in spite of unplanned layovers.

Making layovers (planned and unplanned) is an important aspect of life's journey. Layovers allow us to heal from past experiences, expand knowledge, and receive guidance from Spirit. Even though at times it appears like we've abandoned our dreams, we haven't.

As you have just witnessed, along my life's journey, I have experienced many planned and unplanned layovers and how each one has moved me closer to my final destination. But what is that final destination?

After the painful ending of my business partnership and the dissolution of the business, I made a brief layover in order to pivot and embrace the new transition from partnership to sole proprietor. My work with women facing transitions wasn't over; only my delivery method changed.

When I find myself asking, "What's next for me?", I follow the seven-step "Flight Plan for Life" program I developed for my clients. I begin with a personal inquiry: Where am I heading? Or more importantly, where do I dream of going?

Shortly after I began regrouping professionally, I realized I had outgrown my days of singlehood and dreamed of being in a long-term, committed, monogamous relationship.

After identifying what direction I was heading in, toward a life partner and a business devoted to women's wellbeing, I was ready to create a plan of action.

I made plans so when the pathway appeared, I would be ready to move. I created a physical space in my world for my new man. I purchased a pair of slippers and put them under my bed and cleared out a dresser drawer. When he showed up, his space would already be there. I also needed a plan to vet any potential partner, so I developed a job application for a compassionate companion. All job positions come with applications. Why not have an application for the person you want to fill the position of life partner?

Now that I had identified where I wanted to go and put a plan of action in place, I needed to pack for my journey. Part of the "packing" process for me—deciding what I was taking with me and what I was leaving behind as I pursued my new dreams—I needed to remove the man who was currently occupying my suitcase. His presence was taking up space I needed for my future man. So, I packed my bags with new ideas and attitudes about relationships, and left plenty of empty space.

Having my destination, my plan, and my luggage packed, I needed a force to propel me forward on my journey.

My motivation came in the form of a document that had thirty-four characteristics of my perfect partner. I taped it to my desk so each day, I would see it. Every time I focused on it, I would imagine having someone with those qualities in my life. I would see us dancing together and taking trips together; and the joy that filled my heart motivated me and sustained me as I moved toward my dream.

To help me stay emotionally involved and motivated while waiting for my perfect partner, I purchased a journal and wrote letters to him. Writing in the journal gave me H.O.P.E. (Having Optimistic Perspective Every day).

When I started to have fear about starting a new relationship, I confided in someone who was in a long-term marriage. Her advice proved to be invaluable, helping me move through my apprehension.

Although I panicked when my new boyfriend proposed a ten-day visit so we could get acquainted, I accepted his request. I understood my initial reaction was based in the fear of the unknown. I also realized my happiness was based on the acceptance of the unknown. The day he arrived was four years to the day that I had started the journal. THAT'S NO coincidence!! That's God! You can't make that st*ry up!

And after working for three years to earn my Doctorate of Ministry, I was on my way to launching a new Multi-faith Diversity program when I found myself on another layover writing *The Uncrowned Queen Regains Her Throne*, a book which offered me the opportunity to expose the buried pain that was expressed in the world as an Angry Black woman.

To my surprise (Why am I still surprised?), when *The Uncrowned Queen* manuscript was complete, Spirit directed me to put it aside and remain on my layover. It wasn't time to take off.

During times like this, I call on Psalm 32:8, "I will instruct you and show you the way to go; I will counsel you with my eye on you." God's counsel was clear, and when my dear friend, Amanda, showed up with her new collaborative project, I was ready to take off and continue my journey.

Today, I am in flight toward a new destination/dream, publishing a book, *Thank You for Loving Me Through My Crazy: How to Manifest Your Perfect Partner*! I will transition from writer to Best Selling Author.

Should be easier because I'm so good at transitions, right? LOL

Amanda's Side of the Story

For months before Ahmondra took the stage and took the audience on the "That's So Sad" journey, I was the one whispering those words to myself after every text, email, and phone call that relayed the next crisis emerging as we worked to finalize her manuscript and move it through production. All I could offer was sympathy and the assurance that I would continue doing my part while she was away taking care of a loved one or handling some other business that needed her attention.

I cannot even imagine, I thought to myself one day as I hung up the phone after one of these chats. *So much grief.*

Staring past my computer screen and out the small window at the top of my basement-level office, I breathed into the heavy ache in my chest and let some more of the tears that were always right there fall. *I cannot imagine feeling this type of loss for more than one person at a time.*

Just a few short months before Ahmondra had reached out to ask for support with her book, one of the most important relationships in my life to that point had ended... abruptly and painfully. It wasn't a physical death, but it was a death—of a relationship and of an extremely important part of my life. The loss rippled into every corner of my life, causing me to second-guess my instincts, my inspiration, and my intuition.

It was a painful lesson that was absolutely necessary for my growth as a woman, a friend, and a CEO. But hot damn... it still hurts. I miss them. I regret not handling it with more grace.

I let the tears stream down my face and make space for the tiniest bit of insight and grace to make its way to the surface.

Of course Ahmondra is here right now. The Wind knew I needed her as much as she needed my expertise.

My mind traveled back through the many moments this woman's presence had challenged me, supported me, and nurtured me through some of my own painful transitions.

The transition from my head to my heart was excruciating. I walked into that facilitator training program certain that I would be able to achieve and excel the way I had in all of my academic efforts, but quickly realized it required an intelligence that was underdeveloped in me.

"Amanda, you already said this was the person you need to call to make amends. Don't back down from this and call someone else. Make the phone call. I'll stand right next to you."

I've never known someone who can call me out and kick my ass into gear with so much love.

The transition from participant to facilitator was windy and long. She always jumped in at the perfect moment to save the room before I lost everyone with my robotic recitation of the curriculum or, worse, by exposing a still-oozing wound in a story.

"Amanda, I'm going to take the next lesson and I'd like you to pay attention to the details I'm sharing. We'll talk about *why* I chose this story and these details when we debrief. Why don't you partner with...?"

With nothing but love and wisdom, and oh so much patience, she would allow me to step back into the room as a participant and do the next bit of work necessary to heal my heart so I could hold the front of the room without her someday.

The transition from disconnected distrust to vulnerable receiving was real. There was at least one part of me regularly "acting up, pushing buttons, writing awful emails and 'accidentally' sending them to the whole team," or worse.

"Amanda, we see you. We know your heart. You're going to be a powerful facilitator. Just stay and do the work." Ahmondra didn't give up on me, even though I was ready to do so myself many times.

It wasn't until we did a particular exercise that I finally saw past my own stuff and saw Ahmondra for who she was, and is, in my life. Imagine two long lines of people facing each other, forming a path of sorts for someone to walk through. Then imagine someone willingly closing their eyes and allowing the people who are forming the path to guide them with their hands and their voices, whispering words of affirmation along the way. A journey of fifty steps that feels like a million because you cannot see where you are going, how long it will take to get there, or even the people who have been placed alongside you to support you. It was the perfect mirror for the training program that I was finally completing, and I wept tears of gratitude all along those million (or fifty) steps. And at the end of the path, someone was there to welcome me home to myself with the warmest hug.

When I heard her voice whisper words of affirmation and pride in my ear, I knew: *She is my spiritual mother. This woman has labored alongside me for three years, knowing and believing in me when I couldn't, guiding and challenging me when I was lost, loving me in some of my most unlovable moments.*

The transition from mentee to coach was fun (and only a little painful) because of her. When she contacted me for help with her *Baby Snatchers* manuscript, I got a deeper look into the circumstances that had helped my mentor build her resilience and I loved every second of it. The first draft was so engaging that I lost track of time while I was reading it... on a treadmill... for four hours. Yeah, I didn't walk right for a few days, but we had a lot of fun talking about these characters and making the story even more powerful and engaging.

The transition to respected colleague was truly overwhelming. She and her business partner spent a few hours during the Monetize Your Message retreat, coaching my clients the way they had coached me while I sat on the couch breathing through the gratitude exploding in my chest and let the tears fall. And when Ahmondra showed up to participate in one of my Dare to YES retreats, I watched in awe as she allowed *me* to guide her through exercises that I'd developed to help the room heal their st*ries and manifest their dreams.

Wiping the tears from my face, I noticed the ache in my chest had dissipated and took in a long deep breath before looking back at the notes I'd made during our call.

Well, I'm glad she's going to be back in the country in time for the big event. I can't imagine the stories she'll tell in her ten minutes.

Watching her move the audience with "That's So Sad" a few months later, I smiled and laughed at her masterful approach and the audience's response, unaware of the other massive transition that was about to take place in my life or the important part Ahmondra would play in that one, too.

Almost a year after our big event, I was drowning in the deep end of more st*ry-healing. Actually, it felt more like I was coming apart at the seams. The only person I could think to call was Ahmondra, who quickly invited me to her home to do some of the most important healing work I'd done to date. In true spiritual mother style, she helped me reclaim parts of myself that had been lost—parts that held the keys to the real st*ry that had been sabotaging my life and business.

And, of course, it didn't end there...

When she contacted me again about *The Uncrowned Queen* (which she had subtitled: *The Diary of an Angry Black Woman* at the time), I giggled to myself about the timing. We hadn't talked in a while, and she had no idea that I'd been working through unconscious biases for more than a year after seeing how mine impacted a group of young people and a company with which I was working. I was grateful for the opportunity to witness her personal story at another level through this lens and dig into more levels of that work.

Her most recent book, *Compassionate Companion,* is also perfectly timed. She literally reached out to me the day after I had told my hubby that I'm starting to think—after all the work we've done on ourselves for twenty years—we have the opportunity to start from scratch. And here is the way... just dropped into my lap... the next day. You can't make that st*ry up.

With big transitions on my horizon this year—bringing on a team for my business, starting over in my marriage, and moving across the country—I have no idea what to expect, other than the discomfort that always comes with big changes. What I do know for certain is that I am looking out at that horizon with more tools, skills, confidence, and wholeness because of Ahmondra's presence in my life.

After a devastating car accident, Lori Giesey chose to fight for a full recovery, despite her doctors' prognoses and voices from her past that said she wasn't good or strong enough to do it. Within a few years, she was a business owner again, a marathon runner, a high-adventurer, and a writer. Lori loves helping individuals create and enjoy their own magnificent moments and spending time with her family, especially her grandchildren, who have inspired her latest adventure— a children's book series that will take kids on adventures and give them the tools to live life to the fullest.

There are No Accidents

Lori Giesey

*O*w. Step. *Ouch.* Hobble. *Owie.* Limp. The pain was intense as I maneuvered with my injured leg into the chiropractor's office. But the pain wasn't just physical. The receptionist greeted me with a concerned expression on her face. Acknowledging her, I slumped into a corner chair as if trying to disappear into the fabric. I really did *not* want to be there.

I had been fighting a pain in my left leg during my last several runs. Thinking back, it had actually been nagging at me to pay attention for a couple of weeks. However, I was training for my first marathon; and I just chalked it up to the cold, snowy, and icy weather I had been running in. Besides, you cannot train for a marathon and not have a few aches and pains, right? Generally, it only bothered me for the first couple of miles until the muscle would warm up and the cramping calmed down and all would be well again, or so I thought.

A few hours earlier, I had again reasoned that it just needed to "warm up," but the muscle never allowed me to settle into a solid run. I had stopped multiple times along the way to lean against a light pole or road sign to stretch, attempting to stop the cramping. I knew there was something wrong as I got to mile number three and then four, and it did not go away. In fact, I had cut my run short, hobbling home while calling the chiropractor's office to see if he could fit me in.

Sitting in the waiting room, I slouched deeper into the chair, realizing the last thing I wanted to do was look this man in the eyes and tell him that I was there because I'd ignored him. Only a few days earlier, he had counselled me to take a day or two off and rest. I had literally scoffed at him, as we were standing in the reception area, other patients around me. "I am only a few weeks away from my race. I can't slow down NOW!" He had shrugged his shoulders in defeat and turned to take care of his next patient.

Oh how I wish that I had listened. Why is it that I seem to have to learn lessons the hard way?

Humility is a hard pill to swallow and, apparently, I was not yet ready to partake; as a few minutes later, I balked when I laid down on the table and he again suggested I stay off of it and go see a sports massage therapist he knew. Lost in thought about how I had executed my running schedule with exactness—long runs, short runs, speed intervals, pace workouts and more, all in the freezing cold snowy weather of a Colorado winter—I wondered, *How will "resting" negatively affect all the training I have already endured? It will undo everything!* I concluded.

Begrudgingly, and yet hopeful that he could make a difference, I called the therapist who said he could see me the next morning. I endured both the physical and emotional pain and frustration throughout the rest of the day, watching an internal war raging inside of me. Anger at myself and the situation I was now in, along with fear and trepidation that my chiropractor was probably right about taking some time off to rest, had me wound tight.

The next morning, I arrived at the therapist's office to see if he would impart any good news. After answering a slew of questions and receiving a small amount of massage, I cringed as he taped up my adductor with what felt like an entire roll of kinesiology tape and brightened when he suggested I try a short run when I got home.

Awesome, I thought to myself as I hobbled back to my car. *A day off yesterday and a little tape today, and I will be back at it.* I easily convinced myself that the therapist had told me I would be okay, leaving behind the chiropractor's warning to rest. *Besides,* I thought, *I will only run a mile or two.*

Arriving back at the house, I grabbed my running shoes and started my "short run" after responding briefly to my husband's inquiry of whether that was a smart thing to do. I crossed the street and gingerly headed for the exit to our subdivision.

Turning left, I started up a small hill. The sun was shining for a change and added to my hope that all would be well. About three-quarters of a mile from the house, however, I felt a searing pain shoot through my lower extremity that made me burst into tears. Chastisement mingled with questions raced rapid-fire through my mind. *Oh no! What have I done? Not again! I am so stupid! Why didn't I listen to my chiropractor?* Of course the other side of me was justifying my actions, *But the therapist told you to do it. You were just following his suggestion.*

Having perfected the art of not listening to either my doctor or my body, I had received what felt like the severest of consequences. By not paying attention, I had torn the adductor muscle that might have healed had I given it the chance. Running my first marathon was now non-negotiable, as I was unable to even walk across the living room floor without incredible pain. This injury sent me into a tailspin of emotions, spiraling down, down, down—and back in time, to one of the darkest periods of my life.

No! Not again! was the first thought that went racing through my head. I left the chiropractor's office, head hanging low as I hobbled to my car, opened the door, and drug my body up and into the driver's seat. The mental cries continued internally as I sunk deeper into the great emotional abyss. *NO! I worked too hard to overcome that trauma! I don't ever want to go back there again!* I could almost see myself clawing at the sides of this dark pool of emotions grasping for anything that might help me escape the black, gooey muck swirling around me, tugging on my body in an attempt to pull me under.

Tears welled up, and feeling totally depleted and defeated, I allowed them to run down my cheeks. I crossed my arms on top of the steering wheel, laid my head on my arms, and allowed the pain to come rushing out in a torrential downpour of tears and emotions. I panicked internally, remembering a time long ago that left me broken in every way. All those weeks, months, and years of having to move at a snail's pace, unable to do much more than take care of my basic needs for the day. Now just the thought of weeks and months of immobilization, coupled with the actual physical and emotional pain, triggered that nightmare from my past that threatened to destroy all I had fought so arduously to overcome these past many years.

A major car accident fifteen years earlier had left me with a bulging disk in my lower back and a ruptured disk in my neck, which took the doctors eight months to diagnose correctly. Two surgeries and thirteen months of physical rehab later, I had received a functional capacity evaluation stating that I would probably never work again, and if I did, it would only be part time. They said I would never lift more than ten pounds repetitively and blah, blah, blah. "You won't do this and you won't do that" was all I'd heard for several minutes before I stormed out of the neurologist's office ready to burst into tears.

I had been through so much during these many years of my healing journey. Coming back from the depths of what felt like hell with the "experts" insisting I would never recover from my physical injuries, which was compounded by the PTSD and added to the emotional healing adventure as well.

I **hate** being told I can't do something. My motto has always been, "Tell me I can't, and I will show you I can!" I had no intention of being a couch potato for the rest of my life! I had too much to live for to just lie down and watch life pass me by. That day, so long ago, when I left the doctor's office and declared to my husband that their decided outcome for me was unacceptable, marked the beginning of a physical and emotional journey, and I was so proud of myself and the diligence and training I had accomplished over these past fifteen years. This marathon was going to be another piece of evidence in proving the medical doctors wrong.

I had been documenting my journey and at one point, about twelve years into this adventure, I had decided to write my story for posterity's sake—you know, a memoir. Nothing fancy, just something the kids and grandkids could someday read after I was long gone to help them see that "Life is about choices," and that "You are stronger than you think you are!"

Ugh, now what's going to happen with this darn book? I wondered as I readjusted the ice pack under me.

What I didn't realize is that by making that decision to begin sharing my story, I was embarking on the adventure of my life… literally! I can just see Heavenly Father rubbing his hands together, as I wrote the goal down, and saying, "Okay, Lori, hang on because Here We GO!"

Oh dear! Maybe THIS is what Amanda was talking about when she said I would have to revisit my pain and heal some of my old stories! I mean, there were so many signs that healing my old story was Heavenly Father's desire for me—signs that eventually led me to Amanda. Hmmm. I sunk back into the couch and thought back to my "Come to Jesus" meeting on a mountain trail while running the final eight-and-a-half-mile leg, where Heavenly Father had essentially dared me to start writing. Then there was my chiropractor and friend who had stopped mid-adjustment to tell me that God told him to tell me, "You are supposed to write a book…" even though I had not talked to anyone but my Heavenly Father about it at that point. Then there was the opportunity to hear Amanda share her own writing journey with my accountability group and knowing that she was the one to help me. And during our first session when she asked, "Is this *just a book* or is there something more?" and I heard a voice reply, "More! There's something more!"

I almost giggled as I remembered the shock of those words coming out of my mouth. I'd literally flipped my head from side to side to see who else was in the room and my insides were screaming, *What?!! NO! Where did that come from?* I should have known at that point that my inner soul wanted, no *needed*, this healing process.

I'd made the decision, in that moment, to get the support I needed to create not a memoir, as I had originally planned, but an actual book, with chapters, a cover, and sharing my personal story of my healing journey, my tenacity, and how I was not going to be told to lie down and be still by those who did not really know me or even those that did.

At first, I was elated, after *years* and countless attempts, to watch as the pages of this book began to come together. The words had at last begun to flow off my fingertips with a tap, tap, tap coming from the keyboard as I formed each sentence, paragraph, and chapter beginning with the prologue and working my way through the introduction where I had thought, *Finally, I am through the "accident" part of my story! Now, to cruise through the rest of it.*

Ha, ha, ha silly girl! I shook my head as I readjusted myself on the couch. I should have known that was not how this was going to work. Heavenly Father and I had been on this adventure together, even before my conversation with God on that mountain top. Looking back now, I am positive that God has a sense of humor, and He was very amused at my assumption!

He probably said, with a smile on His lips, "Oh sweet child of mine... You have only just begun this journey. Just you wait and see what is in store for you next." Remember, He had told me to "Hang on!"

Now I don't believe that God causes things to happen *to* us. However, I think He is an all-wise and all-knowing being that has our best interests at heart and, knowing all He knew regarding the choices I was about to make while training for that marathon, He was going to use this opportunity for our next adventure and throw in a little humor along the way. *It is pretty ironic, isn't it?* I hung my head in surrender as the realization hit me. Amanda and I had finished creating the outline for the book a few weeks earlier; and just as I am sure He was the one who had been nudging me to listen to my body, I know He was involved in the naming of the first chapter. He had inspired Amanda and I during our outlining phase to label chapter one, *"Slow Down."*

Oh yeah! You just cannot make this stuff up! It is as real as the nose on your face or the adductor tear in my leg.

So, there I was, broken AGAIN! Sitting on another couch just like the one I'd spent too many months on, writhing in pain, wondering if I was ever going to feel like myself again. Unable to so much as walk across the room without severe pain. Talk about "slowing down." I was physically and emotionally spent. Tumbling and turning, unable to see the way out. But I never was one to let pain stop me if I could help it.

Knowing my granddaughter was disappointed to lose the opportunity to cheer me on, I decided to go ahead and make the trip to Oklahoma City, pick up my racing packet, and spend the weekend with her before I drove the additional miles to Missouri. I needed something to focus on besides me; and while in Missouri, I would help my mother take care of my step-father after his knee replacement surgery. I figured even with a bum leg, I could help out on the days Mom had to work; and it might aid me in feeling somewhat useful.

The doctor gave me the okay to make the trip under one condition. I had to stop every couple of hours, get out, and walk around, and keep the blood flowing, so the leg would not completely stiffen up.

The trip was laborious. Nearly twelve hours after starting, I was relieved to finally see the familiar sight of the big city approaching. I was exhausted, but being with my granddaughter brightened my spirits and cemented the idea in my conscious mind that being an invalid was not on my bucket list. Unable to romp and play, chase and be chased, in our normal fashion highlighted those physical limitations and their accompanying emotions.

Sunday, on my way out of town, I stopped by a friend's house for just a few minutes. It was there I noticed, hanging on her wall, a sign that said, "Be still and know that I am God." *What? Again…?* For the past week or so, I had noticed this verbiage popping up everywhere I turned. These words were displayed in craft stores, on signs in multiple friend's and co-worker's houses in Colorado, in a book I was reading, on social media, and now there it was again in Oklahoma City. *What's up?* I momentarily pondered and then brushed it aside as I had done for the umpteenth time now, not taking notice of the inner turmoil that this phrase brought up inside me every time I laid eyes on it.

The morning of my step-father's surgery was the final straw. Sitting still had been a challenge. Not that I was hyperactive, just that my mind was always on the go and sitting still seemed like such a waste of valuable time. Knowing I would be sedentary for several hours that day, I'd brought my backpack with my heavy laptop along to help kill some time, thinking maybe I would pick up writing again as no inspiration had come forth since my injury; and Amanda was patiently awaiting my next chapter.

Writing had become a non-adventure. On the rare occasion when I opened my computer to my current chapter work, I would find myself staring at the page with my mind as blank as my paper. Or I would become so emotional reading back through what I had written previously that soon I would close my computer and wonder if anything would ever change. How many months or even years would accumulate before this, too, healed? Even more important, and ever

present in the back of my mind, was the real question, *Will I
ever run again?*

This last thought, more than any other, had me "kicking
against the pricks" at the slow down requirements. I had not
taken up distance running until I was forty-eight years old. It
was the one thing that brought peace to my soul and freedom
to my spirit. It challenged me to run faster and further. To
become more. I LOVED to run and wondered how I had made
it so far in life without experiencing its life-changing results.

Mom and I chatted more than I worked and within no
time the operation was successfully completed and mom was
taken back to recovery. Before long, they had made their way
up the back halls to his hospital room and I had received the
message to meet them there.

Boarding the elevator with backpack in hand, I remember
thinking how burdensome it was and wondered if the added
weight was all that great to be lugging around for no good
reason. I looped my arms through both straps to disperse
the weight just as the elevator bell chimed my arrival on the
third floor and the doors opened. I exited the elevator into an
empty lobby; and as I turned in the direction of the correct
hallway, I spotted an entire wall of glass with etching in the
bottom left-hand corner. As I moved forward, the words
became visible. "Be still and know that I am God."

Heavenly Father had finally succeeded in penetrating
my thick skull. Looking up towards the ceiling, I internally
screamed, *OKAY ALREADY! I get it! I am supposed to BE STILL!*
Sighing deeply, I paused momentarily and then turned down
the hallway towards my destination. I wondered if God *really*
knew what He was asking me to do.

Be still... Another deep sigh... Hadn't I been still for the
past several weeks? Moving at a snail's pace was pure torture

compared to the forty to sixty miles of running I accumulated each week, prior to my mishap, that is. *How much more tranquil does He want me to be?* I agonized internally at what this would require while I pasted a cheerful smile on my face, entered the assigned hospital room, and greeted the occupants.

After being hit on the head with the proverbial two-by-four while interpreting the words etched in the hospital window, I determined to do everything in my power to "slow down." I listened intently to hear God's voice and read passages of scripture searching for clarity in an attempt to somehow understand the logic behind this *necessary evil*. Although my prayers for complete healing continued during this time, I now inserted, "Thy will be done."

I began to accept my situation and acknowledge there was a bigger picture, even if I could not yet see it entirely. The edges were smeared and fuzzy but I could sense something there, just beyond the fringes. Like that etching in the window, as I moved closer to God, His purpose came more into focus. I understood that I had to step out in faith and trust the process.

Even now, I am not sure what was more painful, the injury, realizing that I was being asked by both Amanda and my Heavenly Father to go back further into my past, or the realization that eventually hit me that the book was not to be just about my accident journey, but about healing my entire life.

As I wrote, the awareness of that innate part of me that carried me through the abusive relationships, manipulation, and narcissism that infiltrated my life daily the first two and a half decades and then became interspersed throughout my existence every time I had to deal with one of those relationships over the next thirty-plus years grew. It became obvious that it was *that* pain that I had to heal and overcome, at least to a certain level, in order to construct the book that my Heavenly Father had asked me to create. The book He and I both *needed* for me to write.

The struggle was definitely REAL! There was challenging work to be done with every chapter. Always a story or sometimes several stories to heal. They never failed to send me back into my past, which always terrified and overwhelmed me. And yet, in doing so, I found that as I submitted my will to God, He gave me the opportunity to experience joy in healing areas of my life that had been injured and broken both mentally and emotionally since I was a little girl. When the healing eventually took place and I came out the other side, I had always learned and overcome and had definitely become stronger and more self-confident, while adding new coping skills to my tool belt.

Until this realization, I had stumbled to and fro in a state of ignorance at the next layer of healing necessary in order to write the content for *Chapter One*, too enthralled with all my marathon training success to take notice of the physical, mental, and emotional fissures that were appearing until the cracks and crevices became chasms and the ground crumbled beneath me.

Along with "Slow Down" came time for reflection and the opportunity to take note of and mend those areas that were holding me captive to my past. Sometimes I would recognize an old pattern emerging as I dealt with those necessary relationships and implemented new boundaries in order to create a fresh trail to journey on together should they choose to join me.

These boundaries were usually met with much resistance, anger, and emotion from the other parties. I, however, was adapting and creating the skills to recognize and tools to deal with the manipulation, narcissism, negative energy, and abuse.

While all that *stepping back* was going on, I spent weeks, which turned into months, healing my adductor muscle. Many times, as I limped from one part of the house to the other, I would ask, *Is this EVER going to heal?* And I still grieved over my lost race along with my leg that took what seemed like forever to mend.

There were so many areas to heal and repair, most unseen by the naked eye. Each successful boundary implemented was like setting another stone in place, creating a path from which to escape those old narratives my mind had previously convinced me were my reality, about who I was and what I was capable of accomplishing.

Creating this new pathway took time and energy but one day it all came full circle, the physical catching up with the mental and emotional. I had walked across the room several times when suddenly I realized with elation, *Oh my... That did not hurt!* It was the first time in many weeks that stepping on that leg did not cause significant pain. With renewed physical health and the mental and emotional peaks I had climbed and conquered, a new courage emerged and flowed, allowing me to eventually begin again to write.

I was so excited, I thought I might explode. Instead, I chose to use this energy to propel the book forward. With each new chapter there were additional lines to draw that could not be crossed. I was on the mend, discovering who

Lori really was, as I climbed the newly built trails, hiked up mountains, and saw additional vistas that had previously been beyond my reach.

By the next spring, the book was nearly completed when another tragedy struck. I ran smack dab into the biggest emotional barricade I had yet encountered on this journey. Dread and terror quickly consumed me, and all those new skills and tools I had accumulated felt like a child's toy in my hand, utterly useless for the job before me. I put everything on hold, frozen with fear and trepidation, unable to move forward. The cost to that relationship appeared to be too great a price to pay.

I was again ready to sacrifice myself because I just could not see any other way around this enormous boulder that had landed on the incredibly beautiful trail I had worked so hard to build. In one tremendous thud, it destroyed all the peace and serenity, confidence, and accomplishment I had experienced and erected a monumental roadblock in my magnificent adventure that took me to my knees. I immediately stopped the entire process of moving my book through production.

The cause? I had maintained a relationship with the one person who had demanded control over me my entire life. The thought of what this book would reveal and how it might hurt or destroy this person challenged me to my very core.

The old trail emerged and beckoned me towards the cliff's edge with a million, "What ifs..." This thought completely tore down those guardrails I had worked so hard to put in place and threatened to send me careening over the ledge, to the destruction of it all.

I spent the summer contemplating and making excuses. Mad as hell at myself for allowing him to use his manipulative behaviors to gain control over my actions and, in the next moment, sucked into the depths of misery and despair at the destruction my book might cause.

Why do I do this to myself? He doesn't deserve this! Consequences for his actions. But he's still your dad! Back and forth, I oscillated. Justify and condemn... condemn and then justify. Which was it? I couldn't have it both ways. I felt as if I was bungee jumping off the cliff headed for the ground below at an incredible speed only to come to my senses, momentarily jerking myself skyward in an effort to keep me from harm's way. *What am I supposed to do?* I cried out to Heavenly Father.

As summer came to a close with still no resolve, Amanda reached out to see how I was. I shared with her my unexplainable desire to protect on one hand, and yet complete the task that God had asked me to do on the other. With her intuitive magic, she explained how I might find some answers in a new class she was working on for the fall. She explained the workshop and what it would "en-tale."

Twenty-one days of intense soul searching and finding answers through story. The workshop was the first bit of hope I had felt all summer. Knowing I could not continue to engage in this crisis alone, I signed up for the course, with a hope and a prayer that it was the solution I had searched relentlessly for.

The class began November 1, 2018. I spent the time since our initial conversation in deep contemplation over what my intentions were for this class. The day before it began, I wrote in my journal, "The story I want to shift is: Feeling I am not ____ enough." Beneath it I wrote, "Fill in the blank... good, smart, talented... etc.)."

As I worked my way through the course, unbelievable amounts of emotion surfaced as I opened up doors that had been bolted and locked shut for decades. The only thing that seemed to console me were the bars of chocolate and M&M's I consumed as I wrote down and processed old stories, and constructed a new fortress of strength and courage.

Don't get me wrong, I was enveloped in the process to the point of no return and loved the transformation that occurred with each progressive twist and turn. The additional weight I acquired while consuming all that chocolate seemed a small price to pay for the experience of morphing into a stronger, bolder, more determined, and courageous Lori.

I discovered new parts of me I still refer to as, "My Little Girls." Those pieces and parts that had been buried so deep and for what seemed an eternity that when they were finally uncovered and allowed to share their voices, I think the angels in heaven sang.

These new voices were just what I needed to help me set some incredibly firm and life-changing boundaries, as well as show me that Amanda's *Message Multiplier Program* was the "MORE" that had exploded from inside me when Amanda had originally asked, "Is this just a book or is there more?" Even in those first moments, these parts of me that had been crushed in my childhood were trying desperately to be heard.

"More" turned out to be finding those parts of myself—the little girls, like "Feisty Shit" and "Sassy Pants"—that encouraged and enabled me to start building a website with online classes and plans that would eventually lead to a retreat to serve others and help them to find their own inner light, voice, and beauty.

The effort I put into the program also gave me the courage to make two incredibly hard decisions. The first was to get through the publishing of my book. Over the next several months, I finished the editing process on my manuscript, worked with the design team to create the cover, and then had it formatted for publishing. Then… I caved… and decided that although I was going to load it up on Amazon, I would hold off on an official launch. In my mind, I had done all that Heavenly Father had asked. I had written the book and made it available for others to purchase. *Wasn't it God's job to bring people to it that needed it?* I thought as I loaded it up on Amazon July 1st and breathed a sigh of relief thinking I had overcome that obstacle.

The second was a decision to again train for a marathon, demolishing all the mind-fricks and self-doubts surrounding my abilities to run the distance, which had been created with that adductor tear three years earlier. In order to write and make the book available to others, I had put a team together, with Amanda's help, that could assist me through all the different steps. So, to ensure my success for my race, I found a team of like-minded athletes who were all training for the same event—a marathon in Huntsville, Utah. Several of them had run multiple marathons and were now training for a Boston qualifying time, but me…

It would be my first twenty-six-point two-mile race. Therefore, I had no record to break and my only goal was to compete to the best of my ability and complete the distance.

I decided that a time of under five hours was doable with a lot of hard work and dedication. I had run two half-marathons prior to my workshop with Amanda and felt that by completing them so closely together, setting a personal record (PR) on pace for the second one, that I was up to the marathon challenge. Plus, I couldn't think of a better way to lose the extra weight I had gained through the workshop process and holiday season.

"Ugh... What can there possibly be about running, especially a marathon, that motivates you?" some of you might ask. For me, it is the ability to accomplish something most people wouldn't dream of taking on. It is getting up at 0'dark thirty to put in the miles of training while most people are still sound asleep in their beds. It is my foot hitting the pavement and me knowing that I didn't let anyone convince me to spend the rest of my life as a victim of someone else's poor decisions. It is pushing my body to make it through that next lap or mile when I am feeling like there is not one more ounce of energy left in me. And then... It is the satisfaction of completing any of these and walking away knowing that I did it. It is recognizing that, "I can do hard things!" and that "Life is about choices."

I trained hard and smart during that spring and summer, even while spending many hours getting the book ready for publishing, being on family vacation, and at other times away from home. I would rise up before everyone else, and sometimes the sun, to complete a seventeen-mile training run, core workout, or track intervals for speed so as not to hold everyone up when they were ready for the day's adventures. I was determined to accomplish my marathon goal. Nothing was going to get in my way, and Feisty was going to make sure of that!

The day of the race finally came and I was as ready as I could be. I had worked on all aspects of my race from the months of training to shoes that were broken-in just enough not to leave blisters on my feet, hydration, nutrition, and even the right clothes to layer and shed for the temperature increase throughout the race. I had taken all of these factors into consideration.

As we loaded the bus in the darkness of the pre-dawn morning, runners chattered all around us. The breeze was chilly and snow lay on the ground from the storm just two days prior. I sat down next to one of my running buddies, a brief brave smile exchanged between us. The bus soon pulled out and we rode in silence for the next twenty minutes, both of us deep in thought.

"You okay?" she quietly asked as another deep sigh nervously escaped my lips.

"Yeah… I think so," I replied, not really sure what I had talked myself into. This was HUGE. This was *make it or break it* time for all of those mind-fricks that threatened to take over.

We were nearing the start line when she said, "Can I share a piece of advice with you?"

"Absolutely," I quickly responded. I would take any advice at that moment, especially from someone who had run multiple marathons.

"Focus on the current mile," she boldly stated, then went on to explain, "Don't think about what you still have to do or how much you have completed. Just focus on the current mile." Then we disembarked the bus and headed for the tent to keep warm and prepare for the start.

The next hour went by so fast I hardly had time to take the necessary nutrition, pit stop, and head to the start line.

I found my pace runner and could hear them counting down, "Five... four... three... two... ONE!" And just like that... we were off. There I was running in my first marathon. I felt AMAZING!

"Focus on the current mile," I kept repeating to myself as I clicked off miles one, two, three... ten, eleven, twelve... Before I knew it, I was passing the half marathon start line where the timer there and my watch both told me I had just set a personal record for the first half of my marathon.

HOLY COW! I was ready to jump out of my skin. I was so excited. I was a full four minutes faster in this race with another half still to go. This gave me nearly three hours, almost an additional forty-five minutes, to complete the second half. *I really CAN do this*, I cheered triumphantly.

On I went, maintaining that pace for several additional miles. As the road began to flatten out, fatigue began to set in. I completed mile sixteen, seventeen, eighteen. Around mile twenty-three and a half, I began to feel what I thought was a severe cramp in my left hip. I had never run this far in my life, so I chalked it up to the distance.

However, it became increasingly more painful, causing me to interval between running and speed walking. Nearing town, where they had cones set up to keep the traffic away from the runners, I arrived at mile marker twenty-four, and stopped to take in some nutrition, hydrate, and use the port-a-potty. A few moments later, I stretched, retied my shoes, and set off to finish the race.

None of my efforts proved helpful to reduce the cramping. My intervals continued to get shorter and shorter. As I started into mile twenty-five, I would run five to six cones and walk two or three; but near the end of this mile, I could barely run two cones before converting back over to a speed walk pace.

Rounding the corner at mile twenty-six, I could see that glorious finish line. I could hear the cheers from the crowd and the music and the finish line speakers announcing each runner as they crossed the finish line. Determined to "run it in" the last point two miles, I took off to run and was immediately shut down by the pain that pierced my hip joint.

What the heck?!? I cannot stop now! Grabbing my thigh and with tears beginning to trickle down my cheeks, I determined to "chunk" it out to the finish. It was going to be what it was going to be. I would walk as fast as my aching body would let me and that would have to be enough.

I wanted so badly to finish this race strong, but...

The crowd seemed to sense my pain and determination. It was like watching a slow-motion movie as each person I passed seemed to be still as a statue, mouth gawked open and eyes wide as saucers. The silence had me frozen in time until I heard someone cheering another runner's successful completion and someone shouted out to me, "You are almost there! You've got this!"

Only seconds later, one hundred feet in front of the finish line, I took my last step on my own power as my left leg disappeared beneath me and I found myself careening forward, arms outstretched, headed for the pavement.

Two runners behind me, whom I wish I could thank, stopped to help me up. This touched my soul because they took time out of their race to help *me.* Before they could raise me to my feet, I heard my oldest son crying out, panic in his voice, as he ran towards me, "That's my mom! THAT'S MY MOM!!"

The two runners allowed Chris to take over and finished their race. With one arm around my son's neck, a female member of the race committee appeared to assist in helping me to stand upright. I tried to put my foot down but there was nothing there. She signaled for a wheelchair to come and I literally cried out, tears still wet upon my face, "NO! PLEASE... Let me finish my race!"

I leaned forward as if to show her I was determined to finish this race, with or without anyone's help. Of course, my son held my arm tight as I put my good foot down and stepped forward, then I leaned on both of them as a crutch for my bad leg. As I repeated this process, I worked my way towards the finish line. Not exactly the way I wanted to complete it, but in the end, even with the *slow down,* I completed my race in 4:36:19, nearly twenty-four minutes ahead of my goal... AND... I wasn't in a wheelchair!

I *did* cross that finish line and another helper placed the medal around my neck and smiled at the stick-to-itiveness she had just witnessed, as the race personnel chimed in, "Will you sit in the wheelchair now?"

"Yes," I replied, sitting down in the chair and allowing someone to wheel me to the first aide tent.

Again, with help, I maneuvered over to a makeshift cot. Looking up at my son, I said with boldness, conviction, and a new level of courage, "I am going to embrace this moment, come what may!"

Initially, I thought my hip was just dislocated because I felt it slip out of place. Not so. After an ambulance ride to the local hospital, x-rays, and an incredibly inept emergency room doctor, whose bedside manner rivaled, no... surpassed that of my accident doctors, I found that I had broken the head of my femur and would be headed into emergency surgery where they would place an eight-inch rod in my femur and reattach the femoral head with screws to hold it in place while it healed.

What I thought was a major cramp and then my hip slipping out of place was actually the femur head breaking at the neck and sliding out of the socket. People have asked, "Wasn't this painful?"

"Yes," looking back, it was painful in many ways. The so-called cramping I thought I was experiencing, the surgical healing, not crossing the finish line on my own power, but kicking against the pricks has its own painful costs that hurt even more.

I have seen an abundance of blessings by choosing to "Embrace the Moment" at that finish line and beyond. With no need previously for an orthopedic doctor, I randomly chose a doctor in Colorado I had heard about. Unbeknownst to me, my orthopedic doctor in Utah and my random selection had performed their residency together and then served for a period of time together on the medical team for the Navy Seals in training. They knew each other well. Coincidence? I think not.

Of course MY first question was, "When will I be able to run?" They both concurred that it normally took six to eight weeks of non-weight bearing prior to any attempt to put your toes on the ground and six to eight months before either would consider allowing me to even think about running.

By embracing the moment, I believe I allowed the energy that would normally have been spent in emotional upheaval, being frustrated at my situation and the myriad of previous emotions I had felt with the adductor tear, to instead put their intensity, power, strength, and stamina towards *focusing on the current mile.*

After two weeks the doctors allowed me to continue my upper body strength training. At four and a half weeks I was told to start putting weight on the injured leg, and at my three-month checkup they released me completely, three to five months ahead of schedule. A fluke? Again, I think not.

While it was another month until I began to really "run" again, I started with walking, moving into intervals at the track and at seven months, I had completed my first 15K and made plans to return to Huntsville to run a half-marathon the year after my injury and a marathon the following year (2021). The takeaway? Yes, I broke my femur but, in the process, "BROKE THROUGH" kicking against the pricks. Now that's a lifetime marathon win!

It was while recovering from this injury that I launched my book, finished up the website, taught my first online classes, and experienced my first podcast interview. With all this success, you would think that I had finally figured it all out and would settle into my plan.

Hmmm... No, that would be too easy and besides, something was just not jiving. I kept trying to wrap my brain around what I was experiencing but to no avail. It wasn't until the pilot of my *Self-Love* class when, in the middle of the entire four-week workshop, everyone in the class had some family or relationship type crisis that was not related to the work they were doing in the workshop.

One woman's son ended up in ICU, another's daughter's house burnt down, and still another had a major relationship shift. I suggested we put the class on hold and everyone agreed.

Then along came Covid-19 and the "Stay at Home" orders. My race for fall was cancelled, our collaborative book writing retreat was moved to online, and my world imploded! Meeting all of these amazing women, each one doing incredible things in their space triggered my *"Not ____ enough"* button and I felt completely discombobulated. When Amanda asked us to share what we were doing, I felt totally inept.

Breaking the first cardinal rule, I immediately compared myself to all the others; and, of course, found myself coming up short. *What do I possibly have to offer these strong and powerful women who are making an amazing difference to so many? I have nothing! I can't even get my pilot off the ground. I have no real following. I'm such a failure! SIGH...*

I barely escaped without bursting into tears while on the webinar and couldn't hit the "End Meeting" button fast enough. Immediately, my body convulsed into huge sobs of anguish.

Again, you say? I thought you had overcome this nonsense? What gives?

The answer... That took a little more time. However, this go-around, it took a mere couple of hours to pull myself out of the abyss and then another week or so to realize that I have much to give and it is always innately inside of me, immediately available to all. What I have to give is ME and that IS enough!

I get to be who I am naturally. Spreading loving-kindness. Seeing others as God sees them. Perceiving their potential and divine worth and helping them along their journey of discovery.

I knew I was on a mission from God. He had made that very clear by telling me to write my book. What I have recently come to know and understand more completely is this is a continual process. Once we take the step forward to be a messenger, we have a responsibility to continue to grow and heal ourselves so we can help those along our path. We are to be ready for that next level of adventure at a moment's notice and then to "Embrace the Moment."

With each step I take outside my comfort zone, the doors and windows of heaven open and shower down their blessings upon me, giving me more opportunities to help and serve others and in a way that is natural for me. I would not change all that I have gone through these past several years for anything! Including figuring out that I sold more books in July when I first put my book up on Amazon than I did during the actual book launch. It is quite possible that I made the Amazon #1 Best Seller list, but I will never know because I allowed fear to overtake me. A hard lesson to learn but one that I hope to forego in the future.

As I step into the next adventure that is calling to me— writing a series of children's books to help young children realize that "Life is all about choices!" and "You are stronger than you think you are!"—I am determined to bring these lessons with me, along with the two new practices that have intertwined themselves with my heartstrings: "Be still and know that I am God" and "Slow Down!" Incorporating all of this knowledge into exciting explorations, adventures, and exploits my new characters will encounter will give the children reading them the opportunity to learn, in fun and engaging ways, the foundational principles that took me so long to understand and embrace as an adult. I only wish I could be a fly on the wall as they discover, learn, and implement!

Amanda's Side of the Story

"How did it go?" I texted her the morning after her marathon, as I hadn't wanted to disturb her celebration with her family the night before.

"Funny you should ask!" she texted back two hours later. "I finished in 4:36.19 (way ahead of my goal of 5 hours)! Do you have time for a phone call? There's more to the story…"

I sent her a link and we hopped on Zoom, and my mouth dropped open in shock.

"Are you in a hospital?"

Her smiling face nodded in the affirmative as I tried to process what I was seeing. "Yes, yesterday was a lot more exciting than I planned…" and she relayed the entire story of the marathon, the pain in the last few miles, falling to the ground moments away from the finish line, and the story of her son helping her cross it.

Tears poured down my face as I imagined those moments of overcoming despite the challenge.

That's so Lori! This feisty lady just will not stop until she gets what she wants! I mused as I recalled witnessing her book journey over the past five years. *I knew it from that first phone call…*

I held my breath while I read the story of her accident, and I held it again days later while she related the mayhem that ensued with doctors who offered prescriptions instead of solutions over the phone. (Yes, this was before Zoom.) Having watched my dad struggle with doctors, prescriptions, and chiropractors for almost two decades after his debilitating car accident, I was inspired by this lady's feisty spirit and her message about the power of choices in the face of adversity.

Did she just say that she's running marathons now? I shook my head in awe as I hung up the phone and got to work on a proposal.

What she didn't know, and wouldn't find out for years, was that the previous two years had dealt me so much adversity that her message was much-needed medicine. Deep betrayals by people I loved, huge financial losses resulting from my willful blindness to an unethical marketing team, and an energetic attack from a dark magician whose stability was threatened by my work had taken its toll on my body, mind, and spirit.

The interview that put me in front of Lori was the last one I would do for several years, choosing to slow down my business growth because it seemed to be linked to the increasingly painful and terrifying challenges arising. By this point in my work with new and seasoned messengers, I knew this pattern of peak-and-destruction was a sign that there was a st*ry that needed to be healed. Despite all of my coaches', colleagues', and clients' encouragement to scale, I pulled back all marketing efforts and only worked with people who found me through people I'd already supported; and I started digging for the invisible st*ry that was sabotaging my success, my relationships, and now my health.

I was only six months into this st*ry sabbatical when Lori signed on to work with me; and I quickly realized this lady was, and is, a busy lady. Not only was/is she training for marathons, she was/is also an active wife, mother, and grandmother; a non-stop adventurer and traveler; a leader in her church; and an owner of multiple businesses.

She was excited when we discovered the framework for her book, but held her breath as we discussed some of the backstories that would need to be included in the book for people to understand that she was overcoming a lot more than a physical injury after that accident. Accustomed to this resistance, I asked her to just start writing and see what unfolded. We could always cut out the stuff that didn't feel good, but putting it on the page without editing would help her begin to process and heal it. I was thrilled to see her natural writing ability enhanced with a few storytelling tricks I shared, and off she went!

When she called me to tell me that she had injured herself during training, I could hear the stress in her voice. It was more than pain from this injury and disappointment about her marathon plans—I sensed panic.

Hmmmm, I thought to myself as I reviewed where she had left off in her writing. *I asked her to go back and include more sensory details about her physical, mental, and emotional state after the accident. And here she is—facing another injury and the memory of the story of an injury that would destroy her active life forever.*

This was the first time that I consciously witnessed what often happens to clients who are sharing stories that involve physical injuries and re-living that trauma either in a concrete or simply symptomatic manner. It was because of this AHA with Lori that I was able to support a colleague of mine whose brand story writing was stopped dead in its tracks with the onset of migraines. When I asked her about the brand story, she mentioned she had a condition in which her brain was too big for her skull, which caused migraines and required several surgeries to alleviate the pain. Her headaches had returned, and doctors could not figure it out. When I explored the connection between the writing of her story and the symptoms emerging, her eyes widened and she asked what she should do. I wondered out loud what would happen if she finished the writing, and sure enough—her symptoms disappeared.

Connected to the pain and panic of the original injury, Lori was able to finish chapter one and move through some of chapter two before life got super busy again and took her away from writing for a bit.

By the time she was struggling with the backstory in chapter three, I had discovered my own stinky st*ry, and working on how to rewrite it, I found myself shaking my head at the timing. How much detail should she share about her narcissistic, abusive father? How could she tell the stories of surviving that type of pain, considering taking her own life, and having to figure out how to set boundaries with the people in her life who demanded so much and offered so little in exchange? How could she tell the world how little she knew "the real Lori" after so many decades of living for everyone else?

*Is it possible that this lady and her story were put in my path in order to wake me up to the st*ry that has been sabotaging my life? Were her steps to freedom part of my path out of the abusive situation I have been unconsciously living in for so long?*

The answer to those questions is YES.

And, strangely, Lori kinda disappeared the year I started the biggest st*ry-rewrite of my life and then contacted me almost as soon as I had finished setting boundaries, moving out of my toxic environment, and trying to figure out who the hell I was if not the caregiver, fixer, and slave.

We started back into the writing, and I could feel her renewed commitment as she finished the book content and then got stuck in production and launch. I was amazed, at every turn, by her tenacity and loved witnessing her healing journey in the 21-Day Quest From Character to Co-Author. This lady does not back down from hard work, and her insights inspired everyone to dig deeper and go further... to stay committed when it was hard.

It was the strangest and most magnificent moment ever when I finally met her in person at her first retreat some five years after we'd begun working together. Her gentle but feisty spirit continued to shine through and support everyone in the room as she put the final touches on her book and planned for the launch of not just her book but a whole adventure-based business through which she could help others remember who they are and make choices that allowed them to heal and build momentum and a magnificent life.

Everything fell together quickly until it looked like things were falling apart... like they had before... only there was something very different happening this time.

More of Lori was present to her message that every "accident" is an opportunity.

"When they took the x-rays, it showed I'd broken the neck of my femur—a stress fracture—so they sent me to surgery where they put a rod into my femur and screwed it into place." She paused and wiped a few tears. "One of my first thoughts was that this is the sequel to my book." Another pause and wipe. "The second thought was that when I tore my abductor three years ago, I fought the 'Be still and know that I am God.' This time, I am embracing it!"

I shook my head in awe of the transformation that had taken place. Panic had been replaced by Purpose and Peace. Her message was serving her in the middle of a mess.

Of course she healed up more quickly than any doctors imagined and headed back to training, and then another "accident" happened. It seemed there was another layer of healing asking for her time and attention, but she stayed close and connected to the community; and when she was ready, she dove into that next st*ry. Again, I watched in awe as she completely shifted her perspective, her relationships, and her desires around what is next for her.

As she steps into the next season of writing children's books and supporting our community, I'm knowing for certain that it was no accident that she showed up in my life at the moment she did and that she is feeling inspired to write adventures with children at the exact same time that I've been inspired to offer family connection points and develop a children's book offering to my messengers. Why not write their stories that can intervene and reset the course of someone's journey *and* then write a children's book that helps children to learn the lessons now so they don't need an intervention later?

Alyssa Noelle Coelho is a #1 bestselling author, internationally published model, Latin dancer, entrepreneur, and philanthropist who works all over the globe. She has a Bachelor of Arts in Sociocultural Anthropology from the University of California, San Diego. She creates, coaches, and writes to inspire and mobilize individuals and communities to take action toward becoming the answers our world, our planet, and our species need to create a future where every individual—of every race, ethnic identity, sexual orientation, religious tradition, socio-economic status, and cultural custom and language—is able to experience a vibrant and authentic life.

A Journey Back To Love
Again and *Again*

Alyssa Noelle Coelho

"Hi, this is my little sister, Alyssa. She's writing a book!" I gulped at my oldest sister's bold introduction to this stranger and slid my foot into her shin under the wooden picnic table, hoping it would hit her like my heart just hit my stomach.

"Uhm," I barked back, "So nice to meet you. I'm actually not writing a book. My sister is just cute sometimes." I half smiled as my eyes rolled back to her, "I just write poetry."

A confused smile and some small chat later, this sweet stranger sparked a flame I didn't know was already inside of me, "Well, it was so nice meeting you. And hey! You should read some of your poetry at the talent show on Friday! I know I'd love to hear it!"

I was about 3,000 miles from home, spending my August at a summer camp for professionals from all over the world. Just shy of twenty years old, this was my first time traveling so far alone. Had it not been to meet my sister and this band of people she called her tribe, I'm not sure I would have had the confidence to come on my own.

This week was scheduled to the brim with workshops for everything from emotional and spiritual support therapies to business building and book launching to super fun art opportunities and camp activities. At every corner, there were CEOs, Bestselling Authors, Artists, and Innovators who were taking time out of their busy lives to refill their own cups, rejuvenate their creative energy, and connect with like-minded others in organic authentic ways. The expansive energy was gushing so vibrantly, it felt tangible.

It's safe to say I felt intimidated at the least. Once again, for the gazillionth time in my life, I was the youngest in attendance to a group of adults with visions and directions for their lives that were oozing with determination and success. And here I was, having just finished my first year of college and arguably the toughest one of my young life, just trying to make sense of a world where God might not exist.

Having been raised in a Christian home where love and light were palpable, I never felt a need to question what I'd been taught since I was young. There was God. There was Jesus. And there was the Holy Spirit. It was that simple. Oh, and there was an entire history of mythology, doctrine, and ritual intertwined in the belief system. Not to mention a list of do's, don'ts, and other expectations. Shoot, I don't think it had ever even crossed my mind that this was *a belief system*, one of the many in existence. My entire life, it was just the way of being, the right way, anyway. And, that was fine. I wanted for nothing more. Until that first semester of college.

I'd chosen a combination of courses and professors with little idea of the impact they would have on my psyche, my physiology, and every aspect of my life for the months to come. My World Religions course was introducing me to traditions and cultures all over the world that I had no idea existed. My History of Christianity course was teaching me a very different line of history than I had learned in Sunday school. My Psychology Statistics course was showing me just what exactly it means to actually know something and what little capacity we humans even have for that. My Astronomy course... well, let's just say I wasn't exactly the one who got the science genes in the family, and the Theory of Relativity just about rubber-banded my brain to its breaking point. The culmination of these courses drove me into complete bewilderment, confusion, and utter curiosity. My passion for learning and desire for the challenge to expand my understanding for the ways of the world was increasing rapidly. I was learning so many things about our minds and bodies, about culture and tradition, and about community and dogma that completely contradicted the faith I'd been raised in. My years of reconciling the dissonance I'd experienced in conversations with others by regurgitating cliches like, "God works in mysterious ways" was quickly coming to an end.

I began asking questions I hadn't dared to before and doubting leaders and mentors who not only couldn't answer them, but whose hypocrisy directly contradicted their overused excuses. I gradually stopped praying and frantically began studying. There had to be an answer someone before me had found and hidden somewhere in all these books. The fire was kindling within and the friction was obvious in all of my relationships.

And that was just the prelude to this year becoming the toughest of my life. My beautiful and glowing trimester-pregnant older sister woke one morning to her expected infant vanishing from her body. Without any foresight of this probability, I watched her joy and excitement to be a mother fall from her eyes as she too began questioning the existence of an all-mighty being who had the best interest of his children in mind.

Shortly after, I started noticing some unusual signs in my father's behavior: a little more anxiety than normal, a little

more depression than normal, a little more pain than normal.
It took me a while to catch on, let alone really comprehend
that my father's health could be declining, unexpectedly and
rapidly. This man was my everything: my hero, my mentor,
my protector, my guardian, my best friend. I couldn't believe
it. I wouldn't. I quickly realized trying to figure out the *why*
could only turn into a futile and exhausting process. So,
I buckled down, put my emotion on the backburner, and
focused on what needed to be done to support him. I left my
full-time job and design internship to stay home and care
for him. My mother worked full-time and the care was too
demanding. Late nights and early mornings. Doctor's offices
and pain management clinics. I felt no hesitance in throwing
myself alongside him to support in any way I could, but there
was no anticipating the toll it would take on my emotional,
physical, and spiritual well-being to watch my father's health
unravel. My vision was getting quite dark.

The increased time in my hometown gave way for a
timely run-in with an old flame. It wasn't long before we fell
back into each other, and despite our many differences, the
connection was strong. He cared for me with a passion and a
tenderness no one else in my life even knew I needed at the
time. He showed me sweetness and attentiveness. He held
space for me to fall apart and made every attempt to give me
what I needed to get through the day. He didn't care that my
insides were turning on the only truth they'd ever known and
that I was losing control of so many parts of me. He didn't
judge my brokenness or my confusion or my lack of certainty.
He just lovingly supported my search for the answer I needed
to make everything better, to make everything make sense
again. We were beautiful. And we were tragic. It wasn't long
until I learned that the reason I felt so safe being broken with

him was because he was pretty broken, too. He was broken in all the ways I'd come to learn how to support a man: his anxiety, his depression, his pain. Once more, I began putting my well-being on the back burner as I struggled to balance what became another vortex in my life.

I found myself constantly faced with challenges that required coping mechanisms I had already begun stripping myself of. *Why would I pray when I am not even sure who I am praying to anymore? Why would I pray if no one was listening on the other end? Why would I pray if...? What the actual f*ck is prayer anyway?* My parents' disapproval toppled me with shame. My sister's despair pained me with grief. My father's declining health ran me over with helplessness. My boyfriend's chaos sucked me dry of energy. In summary, I was just trying to stay afloat, plugging holes in a sinking boat under a dark thundering sky, still secretly and desperately hoping for a golden hand to reach down and save me.

So... who was I to be sitting here at a table with a stranger talking about a book I was going to write? *Don't people write books to give others answers? What answers do I have? I'm just holding on for dear life.* All I had were my words—my words that toppled onto my pages like tears in stanzas that kept them safer than my skin did. They weren't a hobby or a money-maker. They had no stealth or pizazz. They were simply my tiny, shut down body's only coping mechanism, only release, only hope of making sense of the tragedy that filled my being. It'd been that way for as long as I could remember, since I started writing in junior high school.

That night, Amanda and I sat on the bottom bunks of our cabin and I confessed to her why her hopes for me writing a book made no sense and would never come to fruition. "Sis, everything I thought was Truth has been a lie. I've read all the books. I've watched all the documentaries. People spend their entire lives searching for Divinity, trying to experience it, to understand and articulate it, to show others how to connect with it. Philosophers, priests, scientists, seekers of all kinds... And I haven't found it. I can't find it! I can't even tell if I ever actually had it. It's driving me crazy; and I swear if I just could wrap my brain around this one thing, everything else in my life might make a little more sense."

My sister let her tears fall with mine and reached her hand to my cheek. "Can I ask you a question?"

Helpless, I nodded and dropped my chin.

"What if... there is no answer?"

I stared back at her and sunk into the gaping hole she just punched through my chest. "There... there has to be an answer." My tears had stopped as I realized the desperation in my words.

"What if there's not?" I sat in that for a minute, remembering when I was really young and I used to close my eyes and imagine what it would be like to be dead. I'd imagine stillness so dark and cold, there were no thoughts, no words to fill it. That's what that question felt like. *What if... there is no god? What if... there is no answer? What if?*

After my arrival home and for the weeks that followed, my sister's words sporadically poked at me. And each time, I failed to find an answer. Each time, I struggled a little less to imagine a time and space where I was okay with there being no answer.

And then one night, after a long draining day of caregiving, studying, working, daughtering, girl-friending and all the things, I pulled my old journals from underneath my bed and started reading through eight years of poetry that had poured out of me through my junior and high school years. I puddled in tears as I remembered how rough those years were, how I'd felt so lost, so confused, so empty of answers.

And somehow, as I finished reading them through, I felt hopeful. Because somehow, I was on the other side of those years of anxiety and depression, fear and isolation, drugs and abuse. Because somehow, I pulled through those years when I didn't think I could have. Because somehow, I could look back at that particular journey and see growth and evolution. Because somehow, these pages had semblances of answers that, at this very moment, were exactly what I needed to read. Because somehow, on my bedroom floor, I'd pieced together the timeline and suddenly... it all made sense.

I could vividly see where my disconnection with myself, my body, my heart, my relationships, my divinity, my Love had begun. I could see each stage of grief, of rage, of addiction, of sadness and confusion over losing those connections. I could see the rawness, the beauty in all the steps I took back to myself, each move I made that brought me a little closer to the home that was my body, my heart, my relationships, my divinity, and my Love. I could see the patchwork of lessons and realizations, choices and actions, gifts and healing that threaded through each of these poems in perfect chronology. I could see the inevitability of it all.

Maybe... I did have the answer. Maybe... I was the answer I was looking for.

That night, I called Amanda, "Okay Sis, I get it. Let's do this." I could feel her smile on the other line as we agreed I would spend the next year compiling my poetry into a narrative, producing an epic book, and campaigning it for Bestseller. With Amanda's support, I figured out who my audience was, crafted a unique narrative for them through the chronology of my poetry, designed my very first and very own book cover, worked with editors, interior designers, and campaign managers to perfect it for launch.

That next August, at twenty years old, I launched my book, *CHOSEN—A Journey Back To Love*, with that same community, following a slam poetry performance at the Friday night talent show. The following November, we were scheduled to release it on Amazon and after what felt like a nonstop downhill somersault of delayed flights, category switches and completely misaligned stars, we proceeded to hit #1 Bestseller on Amazon in three categories.

Did this just happen?

Fortunately, this was all the world saw—a #1 Bestseller sticker on my book cover and photos of my post-launch laughing cry. And then... the other photos rolled in. My friends, family, mentors, college acquaintances, high school teachers, professors, and tons of random buyers sent photos of my book in their hands. I imagined them, in their unique pile of broken pieces reading through the same pages where I watched my words clumsily topple from my tears.

Who would have thought?

I have owned and operated my business, Lionheart Creations, for five years now and have been fortunate enough to have supported hundreds of authors, entrepreneurs, and business people launching their missions, their messages, their projects and businesses into the world. Not only have I come to understand the process it is to experience, to internalize, and then to bring forth the entirety of that journey by sharing it with the world, but I have been able to witness mentors, friends, clients, and allies do the same thing. I have often found that our biggest hindrance to believing we have something special to offer the world lies in the disillusion, the belief that we don't have the answers we need to help ourselves and further, help others. This is quite possibly the biggest and easiest lie we get paralyzed by and trapped in—that I got paralyzed by and trapped in.

Working on this book through what at the time was the hardest year of my life, when everything I knew to be my reality crumbled before me, gave me hope. It reminded me that this was a season and that it, too, would pass. It reminded me that I had what I needed to see this season through, that I didn't need an answer from a golden hand in the sky to do so. It reminded me that no matter where the spiraling black holes in my life showed up, that I would grow stronger, wiser, and closer to Love through braving the storm. It reminded me that in trial and process, in space and time, I would grow to understand the things I needed to and would find peace with those I couldn't.

Little did I know at that time that my toughest years were actually ahead of me. Little did I know just how many seasons I had to come that would break me at the knees. That eventually, I would be forced to face moments so dark they tore me right from Love's palm, again and again... Losing my dad before I was ready. Saying goodbye to a soulmate. Traveling the world just to try to understand myself again. Finding purpose in the faces of small children. Then coming home only to lose myself to a master of illusion I barely escaped. Deciding to pursue my dreams of travel, philanthropy, dance, and writing *The Lionheart Chronicles.*

Oh yes, the journey of writing and publishing *CHOSEN* was only the first of the many unique series of experiences to make the masterpiece that is my journey on this planet, my alchemy from tragedy to triumph. Over and over again.

Amanda's Side of the Story

"Do you see it?" I smiled up at her across the small sea of post-it notes between us—mostly-organized chaos on the itchy carpet of a bedroom-turned-office—in time to see a glimmer of understanding spark in her eyes.

On the post-it notes were the titles of poems she had written and words that helped me begin to more clearly see the phases of her journey. In what she believed to be remnants of darker times, I was witnessing a love story. The plot: A young girl finds herself in a dark place, surrounded by villains, cowards, and traitors, and loses sight of who she is, what she wants, and her place in the world. Turning to substances, untrustworthy souls, and her own darkness, her light dims to almost nothing. But... running parallel to that plot, unbeknownst to her, is a second one: Love kept her alive, protected her from worse tragedies, and gave her the gift of words to write herself home.

"I think so?" It was more of a question, but her furrowed brow told me her mind was still warring with the idea of a benevolent force that was working on her behalf and writing in all of the characters and plot twists she needed to return from the darkness.

"What if you just called it Love... not God...? It could be the Love in you, in others, etc.... calling you back, lighting the way..." I offered, addressing her unspoken objections.

My twenty-year-old sister's childhood religion and worldview had been blown to bits in exactly the same way mine had when I attended an honors program at a Christian university that was determined to help me make my faith my own. That meant showing me just how much of it I had blindly accepted as truth and insisting that I answer some of the toughest questions anyone ever asked me, "What if God isn't real?"

Those questions, combined with other plot twists in my life, catalyzed my first dark night of the soul. While I had good mentors, and one good friend, nothing could fix the break in belonging I felt with my family or repair the damage I had done in my early anger stage: "Why didn't anyone teach me how to think for myself, damn it?!?"

By the time this happened to her, some sixteen years after it had happened to me (that's about our age difference), I had decided a few things for myself that had been reinforced by the work I'd been facilitating with messengers for almost a decade at this point. I had so much evidence that there was a benevolent force that seemed to consistently insert the right people and circumstances into my storyline to help me heal and evolve. Whether it was the perfect book "randomly" falling off a bookshelf the day after I'd ask for help in healing my life, or that first client whose message reminded me of what I'd known but forgotten about human potential, or the helpers who showed up at exactly the right time to help me release traumas that blocked me from health and happiness, I had a list that left no doubt in my mind that we are not alone and help is always around the corner. And it wasn't just my list. By this time, I had seen dozens of stories that had reinforced that no matter the pain we see when we look backwards, there are moments of Grace that simply cannot be written off as random happenstances.

I'm just so glad I can be with her on this journey. It was hell to be so alone, I thought as I waited for her to process. *It's no coincidence, I'm sure, that one of the moments I clung to most tightly during this time included her. While cuddling her newborn self on the kitchen floor, after rocking her to sleep, I received my very first message about love and grace. My Co-author used my experience of deep love for this sweet baby to try to help me understand that there was nothing I could do to separate myself from Love... nothing. Sure, I would make mistakes. Yes, I would question and rebel. Of course I would make terrible choices. But Love wouldn't move. Love would always be waiting for me to return again and again.*

"Okay, I really like the idea of the narrative that weaves them all together. Let's try it!" She smiled back at me, again proving that while she still didn't believe, she saw the value of this approach at least for the reader.

What she didn't know, and what I couldn't tell her, while sitting across from her on the itchy carpet was that I was starting another journey back to Love for myself that I hoped would not destroy the fabric of my relationship with her... because I knew it would be the end of my relationship with others in the family.

You see, just days before I introduced her to people at Camp as a budding author, Love had intervened through a friend to say, "Amanda, you are living in the middle of abuse and you need to get yourself and your family out of here." As my friend told me the story of how my son had stepped into my caregiver role and almost suffered an anxiety attack before her eyes in my absence, all of the puzzle pieces connected. In the same way that I had been raised to believe in the Christian God, I had been raised to believe that my role in the family was to take care of my grandmother and make life easier for my dad by doing so. As their physical, mental, and emotional health declined, they began to say and do things that were controlling and cruel. Immediately, I realized the source of toxic stress and all of my physical ailments and allergies, and those of my husband and son. And I knew I had to get us out.

As I had done for years, reviewing and editing her essays and papers, I marveled at Alyssa's natural writing abilities as we worked on her book. Truly, she did most of it herself, and I just witnessed it, heart bursting with awe and big sister pride. She took on all of the book production, developed her own book cover design with limited help from our designer, and trudged the interior formatting path largely on her own once I showed her how to navigate it. But what really got me was watching the way she so easily and organically marketed the book, both online and offline. Her love of her craft, her desire to share, and her enthusiasm about the process of development magnetized more attention than I'd ever seen one author garner without a carefully-strategized campaign. In fact, I was the hot blubbering mess in the front row of the GLP talent show when she leveled the room with one of her slam poems and inspired hundreds of people to help her reach bestseller.

Not only was I proud of her and all that she had accomplished in that year; I was grateful that she had managed to maintain an open mind and heart and relationship with me as I found my way back to Self-Love and moved my family to a healthy new environment... and completely disrupted the family system she was still living in.

Unfortunately, the celebration didn't last long enough.

Less than two months later, tragedy struck when our dad suddenly passed, and I watched her slip away into unanswerable questions and grief. When she called and asked me for a book recommendation, I recommended a book I hadn't thought about for years: *The Way of The Peaceful Warrior.* It was one of the first books that was dropped in my lap when I was ready to return from my dark night of the soul. Full of magic, mystery, and sacred spiritual truths, it had restored my hope and belief... and I hoped it would do the same for her.

I shouldn't have been surprised when she devoured the book and all of the other books the author had written, or when she called to tell me she was flying to Costa Rica by herself for a retreat to reconnect with herself. And I'm not about to ruin the story for you, as she is writing a novel based on those events. All I will tell you is that it's been a true joy to witness my youngest sis and friend return to Love time and time again... and help others, including me, do the same.

Dr. Niki Elliott's professional life is dedicated to improving conditions for students who struggle to live and learn in traditional settings. She moves mountains to help educators, parents, health professionals, and social service providers transform personal and systemic practices that perpetuate trauma and underperformance. In addition to providing professional development and personal empowerment through the Mindful Leaders Project, she serves as director of the Center for Neurodiversity, Learning, and Wellness and as a clinical professor in the LaFetra College of Education at the University of La Verne, where she trains teachers to incorporate interpersonal neurobiology, breathwork, yoga, mind-body techniques, and healing-centered engagement.

Becoming the Thermostat

Dr. Niki Elliott

"Amanda, I don't know what..." I started and stopped, trying to find the words to communicate the latest plot twist in my story of trying to get my message out to those who needed it.

I just don't understand it, I thought to myself. *Feels like going backwards.*

"What happened?" Amanda asked, her voice indicating a little more concern than curiosity.

"Well, after sharing my book and giving the keynote for the winter graduation, I was offered a job at the University of La Verne. They want me to be a clinical professor at the LaFetra College of Education and the co-director of the emerging Center for Neurodiversity, Learning, and Wellness. The offer includes free college tuition for my girls, which you know is a high priority for me and also something I've been concerned about."

With all the hefty investments in moving my work forward, I was hoping to see a big return on investment by now. My girls will be ready to go to college in a few years, and I'm not sure how everything is going to shake out after this divorce is final.

"Wow," she responded and then waited for more details.

"After all the time and money I've invested in developing and launching The Innerlight Method™, it's hard for me to believe that this is the direction Spirit wants me to go. Yet every time I ask, there's a clear affirmation..."

"Maybe this *is* the way Spirit wants to launch your message. I've seen crazier things." Amanda seemed strangely sure that this was all going to work out to launch my message.

It feels like it would be selling out on my work to just drop it now. Why would all of this have happened, just for me to go back into the education system?

Like so many helping professionals and entrepreneurs, my message and emerging work with The Innerlight Method™ was the result of my recovery from trauma—a traumatic childbirth experience and the loss of my baby. Soon after the experience, I began to feel other people's illnesses and emotions in my body and hear the thoughts of strangers standing next to me in a grocery store or at a movie theater. It didn't take long for this to deeply disrupt my life, and I often wondered if I would ever be able to enjoy public events again. I didn't know it then, but I was going to be guided to all of the skills, tools, and teachers I needed to manage my new intuitive abilities, rather than feel like I was a victim of them. I was about to get the educational experience of my life—one that would take everything that I had learned about the body and education to a whole new level.

My passion has always been education and my academic career began with a bachelor's degree from U.C. Berkeley in African American Studies. I was interested in the sociology of education, knowing there were educational inequalities for black students who often weren't perceived to be as intelligent as other children. After completing my bachelor's thesis about the culture of poverty theory and its impact on the educational opportunities available to low-income children of color, I decided that I wanted to build schools that would help non-traditional learners thrive. That's why I decided to attend Teachers College, Columbia University, in New York City, where I earned a master's degree in Urban Schooling and began to teach fourth and fifth graders.

As a teacher, I soon noticed that I would often be assigned to the very bright children of color who had behavior or anxiety problems—children the other teachers didn't know what to do with. I fell in love with these exceptional but struggling children and developed a record of success in working with them. I became even more determined to help create learning environments where these children could thrive as I noticed the issue of inequities in the education system. White children with challenges were often perceived to be smart and bored and referred to gifted programs, while children of color were referred to programs for behavioral problems and not given access to higher educational opportunities. I also became curious about the general population of exceptional children who were often highly-sensitive.

When I came back home to California, I won a Spencer Fellowship to study Urban Schooling at the UCLA School of Education. There I earned my Ph.D. in Education with emphasis on charter school design. My goal was to build alternative, holistic environments that would give bright but struggling children the opportunity to learn.

It was during this time when I lost my first baby, began to experience other people's thoughts and feelings, and started a desperate search for a way to help others without compromising my own health and sanity. When I finally

learned that the trauma had essentially blown out my
nervous system, I began to acquire skills and tools to self-
regulate and heal. Over the years, I developed a proprietary
protocol for balancing my energy while I finished my degree
and began to work as an educational consultant, helping
people build and design charter schools. Ultimately, I became
the founding board president of Aveson Charter School in
Altadena, California; and, when I saw the same symptoms
in the children, I integrated energy balancing into the
educational curriculum for sensitive and gifted children.
As word of my success traveled, I opened the Innerlight
Sanctuary in Altadena, California, so I could offer the benefits
of energy balancing to more children and their families. The
more people I helped, the more my own gifts opened up.

Finding myself at the intersection of my spirituality,
mind-body practices, and neurobiology, I began to invest
heavily in getting this work out to all of the empathic
intuitives who were suffering. Unfortunately, because
science had not yet caught up to explain how or why this
was working, my work in both the school system and a
New Thought spiritual center brought into question the
appropriate place of the work with regard to the separation
of church and state. It was then that I resigned from my
public charter school position and my role as minister, and
began serving children and families with The Innerlight
Method™ full-time.

As I looked for ways to share my work with others, it
became clear that one of the best ways for me to share my
message and build credibility as an entrepreneur was to
write a book. I wrote the manuscript for The Intuitive Mother
but found myself struggling with fear of sharing that story for

years. Plus, I had also two more book ideas bothering me and couldn't seem to make headway with either of them.

That's about the time I found myself in an intimate women entrepreneurs' mastermind, sitting next to a book coach named Amanda and wondering if I'd heard her right. Did she say she'd written her book in *three weeks*? I wondered if she could help me but didn't ask because... well... she didn't appear to like me very much.

Several meetings passed and I kept wondering, *What is her problem? I don't think I've done anything to hurt her feelings.* I did not want to push myself on her, but when the editor of my first book passed away suddenly from cancer, I knew I was going to need support from someone like Amanda. So, I cautiously reached out and told her about the book I wanted to write titled *The Five-Point Bliss Plan.*

"Hmmmm... Is there another book you've been thinking about writing?" she had asked.

Reluctantly, I'd told her about the other one.

"Oh yes, that's the one!" she'd exclaimed, as if she was already tuned in to my author trajectory.

I hired her, completed all of the exercises she gave me, discovered her intuitive gifts of organization, and wrestled with her about how much of my personal story to tell. She won that match, and I'm glad she did. As uncomfortable as it was to put it in there, the feedback on the book always includes gratitude for including my story.

It wasn't too far into our collaborative process that she asked me if I thought she could help her and her family energetically, and I was able to give her the experience that I had only been able to tell her about until then. And, at some point throughout all of this, she warmed up to me and a friendship blossomed. She even decided to become an

Innerlight Practitioner so she could help her empathic clients move through the writing process more easily.

When I found out that she could help me build a curriculum, I began to engage her for support in developing an online course for empaths as well as updating and refining the Innerlight Practitioner curriculum and some of the promotional materials.

The vision was to attract intuitive professionals—people who would say, "Oh, this woman has an Ivy League education and she's developed her intuition? That's awesome!" and then hire me to learn how to use their intuitive abilities to be more effective and avoid the burnout that affects so many helping professionals.

Unfortunately, the work was not growing as I'd expected and now I was at this crossroads.

Do I stop The Innerlight Method™ work and go back to education?

"Do you see any way that this could actually expand your work rather than delay or detour it?" Amanda asked.

"Well, yes. The dean knows about my work and the results that I got at Aveson and how some of the teachers became more effective as they learned how to incorporate mind-body practices. She did mention the possibility of me continuing to run my programs and, if people from the college decided to join, I could simply give the college a percentage."

"Hmmm..." Amanda mused. "I guess if Spirit is nudging you this way, there has to be a reason, whether it's this partnership or something else."

Spirit didn't change Its mind, so I said yes to the offer from the university and jumped in with both feet.

Amanda was right. There was immediate interest in my programs as my graduate students began to integrate some of the mindfulness and energy hygiene practices into their daily routines. They were experiencing tremendous improvement in their physical and mental well-being, they were having less issues in their classrooms, and they were hungry for more. Over time, I began to fold the lessons into my graduate level classes and became determined to reframe the work with more science and research than energy balancing language. Fortunately, science had caught up. Research in neurobiology and trauma-informed somatic practices could now explain exactly why and how these mindfulness practices work.

I scheduled a retreat in Oregon with Amanda and we created a new science-based approach to helping educators and leaders become more powerful healing agents for children without compromising their own well-being. We wrestled a little bit around how to lean into the science without completely divorcing the woo, but we finally found a solid balance. She helped me revamp all of the curriculum in three phases—Intrapersonal Mindfulness, Interpersonal Mindfulness, and Institutional Mindfulness—and make it digestible for the teachers and leaders who were beginning to ask for more of what I was sharing through my classes and the retreats we had been hosting through the university.

When San Bernardino City Unified School District approached me about providing them with year-long professional development for their teachers, principals, administrators, and even superintendents, I was ecstatic. The university had positioned me and established credibility for me and the work I am here to do at a level that I could not have even imagined when the opportunity was first offered to me. Instead of training helping professionals from all walks of life, I was now in a position to bring everything I had learned back to the education system that was my original focus and passion. Instead of helping classrooms of thirty students every year, my work is now potentially improving the lives of the tens of thousands of students who are being taught by the teachers I've trained this year and for the rest of their teaching careers. YCMTSU! Spirit had a much bigger plan.

There was only one problem—the name of my business. Public school administrators told me they couldn't write a check to a company named Innerlight Sanctuary. It was a very difficult but necessary decision I had to make. After a few weeks of meditating on it, Mindful Leaders Project was born, and Amanda and her design team went to work rebranding the website and materials while I navigated the emotional experience of shepherding a contract this huge.

The superintendent of one of the largest school districts in the state of California had asked me to lead them on a retreat with the superintendent himself and the principal of every school present. They hadn't pushed back on the price. They hadn't tried to negotiate me down. They just trusted me enough to ask for the contract and then convince the entire school board to approve it, and then convince principals to attend on the weekend. The doubts and fears reared their heads, especially after dealing with some of the pushback from some colleagues at the university: *Why me? Am I a fraud? Am I making this shit up? Is it really real? Does it really help people the way I say it does?*

I used all of my own self-regulation practices and showed up, and the results were incredible.

Shortly thereafter, I developed a mindfulness practice called The Vagus Nerve Reset and contacted Amanda to help me write a book about it. When she pitched the proposal, I gulped. Another hefty investment and I wasn't sure I could make it happen. I told her I would get back to her and told Spirit I needed to know if this was the right next step. The very next day, I received an email from an administrator from a district I'd pitched many months prior. They'd been unresponsive, and I had assumed that it just wasn't going to work out. In the email, the administrator said they had been working to find the resources to pay me for at least a small amount of professional development for their district, and I gasped when I saw the number. It was the exact amount of Amanda's proposal. You really cannot make that shit up!

We signed the contract and Amanda created all of the structures, but I just could not get around to doing my part. Did I mention that I was working two full-time jobs (the university and Mindful Leaders Project) and running half a dozen teams in addition to being the mother of three children whose needs are such that I devote many additional hours to advocating for their well-being and supporting them as they tackle their goals?

When I kept apologizing, Amanda reminded me delays are normal and they usually have purpose; and then, as we had experienced together several times before, we realized Spirit had other plans. We rode the waves of inspiration and feedback and designed a curriculum instead for those who wanted to learn the new practice and those who would want to coach others through the process of learning it.

If there was one thing we were learning through this process, it was that the science of mindfulness was making it easier to accept the reality that we all have the power to self-regulate, heal, and tune into the intuitive knowings that come in various ways at all times of the day and night—not just when we go to church or sit on a meditation pillow.

From the beginning, I've known that the only way to build this enterprise was to embody my message—to become the thermostat, not the thermometer—but it hasn't always made sense and it hasn't been easy. In fact, sometimes it's been extremely frustrating, especially as I am growing into roles that have required the shift of the once-very-cozy-and-intimate dynamics in my community and leading a team of people like Amanda who move quickly and find themselves waiting on me. Amanda, how many times have I half-joked that I'm not really being a slacker?

But I've realized, it's not really *me* they are waiting on; it's the timing and direction from Spirit we are all waiting on. There is a higher timing involved, and 2020 was an exceptional example of that.

In the first quarter of 2020, we were looking at a busy year full of bigger contracts, retreats, keynotes, and training events than we had ever seen. By mid-March, like so many other enterprises, everything was being cancelled as the pandemic turned up and the world shut down. It didn't look good, and I won't lie and say that I wasn't struggling with fear and disappointment. It was a scary time on… so many levels.

Then, I started to receive phone calls and emails asking how much of my work could be provided online because teachers and students were struggling emotionally and needed support immediately. Time was of the essence as an outdated system struggled to adapt to a whole new approach to learning. In the time span of five weeks, my calendar was full again, I was delivering my work online, and I was looking at a watershed year by the end of 2020. It was the first year in 10 years of business ownership that I was able to pay off all of my debt and pay myself a salary.

Spirit also nudged me to move during this time. Not just move, but buy a house. What? In the middle of a pandemic? Knowing that I had to listen, I started my search and contacted the professionals who could help me. My heart was set on staying in Pasadena, and when Spirit pushed me toward Pomona, I argued. I didn't want to live in Pomona.

"But what if your new man is waiting for you in Pomona?" Amanda asked innocently as I was sharing this frustration with her.

Four weeks after I started looking, I found a home in Pomona. It was an amazing find and I got an incredible deal for it. Four months after I moved in, Spirit told me to walk the neighborhood. Then It told me to strike up a conversation with a young woman I was passing. We walked together for the next few days and became fast friends. One morning, I boldly asked her, "So, where does one go to find a good man around here in Pomona?" We laughed together and then she said, "Oh, wait. I know a guy..." A few days later, she connected me with one of the kindest, most caring, and spiritual men I have ever known. I had to call Amanda and tell her what had happened and all of the YCMTSU details, including reminding her of the fact that she predicted that I would meet my new life partner in Pomona. What we couldn't have predicted was that his parents and mine had attended the same church for years. Seriously?

By the end of the year, I was starting to realize that my bandwidth was about to be completely tapped out. As the result of some keynotes I gave and word of mouth endorsements, I found myself looking at an inbox full of potential contracts that there was no way I could fulfill on my own.

How am I going to get this work to more people and still have a life? I'm enjoying being in a relationship, and I have a short time left with my girls at home before they leave for college. I just cannot take on more, but I don't want to prevent other leaders from engaging in this work.

I called Amanda again and, after some conversation, realized that it was time for me to build a curriculum that could be licensed and delivered to school districts without it requiring my constant presence and energy.

Again, Amanda delivered the framework and the initial curriculum very quickly and then waited for me. Frustrated that I could not seem to get to this very important work, I told her that it was time for her to kidnap me again. She quickly put together a small retreat experience and I flew to Oregon to work on this project, certain that I would be able to complete it while I was there.

But I didn't. I couldn't. Because I could not stop thinking about this dream I have of owning a retreat center where I will live and host retreats and events for mindful leaders. When I shared my frustration with Amanda, she asked if this idea could somehow be related to the project we were trying to complete.

That's when it hit me. All of my "obsessive thoughts" were focused on creating an environment where people would feel safe and nourished.

"Amanda, there's a fourth piece to this framework—Environmental Mindfulness," I started when she sat down next to me at the table. "I'm shocked this didn't occur to me before because environment is everything in the work I do at the Center for Neurodiversity, Learning, and Wellness. I've told you that I have helped many leaders transform their spaces into nurturing environments that soothe and nourish, but I didn't even think to include it in this curriculum as its own piece until now."

"Well, now we know. When's the next time I get to kidnap you so we can write this all out?" she asked with that mischievous smile.

Amanda's Side of the Story

"Can you just ask my book if it wants this piece in there?" she asked.

Grateful I was on the phone and not video, I closed my gaping mouth and searched for an appropriate response.

"That's what you do, right? You communicate with people's messages and books and help them land on the page the way they want to?" she probed.

Dozens of moments of sitting with thousands of post-it notes full of clients' stories flashed through my mind, followed by common responses when I presented my first attempt at their message matrix: "How did you do that... and so quickly?"

And just a few weeks before when Niki had told me that she wanted to write a book about achieving bliss, I'd responded, "That's not the book that wants to be written. Have you thought about other books?"

"Ummmm... yeah... I guess that *is* what I do," I laughed lightly as the realization sunk in. It was the first of many important realizations Niki would crack open for me.

Shortly after we began working on her book, *I Feel Your Pain,* I knew exactly why this woman had entered my life at the time she did. It was the summer that I discovered I was living in an abusive family system and a few months after I had taken on my grandmother's care full-time and gained twenty-plus pounds overnight (no exaggeration). I am an empath, and my body and mind were completely collapsing under the weight of the empathic overload.

I immediately made appointments with her for myself, my husband, and my son, realizing that so much of our strange symptomatology was actually energetic overload. Within just a few weeks, all of us were feeling better, and plans for transitioning out of our toxic situation and into our own space and life were underway.

Once we were settled in, Niki asked for my support in developing an online course to support those who wanted to continue the work beyond the book. That's when my whole life really started making sense. As I began to interact with her content, I realized that trauma in my childhood had compromised my nervous system but also blown open my intuitive abilities, so that I could protect myself from more trauma. If I could somehow hear or see or sense that something was about to go awry in my world, I could get away in time or try to prevent it, right? Well, those intuitive superpowers served me well over the course of my lifetime—keeping me safer than I would have been without them *and* giving me the ability to hear, see, and sense the stories behind people's stories. This was one of the reasons I have been so damn good at helping people write their stories and heal the st*ries that were in the way. But like any superpower, there was a shadow side—a corresponding weakness—that had created some serious messes for me in the past few years of my business. Turns out some people didn't like me eavesdropping on their internal world or their marital stability or... and some of them and/or their partners were just powerful enough to take revenge and simultaneously destroy my financial and physical well-being. The good news was, Niki knew exactly how to help me preserve and even expand my intuitive superpowers but also contain and direct them more consciously.

This realization also helped me understand why Niki and I got off to such a strange and uncomfortable start. As I was reading through her content one day, it occurred to me that I had used this shadowy superpower to quietly read people and situations to assess whether they were safe for me. Niki was the first person I'd ever met who had such a strong and clean energy boundary that I could not "get a read on her." Of course, unconscious to this entire process at the time, all I determined was that she wasn't safe. Consciously, I thought I was being nice and cordial, but her highly-developed intuition knew that something was off. Looking back, it's crazy to me that one of the safest people I've ever met felt unsafe to me at first for the very reason that they presented something so unfamiliar that it felt unsafe.

Two years after we met, I had the opportunity to work on Niki's Innerlight Method™ curriculum and join her practitioner certification program. It just so happened (in true YCMTSU style) that the weekend of the first immersion was only two days after my very first seven-day retreat. As I listened to her share the foundational concepts of her work, I realized that I had actually been witnessing healing and energy balancing for people for almost ten years but that my problem was that I didn't have the energy boundaries to avoid taking on all of their st*ry. So, I was essentially absorbing their pain instead of simply witnessing it. This awareness and the tools she gave me through this certification program completely transformed my own personal well-being; and, when I began to offer these sessions to my clients, I was stunned at how much more quickly and easily they all moved through their writing and healing process.

I have loved witnessing Niki's personal journey as a messenger through all of the wrestling matches that come before the next iteration or expansion of her work. Of course, one of the first wrestling matches I witnessed was in a hospital bed after a terrible asthma flare-up; but as soon as she got the direction she needed, we made that right with some of her favorite food and entertainment. Since that moment when she worried that she was walking away from her message by taking the position to the university, I have watched her wrestle with the next challenges presented and then shake her head in amusement and awe when it all unfolds so divinely. Like the time she came to a retreat to strip all of the woo out of her curriculum and lead with the science. Oh my goodness, the struggle was real, as she refused to abandon this essential part of herself (the woo) and lean into a more challenging and academically-demanding approach. When she told me that her first group of teachers in the district were Christians and were seeking her out during breaks to ask how this science related to their personal religious beliefs, I couldn't help but laugh.

More than any other client I've worked with, I have seen Niki pour all of her money and faith into her mission in obedience to Spirit's direction and be rewarded time and time again. It may not have happened as quickly as she wanted it to, but it happened; and we celebrated it every time.

That part of our story is actually really important. We have both had to see and own the contribution we are making, raise our prices, and negotiate new rates and agreements to what is possible for both of us over the last six years. Once, while she was being stretched to invest for more of my support, I was working through this old st*ry about my value/worth being tied to my performance/productivity and this shitty belief I have that I am a tool for others to get what they need and want. There was one moment where our mirroring st*ries collided, and she created a disconfirming experience for me, even though it created more stress for her. She had called to let me know she would be a little late on her payment; and she must have intuitively heard my panic and the st*ry behind it, because she quickly shifted gears. "Amanda, I cannot be part of you thinking that your current financial situation is the result of a lack of value/worth or even punishment. I am going to make this payment with my personal credit card, so we can both move forward the way we need to." The money was sorely needed at the time, but it was the message she delivered that really changed everything for me in that moment: "You are worthy. You are not being punished. Spirit is supporting us, so let's take this leap together."

That's one of the qualities I admire most in Niki. She has the intellectual and intuitive power to access a level of success and visibility that most messengers seek, but I don't think I have ever seen her misuse it. Instead, she does the work that she encourages everyone else to do. While it has taken longer than she hoped, I believe she is on the precipice of leading a movement that is desperately needed in our world and, more importantly, that she will not crumble under the pressures that come with that level of responsibility and visibility.

In addition to having the honor and blessing of being witness to all of it, working with Niki has given me the unique opportunities to experience dreams that I let go of almost twenty years ago when I walked away from education. For instance, in 2018, she enlisted my facilitator skills for a portion of the retreat she was facilitating for special education teachers, and we were in the car driving up to Lake Arrowhead for the weekend when it struck me.

I was about to facilitate a heroic narrative st*ry-healing session for passionate-but-tired teachers who stayed in the profession instead of high-tailing it out like I had twenty years before, because I didn't have the mindfulness strategies that Niki teaches, just down the street from my childhood home where I had received my message decades earlier. How's that for a YCMTSU story loop?

I had received the message of "grace in imperfection on the road to true to intention," though it would take me years to truly accept and embody it. Then I had been inspired to become a writer and change the world, only to go to the university and decide to become a high school teacher to help young people really learn from history by engaging great stories, only to walk away because of how emotionally and physically unhealthy I was. But then the re-ignition of my message had led me to a transformational facilitator program, which then gave me the platform to support aspiring messengers, which inspired me to create True To Intention and support people like Niki.

Because of all of those starts and stops [and perceived failures and hiccups], I walked into that retreat with the capacity to facilitate transformation at a deeper level than I ever could have if I had stayed in education. Because of that journey, I am creating more impact in the lives of students, teachers, and education systems by applying all of these skills to Niki's work than I ever could have achieved on my own had I stayed. Makes you think that maybe that was the plan all along, doesn't it? Yeah, me too.

Rick Amitin is an International Speaker, Author, Blogger, Facilitator, Creator of The Design to Shine Community, and President of RickAmitin.com, a company dedicated to connecting people to the power of their dreams. Rick is a Certified Behavioral Analyst and a Veteran of the United States Marine Corps. Rick has been married to his wife, Tina, for forty years. Rick is a father, grandfather, and a great-grandfather. He loves the water's edge, a good book, the company of friends, meaningful conversation, and remains a lifelong student.

The Story I Didn't Plan to Tell

Rick Amitin

"**Y**our writing is good, Rick. You've done great work here to harness the power of your message."

I didn't know what Amanda was drinking, but I wanted to Amazon her a case with Prime delivery to keep her stocked. And yet, what should have been a magical moment came with a pause for me. I heard her words, but the feeling that usually accompanies praise was missing.

"Amanda, do you really think this is good? Because... I'm not feeling that from you."

There was a brief silence and a nervous giggle, like she had been caught with her hand in the cookie jar, before she responded, "I think your book is incredible, Rick. But your message has brought my own daddy issues to the forefront. I think what you might be feeling is me holding the closet door of bubbling emotions shut while I'm coaching you. I'm sorry if that's made you feel like I'm not authentically proud of your book and all the work you've done."

Wow! Talk about a defining moment. What could be more affirming than to have your Book Coach experience healing from the book you are writing to heal your own life? Dang, you didn't just appear, Amanda. You showed up, and I will always love you for that.

I was relieved that the disconnect I was feeling from Amanda was not actually between us, which could have derailed our working together and left me reeling from the wounds of my past.

My Story

One of my favorite comedians, the late Flip Wilson, offered
this take on Love: "Love is the feeling you feel when you're
about to feel a feeling you've never felt before." Comedy
can be so honest. Any list of basic human needs always
includes love.

The absence of love in my early years, coupled with the
abandonment by my father and having three step-fathers by
the time I was nine, sent me on a quest for my real identity.
I mimicked whatever masculinity was trending at the time.
I unwittingly attempted to make a father out of many of my
male role models. I ruined some mentors by mistakenly
thinking that was their role.

In every city I traveled to for years, the first thing I did
was check the local phonebook to see if my father was listed.
I searched and searched for him. I even hired a detective
who came up empty-handed. I called all the Amitin's I found
numbers for, and nothing led to my father. Many years later,
I found out that some had lied to me about knowing him. One
woman, who said she didn't know him, had been married
to him; and so I was still looking for him ten years after
he was dead.

By my thirties, I had given up, believing I would have to
live with my emptiness. I married, had children, and captured
much of what I thought I had missed from my father by
fathering my children. But there was a residual effect that
persisted. I never felt good enough, and there were all too
many people there to reinforce the belief. I further advanced

my debilitation by mirroring the patterns of my childhood. If things didn't fall apart on their own, I would tear down what I had built up as a precaution to what I believed was inevitable.

After being in full-time ministry for years as a Pastor and Evangelist, I made the decision to leave the only religion I had known when I could no longer navigate the inner workings of my denomination nor the inner emptiness I was experiencing in my private world. I focused on business for a few years and enjoyed financial success. My faith was never in question; it was more about the packaging that had surrounded my spiritual life and what I was being drawn to. I went back into full-time ministry before determining that my life's work going forward would be expressed in a different domain.

Here comes Enthusiasm!

I'm gonna write a book!

The idea exploded inside me! I thought I'd eaten a firecracker. I'd been thinking about it for years. I mean, really. I've always had something to say, even before I knew I had a convoluted voice. My life story is fragments of truths, lies, and oxymorons woven in clandestine backdrops and kaleidoscope tapestries. *After all, I've been to the circus and lived to tell about it! Not all of God's creations are friendly!* My scars are marks of nobility. I walk with a limp, so I'm trustworthy. And I rely heavily on my immortal humor to sustain me.

I have a story the world needs to hear... a message to heal the masses. Hot Diggity Dog, we're talking "bestseller" here!

I shared the idea of writing a book with my wife and best friends. They gave me enough encouragement that I immediately started organizing my thoughts. A little research told me there are between 600,000 and one million books published each year.

I don't know how to write a book, but how hard can it be? For years, I was an in-demand speaker. I'm almost as at home in front of people as I am alone. Surely after thirty years of developing and delivering messages on stage, I can effortlessly transition this ability to the written page, right?

I decided to put together a collection of mini-sermons, using bits and pieces of my story for the illustrations. I would share my desperate search—as a Christian, preacher, and entrepreneur—to find the father that had abandoned me... only to finally discover God as my heavenly Father.

I created the first few chapter titles, and in just a little over two weeks, I had eight chapters written. It was pouring out of me. *If I had known how easy this is, I would have done it a long time ago!*

Then, I joined a couple writers' groups and began sharing what I'd written. The first round of feedback and edits stole my joy. "You have story killers."

"Whatever, do you mean?"

"Writing is an art, a craft, and you are sending your story in multiple directions."

"Huh?"

I perceived this talk as vital, and I shook my finger at ego, so he knew to behave. Oratory, with its visual influence and emotional connection, is not uniformly transferred to a book. A book is a different kind of engagement. I came to affectionately refer to writing as "catch and release," whereas I look at public speaking as "hook and reel."

One of the other published authors befriended me and offered some support: "When you talk, Rick, I feel it; but I'm not getting that same experience from your writing. The way that you are writing is not how you speak. You really want to write in your own voice."

Writing began to feel like potty training; I soiled myself repeatedly. I reworked the eight chapters to reflect my new understanding of writing with more clarity. I wasn't confident that I nailed it, mind you, but I sensed enough sufficiency to move on. Here's the thing about a learning curve: it's a curve that will never self-identify as straight. Authenticity, as it turns out, is an inside job!

Here comes the Book Coach!

"Amanda is a book coach, and she's very good at what she does." The recommendation came through a mutual friend.

"Really? What's a book coach?" I asked.

"Amanda helps people get their books done," she said with some mystery in her voice.

"That sounds great. I could use some help."

After some phone conversations, Amanda invited me to a writer's retreat she was hosting. I decided to drive from Garland, Texas, to Los Angeles, California, to attend. *What goes on at a writer's retreat?* I wondered about Amanda. *Who is she? How does she fit into my life? My book?* I was the first to get there, and the formal introduction was warm and natural. We connected with everyone else as they arrived, spent a little time discussing what we would be doing over the next few days, and headed for bed.

I am ready to get this show on the road!

The proverbial early-riser, I wasn't surprised to find that I was the first one downstairs the next morning. *Oh, wait! Someone has already been here, and the coffee is ready!* I grabbed the cup with my name on it (*Nice touch, Amanda.)* and seated myself at the breakfast bar. Soon we were all gathered, having breakfast and enjoying small talk. After a quick cleanup, we took our seats.

We spent a few minutes sharing who we are and a little about our projects. It was relaxed and light, and then it was time to get to work. First up, Amanda had prepared a painting exercise for us. *A painting exercise? What does a painting exercise have to do with writing? I hope it's "paint by numbers" because I can't even draw my name out of a hat.* And, off we went into another room where water paints and paper were waiting for us.

"I would like for you to paint a picture of the defining moments of your life," Amanda instructed, "and then a second picture of your life today. You will be using these to introduce your true self to the group."

What happened next is hard to verbalize.

I looked at the paints, and then my eyes landed firmly on the blank paper. So much emotion swelled inside me that I was stunned to the point of not being able to move. That's right, Mr. Tough Guy was crying intensely. Nobody else was having this kind of response. I considered being embarrassed but dismissed the idea. I didn't know what was happening or why it was happening. I could not pick up the paintbrush. A few minutes passed and Amanda made eye contact with me. I read her lips, *"Are you okay?"* I nodded *yes*, but I wasn't.

After a bit, I excused myself and went outside. I needed a talking to, an inquiry, an explanation. I did not like my life, how it looked, and I didn't want to paint that picture. The shame and self-condemnation were tangible. My religious conditioning and self-hatred were too active to allow me to become evidentiary. *Nobody can EVER see what I am looking at but me!*

After I collected myself, I returned, picked up the paintbrush, and painted a picture. I don't remember what I painted. It wasn't much of anything, but it didn't matter. The actual image was the truth that was unfolding within me. You can't make this s**t up!

And so, *The Story* began.

I had become everything I never meant to be—an outsider to my own life. Oh, it began in earnest. I tried to follow the principles of success and righteousness as outlined for me. I attended this seminar, that training, read this book and that one, listened to enough self-help to cure the planet. I searched the Bible from cover-to-cover multiple times, preached my guts out thousands of times—trying to save the world and myself—to no avail. I continuously probed and investigated what was too obvious to see...

Over the next few days, we worked through the details of our stories and messages. There were aha's and hiccups. Laughter and tears. It was fun and baffling. Amanda listened to our stories and then helped create a *matrix*, an outline for our books. We spent considerable time accomplishing this task. She asked a lot of questions. She heard things in my story that I didn't and saw things I hadn't.

Her eyes widened when I told her that my father had abandoned me, and my grandson's father had done the same to him. She nodded when I shared that I was angry, as angry as I had ever been. I understood that the issues around my father had caused immeasurable pain and confusion inside me. She shook her head in understanding when I told her that I lived with, what I call, identity theft. Not the loss of a bank account or credit score, but the loss of affirmation, a sense of worthiness, and clarity. I was more than a little upset this nightmare was about to repeat itself in the life of my grandboy. Her eyes twinkled when I shared that I was, and am, resolved to lessen his potential pain.

Tears fell down her cheek as I told her the story of our incubation and his birth. "Amanda, it has taken me years to be able to interpret my private world coherently. I have been grieving my entire life. Here I was, a grandfather with a precious grandboy who was in desperate need of a man, a man who is whole in his life. I began to parent myself and completed the manhood that had been hijacked in my infancy. I became the *Observer* to my maturation. If it is the last thing I do on this Earth, my grandboy is going to enjoy what I call "Identity Anointing"—the power of affirmation, knowing how to relate to the world with a sense of worthiness, and the kind of clarity that informs him of his competencies so he will know how to prosper. When I held him for the first time, I made sure he heard the words I'd always longed to hear: 'You are loved and wanted. I am glad you are here.' He will need love, examples of authenticity, and an awareness of his instincts in order to thrive. He'll need more than just what I'm able to provide, but I vow to be a man that he can always trust and count on for as long as I live.

She nodded when I told her the term *fast food* was recognized in the dictionary by Merriam-Webster in 1951 and that, while most of us are familiar with the phrase and associate it with drive through restaurants, I came to know *fast food* as an early and even premature life experience. "I experienced rejection, neglect, molestation, physical and emotional abuse, divorce, and poverty before I had the skills to deal with any of them. These are the *fast foods* I'm resolved to do everything in my power to prevent from emerging in my grandboys' life. I am determined to do my part to nourish him with whole foods that will lead to his well-being, and I am desperate to ensure my grandboy doesn't grow up feeling the way I felt."

Somehow, Amanda got all of this story and all of this intention into a *message matrix* that would put me in touch with the deeper meaning and message of my book... and life. And I would become even more intentional toward my grandson.

I left the retreat with zero chapters in hand. I had to start over. My original book was a discombobulated me—a collection of sermons with powerful illustrations that told my story—but not *The Story* that was trying to emerge.

The Real Work Begins

The matrix and I began as friends. Then it turned into a demanding demon. I struggled to stop telling my story and let *The Story* tell itself. I quit with my BS (belief system). I wiped the sweat from my brow often.

The account of my life story was deeply embedded, and it was rising to the surface. After writing all day, I would read what I had written to my wife. We often laughed and cried as I connected my fatherlessness to that of my grandson. I relied on feedback from my wife and friends to guide me, and I also learned to trust my intuition as I traversed the highs and lows of my life.

Full of excitement, adventure, exploration, and occasional frustration, I labored to put my life on paper, determined to be honest, reflective, and transparent. *Nobody's perfect, "right?" How can I be authentic if I don't show my warts?* I comforted myself with a mini-message: *All princes are former frogs. There's no need to croak over sinking lily pads or colossal failures. People need the hope found in what other people have overcome. It inspires a passion for their own lives. I have survived, and people like to hear stories from those who have risen from the ashes!*

I'd had my high-rise moments, too—experiences of grandeur and Ferris wheel views. I'd strolled the boardwalk of intimate ideas and shared transformational lollipops with dignitaries. I'd relished in the feeling of significance, and I'd hugged the shores of contentment. I'd learned the notes, found the melody, and sang the tune. *I have felt the wind beneath my wings! I have a tale to tell!*

I Can't Tell THAT Story

Honesty is not always warm and fuzzy feelings of liberty. I intended to leave some unpleasantries distant. What I didn't understand was that within those details were the intricacies of *The Story* I didn't plan to tell. *The Story* had its own voice.

Bam! That's a huge, hairy, and ugly wart on my nose. How am I able to breathe? Convinced I already had my story, I'm shocked the universal consciousness I call God had a difference of opinion with me. *Imagine that!* The words of mentors and influencers began to pulverize my brain: *"Your life is either a warning or an example."*

Wait, I can't be both? I plunged into the kind of inner work that was unanticipated.

My shame was palpable. *What do I know for sure?* I experienced confusion as self-doubt interrupted my peace. I felt set up by my intention and violated by the simple attempt to make sense of my experiences. *Am I kidding myself? Do I have anything worthwhile to say? Who will buy this as accurate?*

Then someone close to me had to be in the book, and they had a bad case of unhappiness. If I had known a memoir is considered by most to be the most difficult to write, I might have opted for a comic strip.

I had to consider other people and how my story might affect them and my relationships with them. Some people did ugly things to me and it was impossible to make them handsome. And I also had to deal with *my* unflattering actions and critical decisions.

Some memoirs are lighthearted, playful, and don't take a deep dive to manifest. I've read some that were fun, joyous, and made me envious. My book was looking more like spaghetti and meatballs that got accidentally dropped on the floor. The cleanup seemed messier than the drop. *Is it even worth the effort?*

I was so triggered, I could have been the global poster boy. I slammed into my story so hard that I had to put my book on hold for some months. I let it sauté while I marinated and told Amanda I would be back after a bit.

We moved from Texas to San Francisco before I finished my book. It's apropos that I would change externally at the same time I internally culminated. Geography isn't necessarily a quantifier of growth; but being near my grandboy, who is a lead character in my book, played like a harp in heaven for me. Having spent most of our time together until he was five, I was thrilled to be reunited in his daily life, and our time together reignited my passion. He is a connection, for me, to the eternal.

I started writing again with determination.

Here come the Munchkins!

"Houston, we have a problem!" Chapter seven began with a knock-on on the door of my inner sanctuary. It was both an unwanted interruption and a welcomed distraction. *Who is there, and what do they want?* I slid the door chain off of my heart and cracked my mind open, ever so slightly. My worst nightmare came to visit. I didn't invite these voices, and I was not in the mood to entertain them. They were not here to socialize. They wanted to eat the flesh off my bones!

I hadn't walked my path alone. There had been so many people who had moved in and out of my life, leaving watermarks and indentations. I had a severe collection of smiles and frowns, bits and pieces of wisdom and insanity flowing through my equilibrium. I'm a garden of versatility, a mutt haunted by the lack of thoroughbred genes. Yet the echo of promised stardom danced a holy shindig in my hippocampus.

While I heard *The Story* I wanted to tell in the deepest recesses of my soul, my voice had playmates. I was angry. And this anger was blocking my virtue. From the abandonment by my father to the violations at the hands of my perceived masters, it all still stung intrusively. My naïve vulnerability had caused me to promote a few men to father figure status. I wanted a dad, someone to show me the way. I thought I had found such a man on several occasions.

One, in particular, proved nearly fatal. I considered him powerful, influential, and capable of fathering me. For a while, I enjoyed the fruit of my notions. Then the unfathomable unfolded.

Successful in his circle of influence and deemed worthy by my intuition, I was never more willingly susceptible. He contributed to the spreading of my wings. Then, abruptly, we entered a treacherous downturn when his insecurity, that I never perceived or thought possible, redefined our relationship.

I went from being touted as a rising star to being trashed as problematic. This father figure used his stature as a platform for abuse of power, manipulation, and exploitation. The lies told violated my wife and me at an immeasurable level. I crashed, found myself on the outside looking in. My descent transpired so rapidly, I did not foresee recovery.

We moved from Maryland to California, and I bounced back quicker than I had imagined possible. Within a few months, my calendar was filled with speaking engagements six months in advance. I even had an offer to come on as an associate pastor to the largest church in our denomination. Even though I was flourishing, the emptiness I was experiencing was even more magnified. I just could not get over the fact that something was missing. I simply couldn't trust the system I had given my life to.

Writing this chapter rebooted the pain I thought was a distant memory. This experience is my story: the agony of fatherlessness. My hypermasculinity had failed, my conformity had failed, my eagerness to be shaped into a man by other men had also failed. The story of how I obtained my manhood is *The Story* to be told. By necessity, I would have to relive the whole gamut of all my days.

The next few months were days of heavy lifting and polishing the brass ring. I was a dog with a bone. Healing takes time, and I found myself often pausing to understand the changes healing was generating. When I dug into chapter seven, I still grappled with old addictions, ways of thinking, and fresh paradigms. It would take some time before I would fully possess my liberation.

But I had to get my message in print. I made the call.

Munchkins Managed... or Not.

"Hello!"

"Hi Amanda, it's Rick. I need to finish my book. Can you help me? *The Story* is fluttering like a Butterfly. Ain't that funny?" I said, chuckling at our inside joke. I had lost my fear and figured out how I would include some delicate issues, and I prepared myself to be naked in public. Sorry for the visual.

I had labored to rewrite much of the content and was feeling spiffy about what I had written. Amanda hadn't seen the new material, so I sent it and waited for her accolades. What she sent back couldn't pass for a romantic rendezvous.

She graded my homework like a professor who had it out for me, hellbent on failing me one way or another. Evidently, there was some residual not-so-loving energy showing up in parts of my story.

Knowing that she was determined to help me get this book right, I responded playfully with, "I hate you!"

Truth is, I didn't believe her and I told her so, so she offered to share the book with a few of her readers and see if they noticed anything without asking them for feedback on anything in particular. When five people all felt the same disturbance in the force around the same story, I realized she was right. It wasn't the book; it was me that needed more luminosity.

All I had to do was figure out how to resolve these feelings so they wouldn't slap my readers in the face.

The room was still and dark and dreary, with the sun shining across my face. Suddenly, I was aware of every sound in my environment, nearby traffic, the fluttering of birds just outside my window, and the gurgling of my machinations. *How can I be choking on ancient artifacts that passed through my esophagus and exited my bowels years ago?* Every experience leaves a calling card, an emotion, a thought, an interpretation.

This book began as an act of love for my grandboy, but quickly spread to include self-love. And then, even extended to loving others more authentically. *How did this love train leave the tracks? What derailed my intention so absolutely?*

My book and message felt like a kiss with bad breath. *Yuck!* I was now holding seven chapters of a book I wanted to throw against the wall, scoop it up off the floor and bury it without a funeral.

With the door fully opened, the din of every voice I'd ever known used my mind for a racetrack. Every kind word or experience yielded to the traumatic events in my life, those horrible things that were said and done to me. While I held tightly to the positive affirmations bestowed on me, the negativity encapsulated me like a fetus in a womb. I would come to understand why the "rats" have the loudest voices. It's not them; it's us repeating them with our interpretation added for effect.

It's true. I haven't forgiven the bastard-maker or those just like him. Whoopsy daisy, that can only mean I haven't forgiven myself—a requirement for an authentic messenger. Well, I'll be the son of a suck egg mule! Writing isn't fun just now.

As I sat in despair, I felt the love that I had felt when my grandson was born. When I first held him and poured my love out to him, it was at that moment that I understood "love" for the first time. (Hey, we're not talking about you; we're talking about me. I'm a slow learner; what can I say?)

I sat at my computer, looking at my book on the screen and realized I was observing a reverse miracle. My beautiful Butterfly had turned into a cocoon. It was one of those moments of truth thingies, where you recognize the larva is protecting the pupa so the Imago may emerge!

Before I could write another word, I had to confront my imagination; *image-I-nation.* I couldn't paint that day at the retreat because of what I saw and didn't see. What had taken shape and what was trying to take shape were at war.

I was still kicking and screaming, refusing to let go of my ideas and images of separation brought on by the abandonment of my father. All of the time and energy I'd spent vying for a sense of worthiness, value, and acceptability left me angry, confused, and resentful. I found myself in a time capsule where I was communicating with my past, present, and future at the same time. I was holding on to the remnants of my story as *The Story* was telling me that I was clinging to nothing but self-deception. I'd built a nation of images, false gods, a false Rick that covered the idea of The Creator who only creates in His image. *My Father and I are one. I'm not one with the father who abandoned me, but one with the Father who never did and never could.*

And this is where I, as a Messenger, got sick. I'd hear the message and get so excited that I would feed others before I digested it myself. Our reality has to get to us before it can get through us! You have to own it before you can give it away!

Blinking at the computer screen, I realized what had happened.

In psychology, the phrase "bearing witness" refers to sharing our experiences with others, most notably sharing traumatic experiences. Guilty as charged! I had gone from occasionally referencing my suffering to incessantly repeating my perpetrator's crimes until I had perfected my story of victimhood. I provided legitimacy for my excuses. My expository gave me a gloss for why I wasn't self-actualizing.

In writing my book, I had jumped into the perfect storm. *The Story* is ruthless, impolite, demanding, and loves relentlessly. It requires the lead to guide us to the truth. *But what about...? No buts!* I had to come to grips with reality. To bear witness to our own life is proof that we aren't lying to ourselves anymore. *I am the father I never had—and the love I didn't receive.*

After months of having my story pruned, my manhood neutered, and my vocabulary reduced to slightly beyond "Mama and Dada" in an apparent attempt to resolve my pretentious tendencies, I was ready to complete the book.

Here comes the Test!

As I was healing and working on the last chapter of my book, the strangest thing happened. A man contacted me who turned out to be a relative. He had been working on The Amitin Family Tree and had a wealth of information to share. I was astounded by what I learned in a matter of minutes.

One phone conversation led to a few impactful emails. My second cousin was so generous as to send some of the genealogy, names, and pictures. My grandfather's name was Alexander, and my great-grandfather's name was Menachem-Mendel, known as Max. There was quite a list of close and distant relatives.

The next couple of weeks had me reeling with intrigue, and it was a pure delight to be filling in the blanks of a lifetime. I will never forget the email I got from my cousin that opened with, "Welcome to the bosom of your family, Rick." I was feasting on what I thought I would never have in my life.

This information coming to me, out of nowhere, at the finish line of *If Only I Had A Dad,* was surreal.

Then, it happened.

My cousin's emails stopped abruptly. My emails went unanswered. I couldn't understand for the life of me why my cousin disappeared, vanished as quickly as he came. I was perplexed.

The familiar chatter returned: *You're nothing, You're not good enough, People don't love you. Nobody stays.* How I responded to all of this is the validity I needed. I stopped this from penetrating beyond my epidermis. *This betrayal, rejection, or whatever it is has nothing—and I mean nothing— to do with me!*

Images from the one and only time I'd spent with my father came knocking. When he had walked into my grandmother's (my mom's mom) house, I'd hid, making sure I could hear everything. "Where's Rick? Where's my boy?" How I had longed to hear those words!

For nearly two hours, we played, arm-wrestled, and laughed. I sat on my father's lap the whole time. I was in another world. When he got ready to leave, I grimaced in a five-year-old way. "Rick, how would you like it if I was here all the time? We could play ball and go fishing. Would you like that?" You can imagine my "Are you kiddin' me? That's what I'm talkin' A-B-O-U-T!"

We hugged and kissed goodbye. I stood looking out the window as he and my mom disappeared into the night. I never saw or heard from my father again.

Now, here was my cousin welcoming me into the family and opening the door to connections and information when I had given up on ever connecting to my roots. And just like my dad, my cousin had vanished into thin air. You can't... you just can't make this s**t up!

Instead of reliving my old stories of rejection and abandonment and feeling all the feelings connected with it, I was able to witness this experience. I was able to let go of my story and surrender to *The Story*.

Here comes the Prize!

"You did it, Rick. You're finished. We'll get you a proof copy, and once you approve it, your book will be available."

I'm used to mixed feelings, but this was ridiculous. I was packed and empty at the same time. I was relieved that two years of reconstruction were over but a bit dismayed at the dismissal of intensity.

I waited like a leopard, ready to pounce for that proof copy to arrive. I ripped open the packaging and pulled out My Book. It was a beautiful thing, man! Just the way I envisioned it. When I received the picture of Jaden, my grandboy, walking across that bridge in Muir Woods several years earlier, I knew that image would be the cover of my book. I couldn't put my finger on exactly what I felt holding that finished book in my hands. Two years of writing and rewriting had come to an end. I was relieved, enthused, appreciative, and proud.

No one knows what tomorrow will bring, but a grandfather is more aware of time. If I didn't live long enough to impress upon Jaden how much I loved him, I would have created a way for him to know long after I'm gone. He could read all about it.

Here Comes the Send-off!

So much life had unfolded since I had been inspired to write *If Only I Had A Dad: Finding Freedom From Fatherlessness.* I didn't see the world, people, or myself the way I used to.

Through the whole process of writing, I had healed, become a man, and had so much more to offer. By becoming less, I had become more! I'd pierced the veil, and the pain had stopped.

And then...

Within days of my book hitting the shelves, I had a heart attack. As the staff was preparing me for surgery in the emergency room, the doctor who would place the stent asked me a strange question: "What do you think brought this on and brought you here today?"

"I recently published a book, and I haven't sold many copies." I could tell from the look on his face that he had never heard that one before.

"I doubt that's the reason," he said.

I didn't doubt it for a minute.

Even though I had finished the book, it seemed my body needed to catch up to my soul. Asking the right questions had moved me into the unknown. My habits of the three-dimensional world were lost in navigating the new paradigm I was embracing. I had to establish new practices to sustain my growth and avoid the temptation to return to the familiar, which I wanted no part of.

We each have two storylines working in our lives: Fiction and Nonfiction. We enter the world as pure nonfiction, authentic, and the embodiment of love. And then things happen that alter our states of well-being. When we are neglected, abused, or violated, our fictional story begins. Living with the feelings of worthlessness, not being good enough, or being unwanted are some of the characteristics of a fictional life. Those feelings are wrong! All of the positive thinking in the world alone will not return us to our authentic selves. Visualization and affirmations certainly help; but until the feelings of fictional experiences change, well-being is all but impossible. The *feeling* of the lies has to change.

While I had intellectually worked through my message and healing in my book, and made great strides in my emotional renovations, there remained lingering feelings that continued to cut deeply. Those negative feelings blocked my ability to advance confidently toward my dreams. My desire to fulfill my destiny was present. I had vision. What I lacked was my Identity Anointing—the feeling of *knowing* who I am.

I drove for Lyft for a period of time to earn money. It was not, at first sight, a place for me to feel like I was doing what I was supposed to be doing. But as I shared my message with many riders and witnessed people's feelings change right before my eyes, I began to understand my life's work in a completely different context.

As three young people exited my car after a long ride where they questioned me relentlessly, they said, "Rick, that was the best Lyft ride ever." "Thank you for sharing your wisdom." "I feel like I understand life so much better." Finally, I knew the power of transformation. Instead of believing I was off-track, belittled, and an imposter, I used my time driving people around to regain my equilibrium.

It would take a second heart attack before I would own my heart. (I already admitted to being a slow learner, or maybe it's pure stubbornness.) Once I learned that I could change my feelings, no matter how long they had been with me or how addicted I was to them, my life entered a whole new dimension.

We relocated across the country, another piece of the proverbial puzzle. My desire to help others has always been with me, but I have come to understand this desire is deeply rooted in a desire to help oneself. We all need support, community, and safe learning environments that are fun and authentic to reach interconnectedness—which is the object of destiny, being the light of intentional design.

For this reason, I have created the Design To Shine community; because we all are worthy of a rich, rewarding, and fulfilling life. I can't wait to see others replacing their story with *The Story*.

Amanda's Side of the Story

"Amanda, I have an idea…" a dear client-friend started. "One of my oldest friends is working on a book and needs your help, but has a budget. But he's also fantastic at negotiating with car dealerships, and I know you and Ryan are in the market for new cars. Do you think you two might be able to help each other?"

"Oh, yes. That sounds like a win-win for sure. Send him my way."

The first time I talked to Rick, I smiled and thought to myself, *Another former preacher. Another person who walked away from religion for the same reason I did. Sounds fun!* When I heard that he had a nearly-completed manuscript and a beautiful vision of helping others, I asked him to send me the manuscript and said I'd get back to him with a proposal for editing.

As I read through the chapters that felt like a compilation of sermonettes, my frustration increased. Inside of these really amazing lessons, shards of his story poked and prodded me. Knowing that if it frustrated me, it would do the same for his readers, I called him back and asked him some questions to see if he'd be open to bringing more of his story into it.

The hesitation was real, but his commitment to reach his reader with his message was so great that he said yes to diving into his story at the next retreat and weaving it into the manuscript.

As he shared his journey on retreat, I felt something new begin to emerge but couldn't see it until he told me about his first few moments holding his grandson and blessing him with all the words that he wished his own father had said to him when he entered the world.

That's it, I thought as I grabbed the stack of post-it notes.

When I showed him the message matrix, with the story of Jaden running alongside his, I could see that it would take him a minute to wrap his head around the powerful opportunity before him—to share his story and heal some of the wounds that I could hear still festered beneath the surface.

That was May of 2015.

Three months later, we were working through the first few parts of Rick's story—his father abandoning him and the solace he found in the church—when I got the wake-up call of my life.

At thirty-five years old, I discovered that the extent of my own daddy issues stretched much further and deeper than I'd imagined. I realized that I had been trapped in and shaped to adapt to an abusive family system dynamic when I was little, and that it was my dad's choices that had put me there. I finally saw the cause of so many of the sticky st*ry loops in my personal and professional life—the conditioned

belief system that had made me easy prey for every
abuser and wounded healer who had crossed my path and
compounded that early trauma over almost three decades.
Just like Rick, I could look back at my life and see all the
moments I had looked for safety, belonging, and self-worth
in other authority figures and communities, only to find that
they were devastatingly human. (What did you call them,
Rick? Mentors, monsters, and... oh yes, the 3 M's. I almost
died of laughter when you sent me that first draft of your
introduction.)

About the same time I was having my wake-up call, Rick
was experiencing one of his own and decided to step away
from the writing to sort it out. I told him I was eager to help
him when he returned and turned my focus to planning our
escape from the toxic environment that had wreaked havoc
on our health and harmony.

In true YCMTSU fashion, Rick contacted me almost as
soon as we arrived in our new home, almost a year later.
As I worked with him for the next several months, I barely
breathed through the enormous amount of emotion that
bubbled as I coached him and read the details of his story.
In the quiet of my office, I cried for the little boy who had a
beautiful moment with his father and never saw him again;
and I wept for the little girl who didn't know when she had
stopped being the apple of her father's eye. I cringed as I
watched the young man search for purpose and peace; and
I shuddered as I remembered the young woman's pain and
loneliness as she looked for answers to the most important
questions of life. I raged for the two adults who threatened
their elders with their questions and capacities and found
themselves betrayed and discarded as a result. I celebrated
the man and woman who had determined to give the next

generation a fighting chance by giving them everything they wished they'd had.

And then, something happened.

Through the last review of the book, while Rick was working through his unresolved anger, I was doing the same.

On the pages of his book, I witnessed my father's journey. Abandoned by a parent. Abused by people who should have loved him. Maladapting and misbehaving just to survive. Loved by a woman who saw the hero behind the masks he had to wear. A father who didn't yet know how to keep his mess from spilling onto his children.

I wept. I softened. I forgave.

And, the very same week Rick's book launched, my father died suddenly... unexpectedly.

Like Rick, I would never have the opportunity to ask why, to listen, to share in this dimension; but through all of those aha's and tears, I had found enough healing and peace that I could relearn how to hold a truer picture of my own father. He was not just a hero to those whose lives he'd touched. He was not just a villain who inconceivably, and probably unconsciously, stole a few decades of my life. He was a wounded child, an angsty youth, a troubled partner and parent, a seeker and a skeptic. He was me. And I was either going to love and accept him, or I would never be able to love and accept myself.

Renee Beth Poindexter is the founder of Living The Potential Network, a community that works together to create a better future by connecting individuals of all ages and backgrounds with the mentors, collaborators, resources, training, and opportunities they need to unfold their unique potential, so they can be and create the change they want to see in the world. An accomplished trainer, facilitator, coach, and consultant, Renee Beth's experience spans the industries of technology, financial services, healthcare, manufacturing, business services, advertising, and non-profit organizations, providing her a broad scope for designing innovative solutions for social change.

Living (and Trusting) The Potential

Renee Beth Poindexter

"Your mission is too big."

"It's not possible to connect the dots."

"Your message needs to be aligned with one demographic—pick one."

"You can't change the system."

"People are unwilling to face the issues."

"You are setting yourself up to fail."

The voices of others who had heard about my vision for launching Living The Potential Network haunted me as I selected books to take to the retreat.

I need this one to establish credibility for... and this one to help me prove I'm not crazy about... and this one just in case..., I thought to myself as the stack of books grew. *Amanda appears to be the one person I've met who not only grasps what I'm trying to do, but knows it by life experience.* I sure did not want to spend five days on the mountain with the one person who finally understood my mission and vision and then not be prepared.

Fear cornered me. *"You better not screw this up,"* and, *"If she says, 'it's too big and these stories don't relate to each other,' you will be more than ready with your trunk full of materials."*

Trunk full and last-minute personal care items remembered and tossed into the backseat, I headed for

Mount Hood. The drive was enjoyable and I felt more and more relaxed as the sounds of the city traffic disappeared and the happy songs of birds chirped through my open sunroof. I could feel myself slowing down to the rhythm of Mother Nature and noticed the magnificent red-tail hawk that flew right in front of my car as I approached the driveway of the cabin.

The hawk is a messenger, and I am on my way to meet with the one and only person who finally can help me bring my message to life. Wow!

Excited, I knocked on the door, and Amanda showed me around the cabin and then directed me to the room I would call mine for the next five days. As I was making several trips in and out of the cabin, Amanda came into my space, stifled a laugh, put her hands on her hips, and said, "These items need to go back to the trunk. They will not be needed during this retreat."

Panic set in, and the self-talk turned up as I realized I would be letting go of a lot of beliefs about me and my message, and putting these books back into the trunk was just the beginning.

It's worth it, I told myself. *Whatever it takes, I'm going to get this message out and create the change I know is needed in our broken systems.*

My search for answers to the broken system dilemma began after I resigned as a high school English teacher in Sylvania, OH, where I had been employed for six years. I was burned out and knew there had to be a better way to help young people, but I left there with some important questions: How do we as humans best discover our purpose? What does education have to do with it?

Lucky for me, I found some answers when I entered into the world of business and continued to collect them as I traveled across the domains of construction, technology, advertising, financial services, healthcare, and more for the next several decades, navigated a personal healing crisis, and witnessed an amazing learning community in British Columbia.

Over the years, I have interviewed hundreds of people about why they chose to do the work they were currently doing. Many would say they did it for the money, or that their parents strongly encouraged them to follow in the footsteps of an elder. In some cases, they chose the lesser of two evils or, worse yet, never really consciously decided at all. I found out that very few people chose their career path based on what they are most passionate about, or because it naturally fit their core values or key strengths. As I traveled from one workplace to another, it became obvious that very few people are actually engaged in a career that matches what they went to school to learn. All that money for a college education that did not actually prepare them for what was ahead! All that stress and too little joy! Seemed like there had to be a better way.

For me, the answer was always "Change the way we do Education," and it has been confirmed at every turn. Our society's conveyor belt system, and underlying assumptions, are outdated; and the youth know it. In fact, when I interviewed a cross section of students from home schoolers to valedictorians to high school drop-outs, and asked what was missing for them, they answered, "Freedom to explore what I am most interested in learning." Perhaps, if learning *how to learn* became a clear strategy for us as humans, we could be engaged to find the essence of our unique talent and strengths and discover the best way to bring that forward in a livelihood. The process would be more focused on the questions of "Who am I?" and "What is my calling?" With these questions and their ever-evolving answers, the pursuit of learning would be emotionally fulfilling as it naturally unfolded a unique BEING who is the creator of *meaningful* experiences leading toward the answer to the last big question of "What will I do?"

Unfortunately, I found very few people who could see what was so obvious to me—how essential it is to wake up to the facts that our children's lives are at risk more now than ever and that parents have the power to change it all; and they don't know it.

Searching for other like-minded people who shared this perspective led me to homeschooling initiatives, conscious business groups, and non-profit mission-driven organizations. I attended education conferences, became the Chair for the SelfDesign Foundation (now the Transformative Learning Foundation, which is partnered with Antioch University to deliver an Individual Master of Arts program with a concentration in Transformative Learning Communities), and offered to be an Advisor to the Board of Village Home, an organization focused on family as a learning community. While I continued to see parts of an emerging paradigm coming together, it often felt as if people were preaching to the choir in their separate domains.

I, on the other hand, felt compelled to offer a societal call to action that would be heard by a wider audience, bring all of the domains together, and raise awareness for why we should put youth at the center of the transformation. Children are truly the masters of play; and it is very interesting to observe their learning as they create, innovate, and well, just have fun. They ask a lot of questions: Why? Why? Why? And then they play out their imagination, and the unconscious imprinting they get from the adults around them. That's why everywhere I went, adults were tired, serious, and seriously tired of the rat race that they unconsciously agreed to or the effort to change the system without support and resources. They had forgotten how to play and have fun; and when I'd ask them about their early learning experiences or what they were "playing" when they were a kid, they'd light up with enthusiasm.

What if there was a place where I could connect the experience and wisdom of the elders with the playful and innovative spirit of the youth? Would there be a problem in the world that could not be solved if people worked together across ages and domains? I had to find out!

The idea to write a book was pressing at me, and I shared the inspiration with a friend who quickly connected me with Amanda. When I shared my history and my heart's calling with her in the coffee shop, I felt her deep listening and confirmation as she was nodding and giggling at the same time. She enthusiastically shared her own journey as a teacher, an entrepreneur, and most important of all, as a mother. When she told me that her son, Aaron, was *her teacher,* I knew she really heard me. I could feel my heart beating to the sound of her cadence as she spoke about her writing program and how her own framework for helping others came through her experience of witnessing her son's curiosity during the metamorphosis of a caterpillar into a butterfly. She not only was a traveler through many domains, but most important of all, she grasped my intention. Truly, she had been living it. I felt completely mesmerized with the realization that, at long last, I had found someone who resonated with my mission and message. And, I couldn't wait to meet Aaron.

A week later, I met Aaron and Amanda at our local Panera Bread for lunch. They were in the back booth, waiting for my arrival with smiles galore. As I slid into my side of the booth, I sensed an unusually refreshing energy. Although they are mother and son, their synergy was beyond any role identification. As I delved into questions related to a core essence assessment Aaron had taken, I sensed I was in the presence of an old soul encased in a thirteen-year-old body. I made eye contact with Amanda as I was listening to Aaron and she knew that I was experiencing what no words could have prepared me to witness. Tears began to flow from my eyes, aligning with the lump in my throat, confirming that these two beings would be instrumental in unfolding the conscious, loving, lifelong learning community that I felt was my calling to bring forward as part of my living legacy.

A few months later, Amanda was telling me that I had to leave my books in my car.

"Well, what am I going to refer to if not the amazing sources I've studied for decades?" I asked incredulously.

"I want to start with *your story* of navigating education as a student," she said matter-of-factly.

Gulp.

When I reflected upon my own learning experiences in school, my emotions ran the gamut. I remembered feeling that somehow I had to prove that I was smart, and smarter than my classmates. I learned to fear putting my thoughts down on paper, and constantly wondered what answer the teacher wanted. The goal was to please the teacher; and I remember feeling anxious, fearing the red pen and the power these educators had over me.

But then, there was more to the story, and I wasn't sure I wanted to tell all of it. That external orientation had started in my turbulent home with negligent parents. It had affected my decision-making around careers and relationships. And, it had led to excruciating burnout and a health recovery journey that I was proud of, but not sure how it would fit into this book.

No matter where we all are in our learning journey, there is trauma from not going along with the system, or asking questions out of turn, or bringing up uncomfortable subjects. And, if you aren't a scholar on the subject, who is going to listen to you?

As I shared more of the details of my story, Amanda began to see all of the connections between the WonderTree story of a handful of youth achieving incredible goals in a self-designed learning community, my own personal story, my love of nature, and the steps one must take to create change in the world. In no time at all, I was looking at a message matrix and framework that offered five steps to every stakeholder that were grounded in the natural world and easy to remember. First, we have to learn how to Trust the Seeds of Change—the innate wiring, strengths, and dreams we all bring to this world. Once we have discovered them, we must Cultivate a Fertile Learning Environment in which the seeds can be planted, nurtured, and grown. Once we have roots and some fruits, it's time for us to Cross-pollinate Domains and bring people from diverse ages, backgrounds, and perspectives together to look at the problem we are working to solve. Next, we have to create Regenerative Resources and Systems to sustain the growth of us as individuals and of the collective that is emerging around the project. Finally, we can Reach Upward and Beyond with Technology, using it to nurture and deepen relationships and create opportunities to scale our impact.

"Renee Beth, I don't think anyone would look at your near-five decades of work and life experience and say that you have no credibility because you are missing a PhD after your name. You don't need all of those books. Yes, we'll need statistics and some academic support for some of your big assumptions and assertions; but this will connect more with the reader if they stay connected to the WHY while they are reading the WHAT."

She was right. Although I do not have a PhD, I have lived experience from the worlds of business, healthcare, education, entrepreneurship, coaching, and consulting; and I recognize patterns no matter what the domain. Having Amanda reflect all of this back allowed me to recognize that I have embodied myself as a domain traveler, and even appreciate myself for understanding the incredible value that this perspective offers.

I could see how this framework she gave me would allow me to establish credibility in the eyes of others by sharing my story and supplementing it with resources to back up my claims and dreams for creating a new world together.

Collaborating with Amanda reinforced that my message, *Living the Potential: Engaging the Wisdom of Our Youth to Save the World,* was desperately needed. I was so amazed to hear her say repeatedly, "Yes, it makes total sense... how you came to your awareness about natural learning and how youth are our teachers... and how your business experience has reinforced this understanding!"

Both being seen and receiving this type of support were necessary for me to enter the cocoon and be nurtured in ways that I had been hungry for over too many years. Here was the one and only gifted midwife who would guide me through the dissolution process in the chrysalis in order to birth the story that only I could manifest... and only once I trusted myself enough. It was a messy process as I emotionally had to confront beliefs which created circumstances that interrupted my writing process. Doing the deep work of reviewing my life events that had prepared me to become a writer to "free the children," I had to free myself first.

A key part of finding freedom came through practicing vulnerability. I found that I would write pages and pages to get to a point that could have been made without so many words. It took me a while to understand *how* to weave my message and let it come through in a story of what really happened, rather than using the research of experts to document the significance. Despite my newfound commitment to establish credibility from the inside-out, I still found myself over-preparing with research; but after a while, I would catch myself through Amanda's coaching and editing.

I learned through this process that I had been feeling unsafe in the story I was living. I became very aware that this fear had been repeating itself since my childhood. Fear of criticism or being attacked for sharing my truth became more and more real; and I knew I had to face my father issues, and others in my life, where I was not allowing myself to be fully seen and heard due to that overriding fear. After all, how could I be "engaging the wisdom of our youth to save the world" when the little girl in me was still so wounded?

It was time to dig into these stories, and the 21-Day Quest From Character to Co-Author and the st*ry-healing retreat helped me to figure out where I needed to start healing and integrating the wounded parts of me.

The key word is integration. I had developed a process for people to bring all of who they are to what they do and get paid to be themselves, so I knew the power of integration. The opportunity before me in this retreat was *to receive* coaching from Amanda within a group of other messengers who were each learning how to do their own integration. I was in a container of support, rather than providing that for others. I could let go and allow the emergence to unfold rather than trying to make it happen for everyone else. It was unbelievably refreshing!

This retreat quickly turned me upside-down, but the fire kept me focused. Fire showed up in messages and the oracle cards I pulled. Noticing the repetition and theme, I felt the call to a full fire-opening warrior energy to bring my message to the world. I knew I would have to show up to be seen and that would mean making friends with social media, cleaning up the messes that need cleaning up, and being vulnerable and transparent. I knew that being heard now with my message is important and yet many will want me to stay in "their" comfort zone; but I also knew that if I succumb to that, I am betraying my soul's purpose and path. All of me was in agreement that I could not let myself do that and die a slow death. I had to find a way to rise like a phoenix and bring my flame to life.

The final bit of fire showed up on a Saturday night. It was about 10:30–10:45 p.m. and it was my turn to share my story. When I looked around the room and saw people nodding out, for I was the last one, I said, "We can do it tomorrow." Everyone's eyes popped open as they said, "No, let's do it now." I still felt like I needed to rush through it. I was frustrated and hurrying through my story when it happened. Just as I was telling the story of Mark and my first date on the Fourth of July, where we experienced the most amazing fireworks over the Willamette River (I called it orgasmic at the time), fireworks went off... at the end of January. I looked around the circle at the eyes now wide open as people were amazed at the synchronicity of the fireworks going off just at that precise moment. Intuitively, I knew that my story was being validated and I could feel the pressure that had been building begin to release. My book was scheduled to launch in less than a month, and I was feeling overwhelmed with all that needed to be done. Suddenly with the fireworks as a sign, I began to relax into the idea that I was being "taken care of," and that "it was all handled." No need to worry. You definitely could not make that st*ry up!

By the time the third retreat came along, my book had been released and I was ready to focus on the business plan. But first, there were more stories coming up.

The education non-profit that I was the Chair of (and had been for nine years) was going through massive changes.

Name change, shifting partnerships and accreditation woes
along with Board members resigning. This again triggered
my responsibility gene and made me feel alone in my
attempts to work against the core elements of a broken
system. As I stepped up and out of my comfort zone to do the
right thing, mostly by myself, all of my abandonment issues
were triggered. I faced the fear of losing the reins in the midst
of not knowing every day, but persevered with baby steps
to keep the community together as we built a bridge to what
was coming next. It was all a great exercise in trusting the
"emergence" process. I learned that this can be difficult if
we expect to have the answer in advance, which helps when
leading other people who need to know, rather than trusting
the generative process. In many ways, I had to stop worrying
what the future would bring. Instead, I moved to designing
the highest and best outcomes for each emerging hour of
each passing day, deepening the seeds of trust and cultivating
them into the nourishing social field of possibility.

On the home front, my partner Mark was dealing with
health issues that appeared to be stress-related. I did as much
as I could to lighten his load and be helpful in supporting
him to feel better. Even so, I noticed a pattern over time
that the more I tried to help him, the worse he became.
Within me, there was a conflict between my need to focus
on my own stressful issues, causing me to take care of what
I personally needed, and the guilt I felt for not being 100%
present to what I could be doing to help alleviate Mark's
discomfort. I was definitely playing the twister game and
having a distant memory of the co-dependency I witnessed
during my childhood. It didn't help that deep inside I knew
that, in many ways, I was working through my father issues
and Mark was my catalyst. I was being tested to hold my own

focus regardless of circumstances, as I needed to let go and let come... without fear... trusting the organic learning for life that was on its way through me. YCMTSU.

Although I felt guided and courageous in the business of creating a network, I definitely needed others who wanted it to come to life as much as I did. One of my core strengths is being a strategic connector with excellent communication skills, so I knew I needed to be speaking to more groups and be on more stages. However, I was still building the foundation of the courses and events along with the masterminds for both youth and facilitator groups. That didn't leave a lot of extra time to do self-promotion or networking, which I needed. I was definitely spread too thin. Those "I am not enough" gremlins reared their head while we were working on strategy; and as I looked for the root cause of it all, I accessed lots of abandonment issues masquerading as self-doubt stemming from my father-issues. I knew I had to face all of this as part of an initiation of sorts. Becoming my most authentic self. Back to the chrysalis. Emotionally, I was in turmoil.

I was grateful for the improv-induced belly laughter (and even the nose-bleed) that lightened the mood at the end of those three days of st*ry-healing work and woke the next morning, ready to work on my business plan. Generally, I was feeling more grounded and ready to integrate the message with who else might care about it—my primary avatars— and develop specific strategies for marketing, community-building, and leadership development. This included upgrading my website, developing my signature talk, and designing my courses and workshops.

We discussed ways of engaging the stakeholders and landed on some fun and branded events to offer. The first idea was to offer Podlucks—an opportunity for people to gather and commune with good food and share their hopes and dreams for the future. Then we would invite people to The Garden Experiment Workshop—a full-day experiential workshop where they would actually see the power of this framework in action. Then, those who wanted to continue with us could take a course.

My first two courses were under way, and my four facilitators were engaged within the certification process. When I showed the curriculum to Amanda, she asked if she could help me align it with the framework we'd developed for the book. I quickly realized that I had just spent a huge chunk of change with another coach who was an excellent curriculum designer, but who was not intimately familiar with my book nor my message. Amanda helped me to stop re-inventing new wheels and stick with the simplicity of the learning model that I had written about in the book. These courses would simply allow them to deepen their experience and embodiment of each part of the framework. My goal with the courses was to attract other change-makers out there— teachers, parents, grandparents, entrepreneurs, C-suite corporate leaders, and anyone who was interested in youth succeeding in learning for life. Some of them would become guides who would help more adults and youth collaborate toward solving real-world problems.

One of my favorite movie's *(Field of Dreams)* primary theme is "Build it and they will come," and that's what I felt like I was doing. But instead of a baseball field in the middle of a cornfield, I was building a network of people who could support each other and collaborate toward a better world for our children. Independent of any one particular school system, or state, we are actually a free agent for youth everywhere who want their dream idea or project to come to life with a supportive community. I felt I was on track with the vision and that more and more people would be attracted to this movement once they saw what a difference it could make.

By the end of the retreat, I had set a date for a LIVE Garden Experiment in Washington, D.C. just a few months later.

It was time to get busy planning and inviting people to check out what we are doing.

But Life had other plans.

I don't think it was even a week after this retreat that everything changed in a moment.

I was driving at a peak traffic time to meet a colleague on a Thursday afternoon and crossing a major intersection when BAM! I was hit by a car whose driver didn't notice that multiple lanes of cars were stopped for the cross traffic to pass through. It sounded like a bomb had gone off and I felt my neck snap. In shock, I did my best to maneuver my car through the intersection to a safe space on the other side of the road.

My car had to be towed and it took a couple of months to get it fixed, but it would take about six for me to recover from the concussion and other impacts.

It was during this time that Amanda offered to step in and "be my left brain in the business" for a while. There was so much to do to prepare for The Garden Experiment workshop in D.C., which had quickly become a fundraising event and a much bigger endeavor than I could handle on my own while I was dealing with headaches, sleepless nights, anxiety, irritability, and depression. It was a struggle to get dressed on many days, and I missed my happy-go-lucky self.

It wasn't long at all, however, before I began to see this accident as a gift. Slow was the new fast. As I was forced to slow down to heal, I experienced more of the *letting go* to become *more present* to each precious moment. As a result, my energy shifted from trying to be all things to all people to receiving support from others; and it forced me to focus on myself without the guilt of trying to be more than what is humanly possible with an impossible schedule. With this shift, I received more insights, which grounded the vision to come through without fear and anxiety. It may sound weird, but I began to feel lighter with the support in this world and *beyond this world*, that was guiding the unfoldment. I experienced my imagination's formless possibilities becoming crystallized into offerings and contributions without trying to *make them* happen. Turns out that this accident was a wake-up call and a true gift. As they say, there are no accidents! YCMTSU!

I focused on what I could do, which was connecting with others and inviting them to the weekly Podlucks and the big event we were doing in D.C.

Finally, August was upon us, and it was time for our first in-person event. The Howard Gardner School was the perfect location with its eco-friendly classroom building, award-winning native garden and yard, "tiny house" replete with a student constructed active-solar electric system, and a pet pig who greeted us.

Beginning with the end in mind, we had decided it would make sense to create a fun cross-pollinating event for Friday night by hosting a fundraising event that would align a non-profit dedicated to addressing the nutritional needs of at-risk children worldwide that would provide a matching grant approach when connected to another non-profit whose mission was serving undernourished children. We chose to work with Lorton Community Action Center, which provides basic needs and empowers people through self-sufficiency programs, a foodbank, and by connecting people with other programs in the area that will have a positive impact on a family's long-term "health." By aligning two organizations who would not have known each other without Living The Potential Network, we demonstrated how the power of collaboration uplifts all who participate and how "a small group of committed and thoughtful citizens can change the world." (Thank you, Margaret Mead!)

That night, we enjoyed music, wine, and a silent auction and were able to raise over $2,000 and the next day many returned for The Garden Experiment workshop.

We had invited parents, grandparents, teachers, administrators, entrepreneurs, church leaders, doctors, nurses, musicians, authors, non-profit board members, and high school and college students to witness the wisdom of youth and the power of our organic learning model.

The panel revealed wisdom beyond their years. Five youths—three recent high school graduates and two recent college graduates—shared insight related to their schooling journey, perspectives about what worked and what didn't work for them, concerns about the world they are inheriting, and several ideas they have about possible solutions. One of my team members captured their thoughts word for word while the audience leaned forward and wiped away tears. Authentic truths were being shared and, to me, it felt sacred.

After lunch and a planting exercise, it was time to workshop the issues that the youth had determined were most significant. One was climate change (renamed climate survival), and the other issue chosen for the day was the lack of community bonding. Each topic was then facilitated in separate rooms with a youth leader and an adult facilitator. The rounds of conversation for each topic followed the organic learning model: Now that we are trusting the seeds that our youth bring, how will we cultivate fertile learning environments for what's possible? Who and what needs to be cross-pollinated for the best possible scenarios? What regenerative systems need to be in place to go beyond sustaining what exists? And what is the highest and best use of technology to help manifest this new reality?

After each breakout, the two groups came back to the main room and debriefed what they had discovered, and the listening deepened. This intergenerational learning space was breaking down the barriers of separation. We were feeling the energy of collaboration, that wisdom knows no age, and that the answers for the issues were right here right now. And somehow, time was evaporating in plain sight.

At the close of the workshop, going around the circle and reviewing the insights, solutions, and feedback, there wasn't a dry eye in the circle. A synergistic awakening had occurred, and with that, hope was more than a possibility. It was alive and well within an intergenerational learning community where the youth are seen and heard and honored for showing up and co-leading with other energetic change-makers... regardless of their age.

After this incredible event, it became clear that we needed more youth involvement. It was time to build the Youth Advisory Council, but where would we find the youth? After

Aaron, at age fourteen, had helped me design the cover for my book, we didn't interact much. He was in the deep end of finishing high school a year early, which meant thirteen classes and a level of busyness Amanda said she had never seen before. However, he was my first choice to be the founder of the Youth Advisory Council; and he came on board to help me build it, bringing his young aunt and friend from Village Home with him.

We were just getting some traction when the pandemic hit. Fortunately, we were able to take everything online, including our Garden Experiment workshops, and keep the community together and growing. Slow but steady. It was about that time that Amanda suggested I hire Aaron as my virtual assistant, since he is brilliant with technology. As an assistant, he has helped me build the online space in which our network communicates and grows and become a key player on our business administration team. It doesn't surprise me at all that he has decided to be an entrepreneur!

It hasn't been easy. There were sleepless nights. There were doubts. There were plenty of mistakes, frustrations, and tears when enrollments did not happen quickly, community members walked away, and finances fell apart. I learned the hard way to ask for help; and I know that without the help I received from my support team, and from my coaches and healers, I wouldn't have made it through the dark times. I had to use all the tools I'd been sharing with others— breathing deeply, energy healing, journaling, meditation, neurolinguistic programming, and time in nature to help me to stay the course when it was hard. And of course, my work with Amanda and the writing community really helped me to share and be inspired by the other courageous souls on the journey to bring their truth forward.

In the long run, it all worked out—better than I imagined. I have held true to this unfathomable vision for the past forty years; and at times, when it felt like the dark night of the soul, I had to really just get out of my own way. With each quantum leap over the threshold of fear, I deepened my belief in myself.

Today, our facilitators are on track to launch their practicum projects and receive full certification, and our Youth Advisory Council is working on passion projects and connecting with mentors through our Bridging The Potential podcast. We are launching the membership, and there are many exciting projects underway geared toward connecting people of diverse ages, backgrounds, and expertise to solve the problems that our community members are the most concerned about in the world.

As of the publishing of this book, we have just begun working with NEXTReady and several other organizations to expand Community Resilience through Diversity, Equity, and Inclusion. This project was catalyzed by courageous youth who won a lawsuit that forced the state of New Mexico to immediately provide at-risk students and teachers of at-risk students access to digital devices, high-speed internet, and sufficient IT staffing, so that these youth would have access to their constitutionally guaranteed sufficient and adequate education. We are partnering with NEXTReady and other organizations to support the development of a fertile online learning environment for all students and teachers, increasing curiosity, learning, and collaboration in addition to equity in access to education. It's incredible what happens when youth take the lead and adults from multiple domains listen and collaborate toward a solution!

Just a few years after I dragged all of those books into that retreat house, and then all the way back out to the car, I am trusting my own seeds of potential largely because Amanda's community was the fertile environment I needed to nurture them, pull out the st*ry-weeds that would have choked out my vision, and cross-pollinate my dreams with the seeds of potential in Amanda's son and sister to create an ecosystem that will continue to reach upward and inspire others to Live The Potential with us!

Amanda's Side of the Story

I sat in the back while she facilitated the "What are you taking with you?" closing portion of the workshop, staring at my now-bare feet and letting the tears fall softly down my face and onto my lap. In that moment, I was all of those folks in the room.

The youth who questioned the status quo and wanted to do something to make the world better.

The parent who marveled at their child's wisdom confidently on display in front of a room full of adults and experts.

The entrepreneur who understands the power and profit associated with putting a young person's mind on a business challenge.

The teacher who wants to make a difference but is frustrated with how the system doesn't support the students or the teachers.

The elder who wants to provide shortcuts but knows the value of learning it the long way.

The facilitator who has done a whole bunch of work she never wanted to do in order to feel whole and ready for a room like this and then feels like they may implode or explode with gratitude and awe.

I listened to the shares and let the tears continue to fall while I reflected on what I had witnessed that day. Youth sharing their stories and concerns for the world. Adults listening and offering empathy and support. People from multiple generations, ethnic cultures, religious traditions, and domains (education, business, science, engineering, art, etc.) huddled up around tables, developing solutions to problems the youth presented. In just a few hours, we had viable holistic solutions—prototypes for projects that could be taken on by universities, businesses, or communities like this one.

This workshop had been a long-time coming, but I was grateful that I had witnessed Renee Beth's journey from the beginning.

We met at a restaurant during a World Domination Summit lunch break in Portland. I'd just moved to the area and a mutual friend made sure we connected at this event. There was no time to really get to know each other, so we scheduled a meeting at a Panera and spent more hours than we planned talking about her enormous vision and all the ways she had endeavored to achieve it before meeting me. I cringed as she shared stories of other coaches telling her it was too big. How did they not hear this lady's credentials and realize that if anyone could make that huge vision happen, it was her? And the investments she'd already made with no return... ugh. It always upsets me when I have new messengers show up, already tens and sometimes hundreds of thousands of dollars in debt, and struggle to pay the person who is actually willing to get into the trenches and help them make their dream a reality.

I knew that I could help her because I saw how I was all of the stakeholders—the youth, the parent, the entrepreneur, the teacher, and the expert—she wanted to attract to solve big real-world problems.

But it wasn't an easy road for Renee Beth because... well... let's see. How many boards was she running and/or supporting? How many businesses was she growing? How many classes was she teaching? How many mentees was she supporting? I'll save you from the near-anxiety attack anyone who looks at this woman's to-do list and calendar inevitably has, and get to my realization that the only way to help her get this done was to kidnap her to Mt. Hood for a retreat.

But then she brought all the books and we tackled the question of: "Where does a messenger's credibility really come from? Do people want to see what you *know*? Or is it more impressive to see what you *have already done*?"

She made a little progress, but it wasn't until she was part of a cohort that everything really started to move more speedily and meaningfully. Her book was nearly done when, in retreat with others, she saw the core st*ries that were holding her back and began to do the work to heal them. These are stories that so many high-achieving messengers share: "There's not enough time and I'm always late," "I don't want to make this about *me*," and still "I don't have enough letters behind my name to make people listen to me."

We worked through the stories with hours of st*ry-healing exercises, walking along the river, eating everything salty and chocolatey, improv games, and nose-bleed-inducing belly laughter.

Somewhere around this time, Renee Beth met a woman who offered to help her develop curriculum and invested heavily to create a course with her. When we started to talk about the possibility of me supporting her in creating the business offerings, she was dumbfounded when I told her I offer curriculum development. Oops!

This was actually a really upsetting moment for me, as it was one of many occurring at the same time. That's how it goes with me. When my Co-Author wants me to get a message, it comes at me from lots of directions! Renee Beth was the third person in a month to tell me she had invested in another program, to acquire something I could have developed more powerfully because I knew the brand and framework from the inside-out, only to be extremely disappointed. I immediately changed all of my offerings to position myself more truly. I had stopped being "just a book coach" years before, and it was time to show messengers that it's easier, faster, more effective, and less expensive to work with me to develop the book, signature talk, curriculum, and business structure and offerings (and keep it all true to intention) than it is to work with multiple coaches and experts.

Once we cleared up that misunderstanding, we began developing that first Garden Experiment, the change-maker courses, and the infrastructure for her business.

With this type of awareness and support, she launched the book and then it was time for another conversation. We began to look at developing her message-based business and more st*ries surfaced: "People I care about don't understand or support my mission and regularly sabotage my efforts to move it forward," "People are not delivering on their promises and it's derailing the work," "Will there ever be a return on all of my investment?" and "I hate social media but I know I have to…"

About that time, my son was graduating high school and frustrated with his options for higher education. He'd graduated from a self-design learning environment and after his interview at one academy that would have provided a similar environment, he said, "Mom, I really wish there was a place where I could go and just try a bunch of things… and not bury myself in debt. Wouldn't it be great if I could just intern at a bunch of places and see what actually lights me up?" When I told him that's what Renee Beth was creating through LTPN, he said he wanted to get involved. So, he helped found the Youth Advisory Council and then became her administrative assistant because he could do all the technology things that she and I struggled to do. Then my sister jumped on the Youth Advisory Council and began supporting with graphic design and social media; and my other sister jumped in to help develop some marketing videos. Suddenly, my family's previous conversations (mostly in jest) about how we all "share the same brain" and "work so well together" and could "rule the world someday with our collective superpowers" began to take a form I never really saw coming—a team for True To Intention that would increase my joy, reduce my stress, and expand the offerings and value I can provide for clients. YCMTSU!

This expansion, of course, has provided me with similar opportunities to heal the st*ries that Renee Beth and I share, the most important of which are the "all work and no play" and the "I don't want to be a dictator/leader" st*ries. For the last few years, I've witnessed this woman pour every drop of her life force and resources into her mission; and I've had a front row seat to all of the moments of doubt, panic, and rage that accompany this journey for people who know they are here to accomplish an inspired vision and face incredible obstacles and challenges along the way. I know all of those emotions and moments well because I continue to revisit them with every project I approach; and I'm grateful to be able to provide a safe space for messengers like Renee Beth who assume they are the only ones who ever feel this way (because other experts and coaches focus on the hype of what's possible and fail to share the inner work it takes to achieve it). It's serious work to be the type of leader that can hold a vision, develop and maintain healthy relationships, and avoid running ourselves and everyone else into the ground in order to achieve our mission when things don't seem to be moving the way we imagined; but it's the necessary work to stay true to intention and make sure that our success in the world doesn't come at a sacrifice we never wanted to make in our health, sanity, or relationships.

I'm incredibly grateful for the last few years of supporting Renee Beth and how it's not only leveraged all of the superpowers that I've developed over twenty years, but required me to hone my self-care, coaching, and leadership skills so that I can play at the level I'm being asked to play in this lifetime.

Torey Ivanic is a road-schooling mom of two amazing children, traveling homeopath for those seeking natural healing, and lifelong adventure partner to her faithful husband of twelve years. She and her family have been on the road since November of 2020 living life differently. After authoring *No Big Deal*, she asked readers to Open Space for change, and life circumstances allowed her to lead by example. She is an avid reader, seeking social justice and change through encouraging others to get outside their comfort zones and by consistently stepping outside of hers.

Open Space for Change

Torey Ivanic

"Issues Identified..."

"The author needs to take out anything that invades a person's privacy or libels them, or else provide notarized permission, or hide identities. To hide identities, the author must take a pen name and change all other identifying information in the MS (manuscript)."

You're kidding me! You think you've identified issues, but you don't know the half of my issues. I am NOT taking a pen name...

I was so frustrated reading the same email from my hybrid publishing agent AGAIN.

This has to be a form document that they just keep sending me. I told them at the beginning I would use my real name and his. They didn't tell me then that I couldn't. I wrote the whole book, and they never even suggested that it would be an issue.

I had notarized permission from all the significant people in my story whose identities I hadn't hidden. My old gymnastics coach (perpetrator) was in prison for the crimes against my friend and myself as well as several of his Chiropractic patients. The trial documents were public record and I'd sent the publishers that documentation. Of course, I'd gone back through and taken out locations and details that led to others' identities, but I needed to keep the things that felt important to me.

I want to write this story with my name on it! It's MY story! I don't want to hide this story any longer. This is a huge reason

351

*that these stories don't stop. We have to be able to own our
truths and shed light on this shit or it will just keep happening.*

When I told my story to the police, it was hard; but hard
things are usually well-worth it, and this was no different.
Amazing good came into my life within weeks of reporting
the crime to the police.

When I told my story on the witness stand, I asked not to
be photographed and captured on video. On some level, I was
still hiding. Even more good came of speaking the truth in a
courtroom to what seemed like hundreds of strangers.

This story had been dug up and retold so many times by
this moment with the publishing agent's email that I could
see it from a different light. It was finally (yes, FINALLY) clear
to me that I actually had nothing to hide.

*That's the point of writing the book—to shed light on
all the hiding and the damage it does! When I've shared my
story verbally, I know it's helped people see their stories more
clearly. The more I change and omit and sugarcoat it, the less
real it will feel to the readers who need it and the less good it
will do. GAH! I had the rough draft done almost a year ago and
this is where I'm at? I'm done with this publisher!*

As young as I can remember, I had two big life goals: to have
kids and write a book. I loved reading and devoured books,
which was the reason behind wanting to write one. Never
would I have thought that the book I would write would
be one of the hardest stories I have experienced in my life
thus far.

In the spring of 2015, I had already achieved the "have kids" goal. The "write a book" goal was so far off my radar, I hadn't even considered it in ten years. I didn't know many people who had written books, and I thought of authors as magical unicorns who led very different lives than mine. However, I *had* been running my own business for several years and was feeling like I needed more training in business. Instead of going to night school for a $15K MBA, I joined a business and self-development program that kicked off with a retreat in Costa Rica.

Right before I made the international trek, a worship leader at my church was arrested on several counts of sexually abusing teen girls. He was twenty-nine years old at the time; and though he hadn't been with my kids, he'd been singing about Jesus in front of my family for many months. This story ripped open a wound I thought I had sealed up years before and completely upset my balance just before I walked into this professional development program. I thought I was going to show up in all my strength and glory and dance through that program with no glitches. However, when I landed in Costa Rica, I was a vulnerable jello-y mess. The people in my group were incredible; and there happened to be, not one but, *three* book coaches in our group. You really can't make this sh*t up. I had no idea book coaches even existed, but to have three in a group of only thirty-five people? I was hanging out with unicorns, and Amanda Johnson was one of them!

I don't remember speaking directly to Amanda about my story in Costa Rica, but I did tell her that I had always wanted to write a book one evening while we were headed to the dining hall. When I returned to California, we jumped on a call; and I downloaded most of the story to her while pacing around the parking lot across the street from my house. I remember her saying, "It sounds like The Wind has been whispering to you a lot through this story," and I knew from her wording that if I were to write a book, she was meant to be my guide.

It seemed crazy to consider writing a book about my deepest, darkest, dirtiest secret. And yet, the more that I spoke it out loud, the more I saw that it was also a powerful story of justice and hope. Many people admitted to me that similar violations had happened to them and that, even years later, it wasn't clear that a crime was actually committed.

At the end of summer 2015, my husband and I uprooted our entire lives when we decided to move from California to Colorado. I packed and sold a house, and we landed in Colorado in less than three weeks. While there were a few good reasons for leaving California, there were many good people and relationships that we were also leaving. I landed feeling lonely and sad for myself as well as my son who had just started kindergarten. It was a hard transition; but as soon as the ski season started, I felt sure it was the right move. We skied more that first winter in Colorado than we had in years, and it felt so good to be back in the mountains. I loved tearing down the mountain next to my three-year-old "Tiny Turbo" daughter on our days off work and preschool. The book had fallen off my radar again, but it was always somewhere in the back of my head.

Enter 2016. Donald Trump was elected president of the United States. An alleged perpetrator was now in the Oval Office. My hackles were up.

It's time to write this story.

I had always been intrigued by the NaNoWriMo movement where you try to write a novel in a month. I

figured that I could use the energy and momentum of all
the other people writing to see if I had enough stories and
content to make this a book. I started with a letter to my
perpetrator, and the next day wrote a story about something
that helped me heal. This was my way of keeping the light
and dark balanced. I leaned into trying to be as honest
as I could in those letters, telling him all the details that I
remembered about what he said, where we were, how he
touched me, and what was going through my head. The letter
days were hard, and more emotion was coming up than I
would have expected. I mean, it had been ten years since I'd
gone to the police, and eight years since he'd been sent to
prison. I thought I was good with this story. I thought I had
healed this wound. Ah, the naivete of my pre-author self.

I made it through twenty days of writing in November of
2016 and felt good about the ten letters to my perpetrator
and the ten stories of healing or rising above. Thanksgiving
was coming up and I knew I wanted a break from living in the
details of this piece of my life; but I looked at the number of
words I had written, and I knew for sure that I had enough
for a book.

I took December off and started again in January, trying
to write it more chronologically. I wrote, and wrote, and
wrote. At some point, I shared it with Amanda and she
said something to the effect of, "You have some really good
content here." I knew I needed help making it more engaging
but, having never written a book before, I didn't know how
or what help I needed. When Amanda invited me to a retreat
in Minneapolis that would last a full week in April 2017, I
knew it was the right next step. But I could not envision how
I could leave my then four- and six-year-old kids with my
husband who worked a full-time job with a long commute.

I didn't have the support around me to be able to leave, but then Amanda offered virtual attendance! Now, that was doable. I knew it would still be hard, and I would need a lot of help from my husband; but I also knew that he supported me in this crazy goal and would do what he could to give me the time and space to make it work.

I remember hanging out in my basement writing space on Zoom and really wishing I was there in person, but also being so grateful that I had allies in the writing process. Those women held space for me, listened to my icky and disgusting story, and cheered me along as I wrote. I took the movie-watching and chocolate-eating assignments very seriously. In fact, I think I deserve bonus points for the amount of chocolate I ate. Chocolate staves off the dementors, you know.

When Amanda gave me my Message Matrix and I started writing my introduction, I struggled at first. I couldn't figure out how to switch back and forth between the voice in my head and the Torey in the book, and likely my current self. I was so confused about tenses and getting frustrated about grammar. But the magic had started because I finally knew *what* to write! I could finally see how to tell this story in a coherent and readable way that would engage the reader. By the end of the week, I had written a decent version of the intro and a solid rough draft of the first *five* chapters! Five chapters in one week! I never would have thought I'd have that. But, more than that, I was actually having fun with the creative aspects of it. I loved looking back at all the good memories I had from my youth and thinking about the ridiculous clothes we wore and the haircuts we had. Holy shit! I really was going to write this book, and it was going to be good.

I had told a few friends that I was writing a book. At first, when people asked what it was about, I would say "my shitty gymnastics coach" or something to that effect. When I started writing, I didn't even know what the #metoo movement was.

It couldn't have been a coincidence that I started writing the book in April 2017, right when news broke about Larry Nassar and his sexual assault of hundreds of high-level gymnasts. I couldn't turn on the radio without hearing the words "sexual assault" or "gymnast." More and more women were coming forward. NPR was hosting them to talk about their experiences, and I was writing my story and riding the wave of energy from these badass women. I felt like they were giving me permission to write this book or, more so, to yell it from the rooftops. Having gone to the police and testified in front of a jury more than a decade before, I was happy to see that this was getting attention in the media; but I felt like I was just swimming in a pool of stories of sexual abuse of women and especially in the sport of gymnastics.

So, I meditated, walked, ate more chocolate, and stopped listening to the news for a while.

I do well with lists and schedules and decided that Wednesdays would be my writing days. I wouldn't schedule any clients, and I would dig in and write a chapter. Even if I knew it wasn't done, I'd write as much as I could so that I could see the story starting to form and come together. I wanted to see the big picture, even if it was messy and rough. It usually took me a few hours to get something new on paper and then I would go back to the previous chapters and look at Amanda's comments. Sometimes they'd make me laugh; sometimes they'd make my stomach hurt. I'd cringe when I'd see her coaching, "What were you feeling? What did it smell like? How did your body feel?"

Yuck, I don't want to go there in THIS part of the story.

The next thing I knew, it was July 31, 2017—my forty-first birthday—and I was hiking with a friend and talking about the book when I heard myself say, "I'm almost done. I think I only have one chapter left." It finally felt real, and I could see how this day was going to become a focal point of the last chapter. I had come full circle since starting to write the book. At first, I thought I was writing it to other survivors, to help them see that they are okay and it's normal to have repercussions after someone breaks your trust and hurts you. About midway through the writing, I thought I was writing it for my kids, so that I would be a more healed and (hopefully, maybe?) evolved mother for them. By the end of the writing, I had removed so many veils that my opened eyes were fuming at how our jacked-up, misogynistic society continues to tell girls that this is NO BIG DEAL. I was writing it as a story to reveal social injustice and incomprehensibly-damaging societal norms.

Throughout the entire writing process, I was battling with the dichotomy of feeling the need to tell this story truthfully and the need to create a balance in how it might affect my readers. I knew that I wanted permission from my exes whose stories I wanted to include. Once I had written enough, I went through the painful twelve-step work of reaching out to them and divulging that I was writing a book... and they were in it. The majority of them took it well and applauded my efforts. Some were a little more concerned and uncomfortable. Each phone call I made, with sweaty palms and an increased heart rate, left me with a different piece of information about how and why I needed to move forward in finishing this book.

Yes, healing this trauma is hard. Stuffing shitty stories under the rug is what my generation was taught to do, but that's not the model I want to create for my kids. As a survivor and a homeopath, I know it's not healthy. And it's not right. None of the people I talk about in the book have anything to be embarrassed about or ashamed of, except for the sexual predator. It seemed that not everyone got this memo. After all the painful writing work I had already done, I started second-guessing myself. People were reacting differently than I had thought they would. Thankfully, Amanda continued to reach out with support and reassure me that this story needed to be told, even when I wasn't so sure.

Concurrently in the news... Harvey Weinstein, Kevin Spacey, R Kelly (again)...

Just because other people are uncomfortable with my story doesn't mean that it doesn't need to be told.

I remembered the conversation with one ex-boyfriend who had surprised me. We had been out of touch for years, but he welcomed my call and supported my mission. Ironically, I'd called him while I was in my daughter's gymnastics studio. It was surreal talking to my ex while in a gym, and he made me pause when he said, "Don't worry, things will get a lot better when the baby boomers are gone." I hadn't ever thought of the impact that the boomers' generation ideals ("don't talk about it, just move forward") had had on our generation. His perspective lightened my worry and helped me keep moving forward.

By that time, a few friends had already read the book, and I'd gotten good feedback on the readability of it as well as the importance of a hopeful and victorious story on this topic. One friend was so supportive that she offered to help in the editing process and the bigger mission. I had endorsements already from people who I looked up to and respected, and I was building a team that affirmed the importance of this work and would help me keep my momentum when it got hard.

If this wasn't worth doing, my mentors and friends wouldn't be so supportive.

Thanks to the feedback, I started to realize that I'd had to write the original draft with all the details I remembered so that I could get back into my own body and tell it the way I experienced it. As I had more conversations and took some time away from the first draft, I realized that a lot of the stories that were so important to me were not as important to the reader. I started feeling less attached to details that were critical in the writing, and I snipped and purged to give more anonymity to those who weren't key players. My exes were unfortunate collateral damage in the big picture of the story, even though their perceptions were important to me. I was more concerned about my close friend and my family, whose stories were completely intertwined with mine.

This story is mine, but I'm not naive to the fact that it will impact others if I ever promote it.

Fortunately, my family seemed to be fine with me writing the book. My parents and brother had access to early versions and didn't approach me with any concerns, so I (maybe naively) felt supported on that front.

No news is good news, right?

My biggest worry was how my telling this story affected my friend who was also a victim. She had been insanely strong, and her story was the main reason my perpetrator was behind bars for so long. Knowing she had been through so much already, I didn't want my telling of it to cause her more pain.

Of course, it will cause her pain and I'm not willing to publish this book if it means losing her friendship.

It killed me for her to have to relive any piece of what had happened, but I also knew that I couldn't publish in good conscience without her blessing.

Twelve months after starting the process, I sat at my computer, looking at those words again, "The author must take a pen name and change all other identifying information in the MS." I was done. I picked up the phone and called my contact at the publishing company and told him I wanted to cancel my contract.

I am done with you telling me I can't tell my story the way I want! If anyone has a right to do that, it's my family and the people I care about who are a part of this story.

After three or four phone calls with people trying to convince me to stay with the hybrid publishing package, and me adamantly refusing their forceful demands to use a pen name or change all the details, I got out of the contract. I only lost a few hundred dollars, but I had no idea how to do all the things that I had been planning for the hybrid publishers to do.

I'll figure it out.

I had a few conversations with lawyers, one of which thought I should pay him twenty thousand dollars to read the book and write a letter to protect me. Fear crept in for a bit, but other lawyers assured me that it wasn't necessary. I opened an LLC to protect my family in case my perpetrator sued me from prison, but I also leaned into the fact that if that happened, it would just confirm the need for more victim support and justice in this country.

If that happens, there'll be another book to write for sure.

I started to fill the gaps of what the publisher wouldn't do. First, I reached out to an artist friend from childhood about possible cover art, and he nailed the image and feeling on the first try. He knew me through the time this story happened, and it seemed magical that he totally got what I was going for immediately.

Second, I leaned into my editing friend. She was a fast learner and a motivated supporter, so she ended up taking on the interior formatting as well as the final editing. Amazon hybrid publishing was easier than we expected, and it was all starting to come together.

This really is going to happen!

And then my dad died.

Of course, I lost my momentum. Priorities shifted and family wounds resurfaced.

The book wasn't completely done and it was far from a good time to celebrate a book release, so I pushed it back again. Plus, the realization of the misogynistic culture I was steeped in as a child became clearer as I returned to my childhood town and witnessed the societal norms that I had grown up with and away from.

The poster hanging on the garage wall with a half-naked woman with a beer in hand that read, "If at first you don't succeed, buy her another beer."

Is this for real? A rape poster? Oh, wait, yeah, that was the reality of college back then, right?

"What happens at the work site stays at the worksite. You'd better not tell your mom or your grandma what you hear there," my dad's old colleague joked about the way it still was on the construction sites they ran.

Boys will be boys, right? What WAS said there?

The all-men's club founded by firefighters called "The Hose Club."

Fun play on words, right? Wrong.

All these things were blatantly offensive to my forty-something self, but when I saw them through the lens of my younger eyes, I hesitated.

No big deal, right?

I kept working on editing and nailing down the final draft while I grieved and worked through the family dynamics that were coming up.

Finally, several months later, I got the author's copy of the book. On a call with my mastermind group when it arrived, I was emotional just picking up the box. I waited to open it because I had invited some girlfriends over to my house to celebrate with me that evening. Tears streamed down my face as I touched the first real copy of the book. We drank champagne, and I read aloud from a chapter toward the end of the book that was happy and had my kids in it. They were proud of their momma, the author, and my friends were wonderfully supportive. It was time to finalize and publish it.

This book was hard to write, it was hard to talk about, and I was finding it hard to celebrate. In fact, I decided to publish on my birthday to help me justify throwing a party for myself. I chose a local female-owned brewery as the location, and it was both perfectly casual and celebratory. Some random patrons even bought a copy of the book and supported the cause. More people than I had imagined showed up to support me, coming from as far away as Ohio and Mississippi. And my friend, who had wrestled with support and permissions for months, ended up being one of my biggest supporters and even flew across the country to show up for the publishing party! I was surrounded by powerful women and progressive men agreeing that this is a BIG DEAL and it's time to open space for change in our lives, our societies, and our stories.

As if the universe were affirming our cause, names kept dancing through the news: *Brock Turner, Bill Cosby, Larry Nassar, Jeffrey Epstein...*

And to top it off, right after I published, Bret Kavanaugh, another alleged perpetrator, was made a supreme court justice.

This can't be happening!

I could totally relate to why Christine Blasey Ford had waited so long to come forward. Out of sight, out of mind. In the same way that hearing my perpetrator was moving back to my hometown and treating gymnasts from our old gym as a chiropractor, I imagine Ms. Ford was appalled to think this man could be making decisions that would affect all the women in the US.

Even if he is completely innocent, the way he responded and did not keep any degree of decorum makes him unfit for the bench. Damn, our society really does think this shit is No Big Deal!

What would have impressed me is if Bret Kavanaugh had kept his composure and said something like, "I don't remember that happening, but I will admit that things were different back then, and I wasn't as respectful to women as I wish I had been. I never meant to scare anyone or hurt anyone." Just as I would have been impressed and grateful if my perpetrator had owned his mistakes and pleaded guilty to the crimes he committed. He would have only spent four years in prison, none of the victims would have had to testify in court (be revictimized), and he would have kept an ounce of my respect.

The men "defending" themselves from "attacks" on who they were raised to be was one thing. What really took me to the floor were the women who excused these words and actions. Women were vilifying one another when they had no idea what that other women's experience had been. It reminded me of when our local paper had a comments section at the time of my coach's arrest and ninety percent of the comments were supporting my perpetrator, questioning our motives, or calling us all out liars and sluts.

I felt like our society still wasn't hearing these stories or taking this seriously, and I was finding it hard to talk to my children about leadership, grace, humility, and tact with the current leaders in our country and culture.

Once the book was launched, speaking about it seemed like the best next step. I wasn't an expert on abuse prevention, but I was a mom and I was a survivor; so I spoke from my heart about what I thought we as a society needed to change and what to watch out for when it comes to kids. I tried to speak to survivors in the audience by giving them permission to not be okay and to see their own stories as a REALLY BIG DEAL. I did a few speaking gigs in 2019, and even got paid a few times. It took a lot of energy and it took me away from my family; and even though I knew it was important, I had to admit to myself that it wasn't something I wanted to build a business around.

It didn't help that sometimes while talking about my book in small group settings, I would feel the room go cold. The political polarity in the country may have been to blame, even though I didn't see this as a political issue. Maybe my focus on the behavior of the president and Bret Kavanaugh was seen as leaning away from their party, but it was really about my upset that alleged perpetrators were now holding the highest offices in the United States. Whether they were innocent or guilty of the specific accusations really didn't matter to me; it was the way they showed no humility or remorse for behavior that is now completely unacceptable. Of course, many other politicians, actors, priests, musicians, athletes, and others were accused and some even convicted of sexual assaults. It was rampant in our society, and I wanted to see the men at the highest level of leadership taking it seriously, not excusing it by calling it "locker room talk." No one should talk like that, ever.

Watch your thoughts, they become your words; watch your words, they become your actions; watch your actions, they become your habits; watch your habits, they become your character; watch your character, it becomes your destiny.

~Lao Tzu~

I felt good about the way we'd set up my new business, Open Space, to be whatever it needed to be. If I'd learned anything in my own healing and transformative work, it's that you never know what might come next. I had ideas for retreats, workshops, and fun interactive camps. I took opportunities to speak when they came to me; I had a decent website up and running, and I really enjoyed running masterminds for entrepreneurs. But I knew what it would take to build out the business and promote it the way I really wanted to, and I was sure I didn't have it in me at the time. I decided to take some time to focus on my family and feel into what was next. I even went to Mexico for my 200-hour yoga teacher training that I'd postponed more than ten years prior. My return flight to the US was March 6, 2020.

Then Covid hit.

I had already planned to pull my fourth-grade son from public schools after returning from my yoga retreat; coincidentally, his first day of homeschool was the day that everyone came home because of Covid. The last few months of the 2020 school year, I watched my second-grade daughter stare at a computer screen all day while I taught my son for several hours each morning before we went out to play. Homeschooling seemed infinitely better than virtual learning for this age group; and my daughter agreed that if her next school year looked like this one, she'd rather homeschool too. We did the best we could with the weirdness of Covid, but I was itching to make a big change.

I had already been thinking about a new book, and the Covid situation really amplified my thoughts about women and their need to pursue and follow their passions to stay out of adrenal fatigue and overwhelm in our current society. Not only my homeopathy clients, but random women I met on the beach were unhappy and didn't know what to do with themselves. It seemed like so many women felt stuck and slightly dead inside, and I felt like I knew a way out. I thought maybe it was good enough for a second book, so I reached out and brainstormed a little with Amanda.

After hearing my own voice say that our current societal norms were the problem, I realized that my husband and I were steeping our children in those same norms every day.

My husband and I'd already had a plan to take the kids on a year-long sailing adventure in the Caribbean when they were nine and eleven years old. Since sailing seemed nearly impossible given my lack of ability to sail on top of Covid quarantines and lockdowns, we opted for a travel trailer.

We sold our house and sold or gave away everything that wouldn't fit in my sister-in-law's crawl space.

On November 3, 2020, we took off into the night to head south to warm weather. It's been more than a year now, and we have driven thousands of miles. We've touched whales, spoken Spanish, and climbed cliffs. We swam and stand-up paddled in the Sea of Cortez, Gulf of Mexico, many rivers, and the Atlantic Ocean. We are living the life of Open Space in a 250 square foot travel trailer. We are outside more than inside. Our feet are bare more often than shoed. We have hard conversations when necessary and the kids are experiencing things that I didn't until well into adulthood. We are slowing down in some ways, but sometimes it feels like life is on fast-forward because we are doing so much and moving so often. We meet new friends and then have to say goodbye. We find new favorite places and then move on to look for more. We watch the weather and plan projects, museums, or movies for the rainy days. We are together. We talk. Sometimes we yell. Jay and I still carve out some hours to work each week and we help facilitate new experiences for the kids. We are living in Open Space and, for all of my frustrations with our society, this adventure is showing me that there are some positive shifts happening in our society.

For instance, my kids went to a camp last summer that offered an optional class to prevent abuse in sports. Nothing like that existed when I was little. Ideally, next year it will not be an add-on but part of the standard curriculum.

Of course, there is the #metoo movement that has given a lot of survivors support and hope just knowing they weren't alone. It is a powerful resource in deconstructing the rape culture in this country and I was thrilled to put my book in the hands of its founder, Tarana Burke, when I met her.

Our media seems to be starting to get the clue, too. I am grateful to see that most television shows and movies now often portray women in strong and powerful roles instead of perpetuating the blatant and awful sexism that was the norm in the movies I grew up on.

Even politicians are beginning to do something. A bill was recently signed to give more money to victim support rather than just perpetrator rehabilitation.

During the 2021 Olympics, Simone Biles, a prior Olympian and one of the many victims of Larry Nassar, put her mental health before winning (or even competing). She now knows that she is in charge of her body and her health and she said, "No." This is true leadership. What Simone did may seem logical, but it is monumental in the sport of gymnastics. Many of the gymnasts who already had some fame and notoriety before Nassar was convicted are using their pre-built platforms to continue this conversation and even speak out to the FBI.

Maybe people are seeing that it IS a BIG Deal?

There are many positive societal shifts happening as the divine feminine is creeping in slowly and powerfully while the toxic masculine sputters to its inevitable demise. When I sit with the situation and listen quietly, I see the movement that I want to happen unfolding in real time. I hear conversations about consent, gender equality, gender identity, and sexuality that I never heard as a child. I see open-loving humans standing up for what they believe in and gently saying that it Is a Big Deal. I also see the backlash of the old ways. I see the yelling and the stomping and the "This is how it's always been, what's the big deal?!" attitude which gets way more press. Yet, the change is still happening. It hasn't been stomped out. We're slowly and quietly opening space for change, and I'm going to continue doing my part— whatever that ends up looking like and however often I feel like crawling into a hole. The world needs me and all of us to understand THIS IS A BIG DEAL and then do what we are called to do about it.

Amanda's Side of the Story

"Amanda, this is actually FUN!" Torey stunned us all with her exclamation.

She's writing the story of being groomed and abused by her gymnastics coach. How could any of that be fun?

It was day four of my first seven-day retreat. After many years of witnessing people do extremely transformative st*ry-healing work while organizing their content and then struggle to get into the writing on their own, I'd decided to extend my retreat to help them find some flow in the writing and experience the writing partnership process.

It was working. These ladies were writing like crazy, and I was getting a front row seat to all of the reasons people start and stop writing. Sitting across the table, I watched one client's shoulders bunch up to her ears and her breath rate quicken while she typed out the beginning of her story. Another one was up and down frequently, preparing warm drinks and grazing the yummy snacks. It was a little tougher to get a read on Torey over Zoom, but she seemed to be managing herself well with physically-active breaks.

And, as she said, she was having fun, and I discovered why when I started to read her content. Her biggest stress about writing had been engagement. How could she really engage the reader and take them on the journey? Well, after I showed her a few storytelling hacks, she could *feel* the difference and *knew* this was going to grip her reader the way she had hoped it would.

The most important part of supporting Torey through the content development process was going further back in her story than she anticipated. To me, the story didn't begin with the first violating word or touch. The questions I knew we needed to answer were, "How does this happen right under the noses of caring adults?" and "What primes a child to quickly and easily fall prey to predators?" The first question is one I was certain the reader would ask, and the second was going to be an important part of the readers' ability to heal.

I knew this because I had just lived it.

There was no coincidence that Torey and I met in 2015, just a few short months before I woke up to the reality that I was living in an abusive family system. And, it's no coincidence that she wasn't ready to dive into her work with me until the beginning of 2017, just three months after my perpetrator had died unexpectedly.

My father, likely in an effort to protect himself in many ways, had groomed me to take care of his mother. I'm not sure how much of this was conscious or intentional on his part, but it is what happened. Because I loved my grandmother and wanted to spend time with her, it didn't even occur to me that I was being (ab)used. He'd set it up in a way that appeared to be a "win" for everyone. Gramma would be managed. He wouldn't have to do it. And I would have all of my needs for shelter, food, and education met as long as I played my part well. The problem was that it wasn't really a win for me in the long run because the grooming had included messages that completely disempowered me: "If you don't take care of her, she'll have to go to a home (and will hate you forever)"; "You take care of her and she'll take care of you (cuz you can't take care of yourself)"; "If you don't stay for just a little longer, everything we've been working for will fall apart (and be your fault)". When I first woke up to this, I wondered, "Did he ever really love me? Were the regular gifts and affection just grooming—motivating me to do what he wanted me to do?" It took a while for me to realize they both really *thought* they were loving and doing well by me while also admitting that the damage was real. And, looking back further in my story, I realized that damage had been done long before I was put in this role. I had been primed for this. In truth, my sense of self-worth had been compromised and externalized since I was teeny. I was good/worthy if I behaved. I was good/worthy if I performed or achieved. I was good/worthy if I didn't ask too many questions, speak out of turn, or challenge the status quo. None of that conditioning was done with malicious intent, I'm sure; but it happened nonetheless.

Because I had done some of this victim recovery work, I understood the propensity of all of us victims to "take all of the responsibility" and "believe it's our fault," or shifting all of the blame to the perpetrator alone. When we do that, we fail to access and expand the innate power we have to stop being prey and become whole. My goal was to help keep Torey's readers from falling into these traps. To me, it was just as important as witnessing how she gathered all of her courage to take him to court, testify, and put him behind bars.

It wasn't long before "That was fun!" was replaced by "Amanda, this book writing process is like a freaking 12-step program! You won't believe the conversations I'm having with my exes about this." I marveled as I witnessed her work "the program" and then hold her ground with the publishing company. This feisty lady was absolutely determined to live her message at every turn.

Neither of us had any idea that this was the perfect setup for what would transpire next in my world.

While I had liberated myself from the abusive family system and was gaining ground with the internal work required to reclaim my sense of self-worth and power, I was waking up to a lot of the other ways in which I had been conditioned to "play the part" and beginning to say, "No more." New layers of conditioning in my spirituality, my marriage, and even my finances began to crop up and demand something more from me.

In 2018, I saw something in a credit card statement that caused me to question the validity of some of my credit card debts and began to dispute them. One thing led to another, and a few lawsuits were filed against me. Fortunately, I had allies to help me learn how to defend myself and, more importantly, to help me integrate Torey's message at a completely different level. Around the time she published her book, I was on the phone with one of these allies informing him that I had won one of the cases. When I read the content of the letter to him, he cleared his throat and said, "Amanda, you're still not getting it. They said *they* believe that debt is valid but will not continue collecting at this time. If you don't object to their statement that it's valid, it's as good as consenting to it. They'll come back for you later. If you're not objecting, you're consenting."

Boom. Something inside me shattered.

I quickly ended the phone call and curled up in bed as this message reverberated all the way through me."If I don't object, I consent…" Every challenging situation in my world quickly came into crystal clear focus. The reason I was *still* in that tangled mess with my family—I didn't object.

The reason my husband and I *still* circled the same relationship drama repeatedly—I didn't object. The reason I *still* struggled with some of the beliefs that held me hostage in my relationship with my Co-Author—I didn't object.

And so, I was consenting to more of the same… *allowing* lies to be "true" instead of telling my truth, *allowing* others to take advantage of me instead of doing what was necessary to keep them from hurting me again, *allowing* unnecessary drama to continue instead of renegotiating healthier agreements, *allowing* perpetrators to continue preying upon me instead of objecting and insisting on justice the way Torey and all of those women did.

But objecting wasn't as easy as I thought it would be. I was worried about how the people around me would deal with my objections. I was afraid they would think I was overdoing it. I was terrified they would leave me… or punish me. And you know what? Some of them did. Sometimes, it was because they didn't want to grow with me and recalibrate our relationship; and sometimes, it was because I just wasn't very good at objecting yet.

While this legal process has been completely overwhelming and depleting, it has taught me some incredibly valuable lessons about objecting. Good objections require knowledge of "the ideal" and clarity about how "what is happening now" falls short of it. Of course, we need to understand the rules of procedure and how to conduct ourselves respectfully *while* we are objecting and working to move things closer to the ideal. They require precision of language—that we avoid making assumptions or creating stories about why people have behaved the way they have, and stick to the facts. As I was learning all of this, I was applying it to my personal path to freedom in my relationships, in my business, in my industry, and in my culture. I found that "working it from both ends"—micro-objections in my personal life and macro-objections in the culture—really helped me to understand that *every single objection matters, no matter how big or small it seems.*

Every single violation of our personal power and space is A BIG DEAL, even when they are well-intentioned or unconsciously perpetrated. And that happens all the time. Think about how easy it is to violate a child's sense of safety, belonging, and sense of self when we are over-tired or stressed. We'll do anything to make them comply and behave, so that we can do what needs to be done, right? But when we deceive, manipulate, shame, or force our way, despite their objections, we teach them something about objecting to what doesn't feel good or make sense. We teach them that their objections are inconvenient, irritating, or wrong; and then we wonder why they don't have a voice to speak up when they find themselves in an abusive situation.

Torey's story and message that any sexual violation is A BIG DEAL is so incredibly important, and I believe that part of the reason for the overwhelm of any messenger addressing the topic is that it's only one part of an even bigger conversation about consent that touches every single area of our lives. We don't really want to believe that we have been deceived, manipulated, or abused. It hurts to admit that the people who loved us and were responsible for our well-being inadvertently primed us for (ab)use. I don't think any of us are really *eager* to do the incredibly tough inner work required to reclaim our voice and power. And even fewer of us know how huge of a collective problem this is in our culture, let alone how to address it powerfully.

But it's the truth.

Our parents and ancestors have gotten a lot of things wrong about gender, race, sex, relationships, spirituality, money, and all the things. And we are the inheritors. Those faulty beliefs run through our DNA and have to be brought to the surface, faced, and healed in order for us to move forward personally and collectively.

It's not easy work, but I think we can all learn a lot from Torey's example.

I love that she shared how hard it was to tell her story the way it needed to be told and hold her ground when others tried to convince her she was wrong. I love that she saw the mirror experience of what was happening in her individually and for all of us collectively. And I love the fact that she has been so honest about the open space she is in right now.

I believe she is living in the tension all messengers have to face—between "the call to do more at the macro level" and be part of shifting the cultural paradigms that allow horrible atrocities to continue *and* "the responsibility to focus on the micro level" and live our own lives to their fullest. In my mind, it's a sign of healing and messenger maturity—not failure or fumbling—when we stop "all or nothing-ing" ourselves and just take one day, one situation, one objection, and one moment at a time. She is living her message in the way that feels the best and makes the most sense at this time—being a wife and mom who is raising children who are strong, healthy, and know how to object because they witness their momma living her message every day; serving as a homeopath, who is helping people find their own empowered way to heal their bodies; and being a messenger, contributor, and ally who objects publicly when the opportunity is presented and supports worthy projects with her extra time.

It's the only way for us to be whole and move our world closer to wholeness too, and I look forward to seeing how wholeness continues to unfold in and around her and because of her.

Michelle Ann Collins is an international best-selling author, certified yoga therapist, grief educator, Ayurvedic lifestyle teacher, Reiki Master, and wellness coach. After suffering a series of heartbreaking losses, including her mother to cancer, her divorce, and her second husband to suicide, Michelle immersed herself in the healing arts. She now shares the tools she developed along her journey, teaching that post-traumatic growth is possible and that everyone, no matter what they've experienced, can live a fulfilling and joyful life. When she isn't writing or teaching, Michelle can be found hiking the Oregon forests or paddle boarding on the rivers near her home.

What If the Obstacle is the Path?

Michelle Ann Collins

"**Y**ou have a message, a story, an experience that will help people when you share it, but you don't know how to get your message out there..."

She's talking about me. How does she know that I am compelled to write and share my story when I haven't really even met her?

I was in my favorite local coffee shop, attending a workshop with Amanda Johnson, discovering why she was referred to as the "message whisperer." After a year of reluctantly and unskillfully wrestling with writing a book, I had decided I needed professional help if I was ever going to finish it. I had discovered the huge difference between wanting to write a book and actually creating a useful product for people. Amanda had coached many bestsellers, out of a variety of experts, mostly in the genre of my book—transformational non-fiction or personal growth. I was hoping she could help me organize the mess of chapters, stories, and ideas I had written in fits and starts over the last year and develop them from mess to message.

I arrived at the workshop a bit late and slightly breathless, pushing my way up to the crowded table where a small determined group of eight ladies had their laptops poised and ready. Except for the woman who actually brought her *desktop*. I couldn't stop looking at her mess of tangled cords and even a CPU—a real-life embodiment of my disorganized mess of a book, right across the table from me!

I was relieved to shift my attention when Amanda began to speak. Not long into her talk, however, I felt a pang of anxiety because I realized her presentation included so much more than "how to write a book."

This was a self-inquiry workshop. This was a "Where have I been and how did I get here?" workshop. This was a "Your message needs to get out into the world and help others" workshop. It wasn't about writing. It was about shining a light on my darkest places, reviewing my deepest challenges, and opening them up for sharing in hopes of helping others. After introductions and some full group and small breakout group exercises, we took a short break. I grabbed the opportunity to speak with Amanda privately and quickly discovered some of her magic is her deep listening. She simply asked, "What brought you to the workshop today?" and then smiled calmly while giving me her complete attention. Her intense presence made me feel as if there was nothing else in the entire world other than me and my answer.

I bumbled on about my experiences in a somewhat coherent yet somewhat chaotic story, explaining that I felt compelled to write, but that I was failing. Then I fell silent. Continuing to gaze intently into my eyes, she asked, "Michelle, what is getting in the way of you finishing your book? What is your biggest block?"

I wasn't entirely sure at first but, in the silence, with her supportive presence, the answer became clear. I explained to her my biggest block was probably "that look"—the one on people's faces when I tell them what I've been through. "The first question everyone asks when I say I'm writing a book is, 'What's it about?' When I respond with, 'Surviving your spouse's suicide,' there's usually an awkward pause.

They take a step back, and instead of looking intrigued or asking further questions, they actually lean back, look down and get very uncomfortable. As an empath, I can feel their discomfort; it's as if the subject was so hot, it might burn them. That is usually the end of the conversation..."

And of any hope for what I thought I needed at the time... support for the project and encouragement that writing this book will help people, I thought to myself.

"If sharing my story makes people feel bad, how am I helping them? I want to write this book. Actually, I *need* to write this book, to give meaning to my suffering and the hard work, skill development, and emotional evolution I've experienced to survive and grow through trauma... Finding meaning is an important phase of the grief process."

I didn't know Amanda well enough yet to tell her the original inspiration I had received to write this book. More than a year earlier, I had received a message from beyond... call it God, Universal Consciousness, the Almighty, Divine, Source, or The Universe. I call the source of my message Spirit, the non-physical unlimited world beyond our five senses' ability to experience. The word Spirit can be found in inspiration, as the breath is the meeting place between the physical and the divine. The message I received from Spirit was crystal clear, and I knew I shouldn't ignore it, as much as I wanted to.

The previous four years of my life had been an arduous rollercoaster. I had finalized my divorce after twenty years of marriage to the father of my children. After one year of grieving the divorce and struggling to manage a household on my own with nearly full custody of my three adolescent girls, I'd met Glen, the love of my life and the man who I believed would save me from all of life's pain. Completely swept up in each other, we married only ninety days after we met. Less than two years together and he was gone, leaving his three biological children fatherless, his three step-daughters in disbelief, and me a suicide widow, barely clinging to my sanity while struggling with shock, grief, and eventually PTSD.

On the one-year anniversary of Glen's death, I stood on a rocky beach in Maui, his ashes in my hand, remembering our snorkeling adventure off this same beach. Glen, a talented storyteller, told the funniest story about that day. He would smile his big goofy infectious grin, add in fun exaggerations, props, sound effects, and his usual humorous spin, and weave a hilarious tale about how he had saved my life from a turtle that was trying to kill me. He referred to this act as the most heroic of his life. This was especially ironic considering he was a retired Navy Seal.

Spreading his ashes off this beach felt right. I performed a short ceremony and did my best to say goodbye, tears flowing into the ocean as I sobbed through every feeling imaginable: guilt, shame, anger, sorrow, and anxiety. And, when a sneaker wave knocked me onto my butt while I was trying to wash the last few ashes from the bag that held them, I experienced a tiny bit of joy.

Glen's presence was so strong that day, it felt as if he were sitting next to me in the car on my way back to the condo, and I wished I could reach out and hold his hand. I felt his love and I felt lighter. Along with his ashes, I had truly released some emotional weight; and, as I drove, I contemplated my experiences during the year since his death—how I had learned to survive one day, sometimes one breath, at a time when grief and trauma overwhelmed me. I even allowed myself the grace to admire how I continued to tenaciously step forward inches at a time through the grueling journey of managing Glen's estate, which, one year after his death, was far from settled.

There was a long line of slow traffic, and it was difficult to keep my eyes on the road as my gaze was repeatedly drawn to the gorgeous sparkling blue expanse of ocean along the highway. As sunlight danced and played on the waves, I replayed the morning over and over in my mind, watching his ashes spread slowly into the ocean and being visited by a turtle who swam directly into the cloud of ashes before they dissipated into the endless blue. Glen had told me clearly that he wanted to be cremated and spread at sea, and I prayed this had been the send-off he wanted. I sent love to everyone who loved Glen. In spirit, I had brought them to this ceremony as well.

Suddenly, I was startled out of my reverie by a sound that I wasn't even sure I heard. It was either a low hum or deep boom, almost too low to perceive; but I could feel a vibration in my chest and lungs as if a gong had been banged inside of me. I looked around, baffled. And then I heard it, a strong clear voice, coming from above my head and dropping like a stone into my chest. I held my breath as I received the message.

"You need to write a book. Put your experiences into a form you can share with others and spread your message of resilience and joy. People are waiting for and need your help. To continue your healing and growth, you need to help others. Write a book, How to Survive Your Spouse's Suicide.*"*

"What the fuck?" I said out loud to the voice as I started to cry. "A book? About this?" I shook my head violently, tears flying in all directions, as I almost drove off the road. "No. Just no. Writing about it will force me to relive it. I can't do it, I'm too deep in grief, PTSD, anxiety, and insecurity. Putting those experiences into a book? Impossible."

Of course, I knew better than to argue with a message from Spirit. Well, I guess I argued a little.

Writing remains one of the great loves of my life. For as long as I could remember, I wrote poetry, songs, and countless long rants in my journal to process experiences and release emotional pain. My published works included content for newsletters, websites, blogs, and scientific research papers; but I had never published anything so personal. I love to write and have always been told I was a good writer, so writing a book didn't seem impossible. In fact, I'd been working on a how-to health series when I'd met Glen.

But this book is a completely different project. Writing about these experiences. How will I find the strength? I saw the research that writing is healing, but I don't know if I can do this.

An hour later, I sat on the tiny lanai in my rented condo, overlooking the exquisite ocean—a perfect setting to support writing—and thought about how to put my experiences into a book. I poured myself a strong drink, which at the time was my answer to all discomfort, and sat looking at the waves. Eventually, I opened my laptop and began putting together an outline. Suddenly, I felt my energy rise. I was flush with clarity and purpose. Words poured from my fingertips, and I was in the flow. The ocean waves nearby cheered me on.

Maybe I can do this! Okay, Spirit, I'm going to make this happen!

The next morning, my bubble of exuberance popped when I received a call from my brother...

"Miss, where are you? Are you going to be back in time for the funeral? I'm flying up tomorrow."

My closest aunt had passed away unexpectedly at age 70, and I needed to get home immediately.

Greeted by new grief and still consumed by estate turmoil, I struggled and failed to write at home. I lost focus. I tried to find help by joining a writing group; but other than poetry, my writing was more like an intricate process of avoidance. I felt like a fraud.

Who am I to write a book about surviving suicide loss?

I had never had such a difficult time with a writing project and felt completely blocked. The facilitator of my writing group recommended I receive a reading from a renowned Human Design Facilitator to help determine what was in the way of my writing. Human Design combines astrology and astronomy with modern science and provides a deep look into who you are and why you are here. The complexity of the information tied to the alignment of cosmic bodies on the day I was born astounded me.

After we reviewed my chart for over two hours, my eyes couldn't take in any more. Completely overwhelmed, I asked, "Is there a bottom line here? I can see this is something I could study for years."

I'm more confused than I am enlightened. To me, this chart looks like I dropped a box of spaghetti noodles on the floor.

"Michelle," the reader said patiently, "your purpose in this life is to live in joy, so you can demonstrate to others that joy is possible regardless of circumstances. You, dear lady, are designed to inhabit joy."

My reaction was less than enthusiastic at that point after years of grief and trauma. I couldn't have felt further from joy. But deep inside, I felt she was right and I had a strong desire to live in alignment with my purpose. Eventually, when I gained an understanding of how to live my purpose, I chose to name my business Inhabit Joy.

Soon after the reading, I joined an author's workshop delivered by a famous publishing house, and during one of the lectures, I was intrigued by an author sharing her writing journey. After struggling to get her message out, she realized, when she was writing her first book, that she didn't want to just reach out to people living with cancer (like she was) or cancer survivors. Her message, she felt, was for a bigger audience. I felt like she was giving me a message too, and I took her words to heart.

Perhaps I'm uncomfortable speaking about suicide loss because this is not my audience. I could help a much broader group with my knowledge of yoga, Ayurveda, meditation and mindfulness, grief, and trauma survival.

Resistance and insecurity, what authors call "imposter syndrome," led me away from my mission. The clear message from Spirit was becoming murky. Relieved to be moving away from the uncomfortable task of authoring a book on suicide loss, I felt more comfortable writing about living a joyful, healthy lifestyle and spreading my message about how to strengthen resilience and meet challenges as growth opportunities. Unfortunately, moving away from my calling led me to a loss of motivation.

After many more starts and stops, insecurity and uncertainty, I was struggling with self-doubt and making no progress. I knew it was time to get some help if I was going to bring my message to the world. Stuck in disorganized files and folders on my laptop, my experience was helping no one. Spirit supported me to move forward when I met a friend for coffee one day and, while describing my internal war between the urge I had to write the book and my resistance and fear, I noticed a flyer for Amanda's workshop. I took it as a sign of encouragement from the same source that sent me the message to write my book. I hoped, by attending Amanda's workshop, that I would find the help I needed to get the book moving.

When the break was over, Amanda asked if she could use our conversation as an example and share my story. Her question filled me with fear. Was I ready to be exposed? After a moment (which felt like an hour) of vacillating between freezing and sweating, I took the plunge.

What am I here for if not that? If my message of joy and resilience is ever going to get out, it has to start somewhere.

So, in front of eight strangers, with the kind and caring eyes of my future mentor softly encouraging me, I began, "Sharing my story to try to help others who suffer is the only way for my journey to make sense in the world. The only way to keep me from the paralyzing pity party, sorrow, or bitterness I could wallow in forever if I chose..." I explained that I felt compelled to share my experiences because if I can help others to become more resilient and live more joyful lives, it will bring meaning to the grief and trauma I endured.

The looks on the faces of the ladies were not the looks of horror or pity that I had feared, but of intrigue, compassion, and earnest support. They didn't lean back; they leaned in.

"Well," I beamed at Amanda as the other meeting attendees filed out. "I'm sure you can help me get this project unstuck. I want to hire you to help me get my message out. It felt so good to share and feel supported by you and the group. I'm more sure now than ever that I am going to get this book written! What's next?"

The knowing smile Amanda gave me in response to my enthusiasm made me feel like I might be signing on for more than I realized. Eventually, I learned that was absolutely true. I had no idea what was coming.

To take a deep dive into clarifying and sharing my message, I signed up for a week-long writing retreat that Amanda was offering. I was ready. It had been two years since Glen's death and over a year since Spirit gave me that clear and powerful message. I had done a lot of work in therapy, studying grief and trauma, writing, healing, and growing. And, through daily meditation and spiritual studies, I had discovered the true meaning of joy and how to live in it fully. It was finally time to share my story with the world! Or so I thought...

I was absolutely thrilled when I found out Amanda's "Message Matrix" retreat would take place in the forested mountains along the Sandy river just outside Portland. I knew this beautiful area was the ideal setting to connect with nature and develop my budding messenger. I write really fast, so I had the secret aspiration that my book would actually be finished by the end of the week!

Retreat day dawned; and I was filled with the electric energy of excitement as I dug through the sea of moving cartons from my recent move, looking for a reference book I wanted to bring.

I'm doing it. I'll come home with a draft and be published in a few months! Now, where is that book I want to bring?

The last time I had seen the book, it was on a bookshelf in the dining room that I used as an office in my previous home—the "room of gloom" so named because it had been where I spent tortured hours working on Glen's estate. Friends had helped me pack, so I wasn't sure which carton held the contents of that bookshelf. I finally found the right carton, recognizing items from my office bookshelf. I tore through it, tossing everything aside trying to find the book when a small purple box delicately decorated with a white floral pattern caught my eye. I froze and stared at the box. It was from my favorite jewelry store in a village near my home. It contained the last gift Glen had given me.

Near the end of his life, Glen had begun to lose his battle with mental illness. He was irrational and he had gotten violent; in fear, I'd asked him to move out. Initially, he was very angry and he'd threatened me. But as I stood my ground, he eventually moved to an apartment just a few blocks away. He showed up at our home frequently, and often frightened or angered me with his surprise visits.

I held the beautiful box to my heart and remembered Glen's words during his last unannounced visit: "This is a gift for you. Don't open it now, you'll understand when the time is right." He had begged me to welcome him back home and handed me the box. I told him no, that I loved him but I couldn't be with him while I was afraid of him. When I tried to refuse the gift, he put up his hand and demanded that I take it. "Just keep it somewhere safe until it's time." I accepted it reluctantly, and he wrapped me up in a tight hug. I breathed into him, love and desire pouring from every cell in my body, but pushed away, remembering my fear of him.

Reluctantly, he left without further incident. Distressed by his visit, I didn't even open the box. I threw it into my office bookshelf and put it out of my mind. Two weeks later, he ended his life.

I stared down at the box in my shaking hand, tears threatening, wondering if that was the last time I had told him that I loved him.

I wish I could have done more. Everyone says it's not my fault, but I still wonder. Could anything have helped? The question I had asked myself thousands of times for over two years haunted me.

I took several deep breaths and cried. Emotions are energy in motion, and I had learned through therapy and yoga that allowing and moving emotions through the mind and body was the only way to process challenges and eventually heal. So, I let the tears flow, hugging myself as I thought back on all the amazing adventures Glen and I had during our too-short time together. So many great memories, and so many difficult ones.

When my tears stopped, I returned to preparations for my retreat. I quickly found the book I was looking for and was just about to throw the jewelry box back into the carton when curiosity stopped me. I was filled with shame for not accepting this box more appreciatively. As this was his last gift to me, I prepared to have total appreciation for it.

I will cherish this gift... I took a deep breath and slowly opened it. I did not immediately understand what I was looking at. The box contained two dull bronze metal cylinders. *This certainly doesn't look like jewelry.* I picked one of them up and, noticing it was heavy for its size, I examined it more closely. It was flat on one end and narrow on the other where it came to a curved tip...

I sucked in my breath as understanding hit me like a sledgehammer to the gut. I was holding a bullet. My legs buckled and I dropped to the floor on my knees. Pure panic set in as I dropped the bullet back into the box and slammed the lid. "OH MY GOD!" I screamed as I threw the box across the room as if it had burned me. I gasped for breath, unable to get any air in. My entire body started to shake. I called upon all the strength I had to stay in my body, to stay in the present and not go into trauma induced shock or dissociate. Relying on the hard work I had done in trauma therapy during treatment for PTSD, I knew what to do. It took a huge effort. This trigger was so strong and had caught me so off-guard, I wasn't sure I could hold on. I reached for a tool from my "PTSD trigger toolbox" and used all of my senses to connect to my current surroundings. *The floor feels cool. My hands are shaking and cold. My breath is quick. I see my favorite books on my bookshelf. The trees outside the window are gently moving in the slight breeze...* On and on, I went through the sequence I had practiced hundreds of times with my therapist and used whenever I was faced with triggers. Disconnected from time, possibly a few minutes or maybe an hour later, through this somatic sensory practice, I fully reconnected with my body and managed to find the strength to get off the floor.

I walked hesitantly over to the box, and took the bullets back out, and stared at them.

"You'll understand when the time is right," he had said.

NO, Glen, I do not!

I called a friend, one of the last people Glen confided in before he died, described my discovery, and asked, "What do you think he meant by that? I absolutely do not understand!"

"Michelle, I think you do understand. The gift he gave you was the gift of your life. I believe those bullets were meant for you and him, and the day he gave them to you, he had decided he was not going to go through with his plan of murder/suicide."

I sucked in a quick breath, "Oh my God!" dropped my phone, and dissociated. Part of me was packing and getting the condo ready for me to be gone for a week and part of me was watching from afar, in shock, not feeling anything. The dissociation I had battled when I found the bullets was now protecting me from being consumed by terror.

The gift of my life....

I finished packing in a dissociated fog and somehow managed to get out the door to pick up one of the other retreat attendees for the drive to the mountain cabin. Of course, I could not have predicted that I would be struggling with a trauma response on the day of the retreat. Instead of doing what I needed to recover—stay home in my safe place and process this new trauma with my therapist—I was committed to driving for hours with a stranger to an unknown place.

Even though I haven't met her in person, as another messenger who is preparing to share her story with the world, I'm sure she will be a good supportive listener and the car ride will help me start to stabilize and process this traumatic experience.

Unfortunately, all of my hopes for support were dashed only moments after I picked her up. She was processing a recent traumatic experience of her own. I didn't understand this, of course, and I was so needy and raw that I opened up to her about the discovery I'd made and how it was affecting me. A very poor choice on my part. I had learned I need to be careful when choosing with whom I share my vulnerability, but my need overcame my judgment at that moment.

When I finished pouring out my story and my tears, I waited for the support I so desperately needed, feeling anxious and exposed. Instead, with little acknowledgment or validation of my trauma, she went straight into talking about her own issues. I tried to listen attentively and actively. It didn't work. I was so hurt, I could only feel frustration, raw vulnerability, fear, anxiety... trauma. I wanted to scream at her, "Did you hear what I just said? That my late husband had planned to kill me and then had given me bullets as a gift?" I needed to be seen and heard, for my trauma to be witnessed to begin processing. She was unable to support me, and I felt sick and heartbroken. I was barely able to drive, much less help her, in such deep need of help myself. I used all of my strength to keep my breath steady and my eyes on the road, hoping that if I could just get us there, Amanda, whom I knew was a strong and calm support, would somehow make this all better.

The first evening was mostly resting and getting to know each other and the home we were staying in. I moved through the exercises, still barely connected to where I was, feeling numb and distant.

The retreat was inspiring, but equally as difficult. Opening up in front of the group while we all worked on our Message Matrix—the foundational exercise from which we would transform our life experiences into our message—would have been difficult under the best of circumstances, but this group did not provide the safe space I'd anticipated and needed. In fact, I was continuously wounded by the unspoken hostility I felt coming at me unexpectedly from across the table. I had to dig deep into my inner toolbox to manage my anxiety and keep writing.

Overwhelmed by the combination of the recent traumatic event I had experienced, and the unsafe space I was in, I frequently had to interrupt my writing to practice calming and centering. I was able to keep going because of these practices; and I also found respite in movies, chocolate, the physical practice of yoga, and an occasional walk along the river. I practiced mindfully being where I was in the moment. I focused on the warm air and the towering pine trees, the call of a bird, the rush of the water over the rocks.

When Amanda and I ran into each other outside during a break, I asked her, "Amanda, is there something weird going on here? Is it that I found those bullets and then, with no time to process, came here to write my stories that is making me feel so anxious? Or is there something more?"

"Michelle, you're doing great. And your intuition is right. There is more going on here. We have multiple fresh traumas that are colliding and compounding each other. I'm doing my best to balance the energy and help you all feel safe. But I'm starting to realize that all this work to create safety for others might make people who are accustomed to lack of safety freak out. I'm inspired by your tenacity, and your ability to be productive and keep writing even in these difficult circumstances."

Amanda's support kept me going, even when I ached to hide or to just pack up and leave. Only later did I realize how much growing and developing I was forced to do while trying to create in that hostile environment. As difficult as it was, this experience was another critical step on my development path.

"The mind adapts and converts to its own purposes the obstacle *to our acting. The impediment to action advances*

action. What stands in the way becomes the way." Marcus Aurelius, Meditations, Book 5.2

This quote that I found during the retreat reinforced that being in joy is not the goal or something to be obtained by getting out of the present moment.

Joy and resilience. If you are going to teach these things, you need to know how to live in them, even when circumstances are hard. It's okay, Michelle. You know what to do when you don't feel safe, I coached myself many times a day. I reminded myself of all I had learned, that even when things are difficult, joy exists along with challenges. If I could connect to those things, I could remember that joy is internal and eternal: that we all live in joy, we just need to remember it's there. A challenging practice indeed.

On days one and two of the retreat, I powered through the Message Matrix exercise, getting in touch with all the most significant stories of my life. Creatively writing about the most formative events in my life was like putting my entire emotional history on display. Fortunately, this wasn't unprecedented work, as I had done a great deal of introspection, exposing, reviewing, and healing of my stories in yoga teacher and yoga therapy training, and of course, in my therapist's office. Still, I was surprised during the retreat, when I explored the most impactful experiences of my life, to find how they had directly shaped me and my worldview. I was also surprised how many of the big impact situations were "negative" or difficult, like car accidents, sexual trauma, deaths, and estrangements, rather than chosen or "positive" like marriage and babies.

"The impediment to action advances action..."

Michelle, look at how far you've come, I cheered myself on as I realized Amanda and Marcus Aurelius were right—

this was another opportunity to heal and grow. I needed to celebrate the fact that with every trauma I've endured, I've grown through it, acquired more tools, strengthened and evolved emotionally and spiritually, and developed greater resilience.

As I wrote, tears falling into the keyboard at times and belly-laughing out loud at others, I did a lifetime's worth of processing and an extraordinary amount of healing. Some of the stories I wrote during retreat week were given the witnessing they needed and were actually healed. Others were buried so deep, they weren't ready to heal but were invited to the surface where they would be more accessible for future writing and therapy sessions.

Although I didn't have a book at the end of the week, I was much more clear about my message, which had expanded to include resilience and the fact that it takes a certain amount of challenge and stress to create it. Effort is required. I was empowered by the knowledge that I was capable of sharing my message in an accessible way. I had also worked with Amanda to tease out which of my stories were simply therapeutic writing (most) and which would actually be helpful to others.

Even with all of the successes and growth during the retreat, when it was over, I felt exhausted from how much energy it took to keep myself writing about such intimate things while feeling unsafe. Amanda did her best to create a safe, supportive space; but it was impossible.

Relieved to be home, I dove back into my busy life of teaching and working with clients and put processing the layered trauma of the retreat and the discovery of the bullets on hold. I needed a break from deep emotional work, but that was not a path I was able to choose. Only two weeks later, my life would take yet another turn that left me wondering how I could possibly write a book about living in joy and overcoming challenges when I continued to be overwhelmed by them!

My brother had a near-death experience and had been suffering on a ventilator and in the ICU for over two weeks. I flew to Phoenix, AZ, to be with him and help his family manage all of the various doctors and therapies and research long-term care facilities. Seeing my brother like this was devastating. I spent hours by his bedside, thinking about the vibrant, fun-loving man he used to be, worrying about his comfort and his treatments, and praying for his recovery. Once again, I dug deep into my emotional well-being toolbox and practiced yoga, meditation, and breathing every morning before going to the hospital, and took frequent breaks to walk through the cool starkly lit halls. When I felt myself falling apart, I went outside to find something in nature with which to connect.

After my brother had been moved from the hospital to a care facility where he could rehabilitate, I went back home. Exhausted again, I needed time to heal. It took months for him to recover, but he did, and my recovery paralleled his. I had to go deeply inward to strengthen my resilience and develop even more coping mechanisms and healing tools. I worked a lot on acceptance, realizing I had no control over my brother's illness or his recovery. It was frustrating and challenging work.

Eventually, I started writing again. Slowly my writing was becoming a manuscript offering readers tools to build resilience and live in joy. I could see the light at the end of the "shitty rough draft" (as Amanda called it) tunnel.

I'm finally going to get this done! A draft, then a book, then publication!

Of course, Spirit had other plans...

As I was closing in on completing the draft of my manuscript, I began to feel pain in my right arm. At first, it was only when I was writing for many hours at a time, but it increased to the point that I could barely move my wrist or shoulder; and I was diagnosed with bicep tendonitis, wrist arthritis, and a frozen shoulder. I tried to keep working through the pain and keep writing to reach my self-imposed calendar goal.

I am going to ignore the pain and get this draft done! I don't care how much it hurts; it's been long enough! I powered through the pain (ironic for a yoga teacher), determined to get the draft completed. Of course, that wasn't going to happen. Just three days before reaching my finish line, I was struck with a stomach illness. Long days and nights in the bathroom and a slow recovery stopped my progress again.

I was forced to let go of my self-imposed completion goal.

Another obstacle? This is never going to end. I feel like my body is giving me messages to stop writing, or at least that writing a book is going to take more resilience and pain tolerance than I can muster. If the obstacle is the path, how can I get it to turn into a book?

In complete frustration, I called Amanda one day and asked, "Has writing a book ever actually killed anyone?"

She laughed, but the laugh wasn't joyful. She deeply understood my suffering and knew I was going through exactly what I needed to go through, to *grow through*, to become the messenger I am meant to be. She reassured me, but, of course, couldn't speed up the process. These challenges were here to teach and strengthen me. I had to learn and grow until I could accept the teaching that these obstacles were giving me.

Trying to finish my book somehow seemed related to the continuing series of disasters in my life. Every time I got close to finishing a draft, some health or family crisis would force me to put the writing on hold so I could heal. I needed to accept this as part of the path.

The obstacle is the way... more learning and growing to do. The learning and growing is the path? I'm beginning to understand this, but how does that understanding help me finish the book?

Committed to healing and getting my writing into the world, I kept trying—new coaches, new programs, new doctors—but nothing worked. Each time I came close to finishing a draft of my book, my body would rebel, and I would find myself too sick or in too much pain to go on. I struggled with depression, anxiety, loneliness, brain fog, and a host of other physical and mental/emotional challenges. Illness followed illness, and I spent strings of days in bed and months in ill health. I compelled myself to keep going.

"The impediment to action advances action..."

I kept growing through these challenges and worked hard to develop love and compassion for myself and my labyrinthine journey.

After nine doctors, more tests than I could track, and no clear diagnosis, I slowly began to find a way back to health. I finally had enough energy to think about writing again, so I posted on social media and published blogs but didn't revisit the book. Toward the end of 2020, I reconnected with Amanda and asked her for help. I explained what I had been through and that, due to my poor health, my book was at a standstill. She offered support and invited me to come to a weekly writing group; and when she encouraged me to write a chapter for this book, I said yes because it seemed like an easy project.

Well, of course, it wasn't easy; it became yet another obstacle. But as I powered through it, I reached a new level of understanding. Part of my message *is* this exact journey. The path, including (or especially) the obstacles, and how I process and integrate them, is my story and my message.

Amanda and I reviewed my most recent manuscript, which had been constructed and deconstructed four times, and organized a way to work the draft so I could finally see the whole book coming to life. Closing in on the finish line once more... or so I thought.

Once more, I became too ill to write. This time I was suffering COVID-like symptoms. I had a high fever and aches for days.

Late one night, while I was too uncomfortable with a fever and chills to sleep, curled up in a ball on my bed shivering, I closed my eyes tight and prayed. I begged my guides, Spirit, the Universe, God, angels, "Please help me. How can I proceed? Why do all of these obstacles keep blocking my path? Why so many setbacks? Why so much suffering? What do I need to do to heal and move forward?"

Immediately, and very clearly, I received my answer: *"Write a book.* How to Survive Your Spouse's Suicide."

Just like when I was in Hawaii, almost four years earlier, Spirit was clearly telling me I needed to complete that task.

"Okay!" I growled through clenched teeth, startling my cat who had been sleeping on me, she scratched me and jumped off as if to give the message an exclamation point. Reluctantly, because I was fully aware of how difficult this was going to be, I committed, "Okay, I'll finish that book!"

As soon as I felt better, I told Amanda about my experience. She didn't even bat an eye. "Well then, I guess that's the book we will work on first. You can't argue with your Co-Author. I mean, you can but I don't recommend it."

I found all my notes and began working on the suicide loss book. Soon, I felt my creativity flowing.

This is going to help people! I can do this!

Words were flying onto the page, and I was making steady progress. Even though it was an exceptionally difficult topic to write about, it felt good to be following Spirit's intention for me. Finally, I felt in alignment with my purpose and with Spirit. I was in the flow.

My journey continues to hand me challenges, and as I meet each one, I use my multilevel toolbox to grow through difficult times and expand the scope of my ability to support others. Mindfulness and my spiritual practices allow me to observe the suffering I have endured and witness each challenge as an opportunity for growth. Each obstacle transforms into the way and, in that transformation, strengthens my resilience. I practice living in joy as much as possible but also welcome all feelings as part of the fantastic experience of being human. I see my journey as a gift, challenges as growth opportunities, and obstacles as the path. I bring meaning to my experiences by sharing my story and supporting others who suffer, and I cannot wait to launch my book, *Spouse/Partner Suicide: A Mindful Survival Guide,* soon after this one.

Amanda's Side of the Story

This is either going to be magical, or it's going to be a triggering nightmare, I thought after hanging up the phone with one of the other new clients scheduled for Michelle's retreat.

The synchronicities were just too intense. Stories full of depression and touched by abuse and suicide. One of the most important characters in the other woman's story was named Michelle. (You can't make that shit up.) And both were coming from more eastern, integrative spiritual experiences.

I thought it was so awesome that Michelle offered to do an airport pickup, but I wondered if that was a good idea when I saw her face upon arrival.

Uh oh.

Uh oh was right.

Before the first exercise was over, it all started to unravel. This other client was triggered and I could see it affecting Michelle.

What happened? I did everything I knew to do. I cleared the energy in this cabin. I set intentions and infused the space with what I wanted everyone to experience: safety, love, belonging, and ease. I facilitated community agreements.

For the next several days, I struggled to figure out what the hell was going on and remedy it. It wasn't the first time I'd facilitated triggered clients, but it was the first time I was dealing with someone who seemed completely incapable of seeing her behavior and self-regulating it. Every time I asked her a question about her story, she saw the face of her abusers and reacted with some energetic violence. This energy permeated the space and the experience of the other participants to the point where I really just wanted to end the retreat and go home. Instead, I kept witnessing energy balancing sessions, using all the skills and tools I had, and asking for some sort of supernatural help or insight.

I'm not sure which day it was, but eventually, I understood the first lesson this experience was teaching me. In all of my attempts to make the space safe for others, I had never considered the possibility that some folks are so accustomed to feeling unsafe that true safety actually feels like a threat to their *normal.* That made perfect sense with regards to this one client whose story did not include any sense of felt safety. Immediately, I remembered my own first experience of safety in a new community and how I, too, completely spun out emotionally and misbehaved, as if I needed to test the boundaries and see how far I could push all that unconditional love and non-judgment before it became unsafe.

I'll have to let new clients know this is a thing—that if they've never really felt safe, this might actually feel terrifying to them. Maybe give them some scripts and tools to help them ask for help and self-regulate as they try to settle into real safety.

I was seriously impressed by Michelle's fortitude, attitude, and resilience. She was obviously struggling to maintain her balance, but she was staying focused and productive and working through all the tough feelings and conversations that came up as we worked through her story. When she asked me about this other participant, I did my best to explain that these groups that coalesce for retreats tend to have some divine intention to them. Maybe this was a powerful opportunity for Michelle to prove to herself that all of the skills and tools she'd acquired and was getting ready to share with the world were just that powerful. It was my best guess, but I still wanted better answers.

A few days after the retreat was over, I checked on the participants and was grateful when Michelle told me how disappointed and upset she was that the retreat had not provided the safe space I'd promised and she'd expected.

As I hung up the phone, I asked again, *What in the world happened? What else am I supposed to learn here?*

That night, I was scheduled to be online with one of the communities I belong to and support; and something the facilitator did while setting the safe space triggered me... intensely. In their attempt to create more safety for the space, they had breached mine. It surprised me, as I'd never experienced that in any community before. I used all of my skills and tools to self-regulate, but I barely made it through the call.

Shaking with rage, I remembered this other client's reactions at the retreat; and the answer that would completely change the way I would run all of my events from there on out finally came.

I think I'm upset because of how much responsibility that facilitator took for my safety. Trying to cover all the bases actually created more stress for me. It put all of the responsibility for other people's safety on me.

As soon as I realized it, the shaking stopped.

I wish that facilitator would have said, "I'm doing my part to bring a sense of safety here. I've cleared this space. I've trained the support team. I'm doing my own work to manage my biases and the energy in the room. If I witness a breach, I will address it. If I inadvertently compromise the safety, please bring it to my attention so I can resolve it. If I don't see a breach, then it's up to you to take responsibility for your

safety—kindly bring awareness to it, ask for what you need,
assume that everyone here is doing the best they know how,
and be open to resolution."

While I have wished repeatedly that I could give Michelle
the experience we both expected, I am so grateful for that
terrible week and Michelle's honesty about it. It catalyzed
an important and necessary paradigm shift around safety
that has changed the way I do business *and* the way that I do
relationships. Despite our best efforts and intentions, none of
us can create perfectly safe environments around us to keep
ourselves and others safe. It's up to all of us to figure out how
to create that safety within, communicate to resolve when
breaches happen, and model it for others.

Lori Bonnevier is a licensed clinical social worker with degrees in social work, human services, psychology, and child development. She has experience as a child welfare caseworker, a preschool teacher and college professor, and a facilitator for the state mandated class for divorcing parents. Since 2002, her clinical practice has focused on providing child custody and parenting time evaluations, and testimony as an expert witness in the circuit courts. Having expanded her practice to include consulting, coaching, and speaking, Lori is sharing her message of Child-Focused Choices with a larger audience. She lives in Portland, Oregon, with her two children.

The Choice and Courage to "Look!"

Lori Bonnevier

Seated in a wooden rocking chair in the cozy retreat cabin, I looked around at the unfamiliar faces of the women gathered before me, awaiting their reaction. I wondered if they (or I) might run for the hills, while secretly hoping that maybe they would have the courage to lock arms with me. Broken, sorry-ass me sat there, wishing we could group-hug this out. But everyone was silent and still, apparently paralyzed by the words they'd just heard spill out of my mouth. Wiping tears from my wet face, I made eye contact with the sweet book coach lady.

Did I just wreck her? I wondered, thinking my ugly story—the story I had buried deep and never-ever shared with anyone before now—might have been too much. *Good gravy. What did I just do? Did I really say all of that out loud? That story has absolutely nothing to do with writing a book for parents and children navigating divorce and restructuring their family system. Stupid move. Stupid, stupid, stupid. That secret was not meant for sharing, especially here with a bunch of strangers.*

The idea of writing a book had been with me since age seven, when I submitted a short story to a contest at the local summertime fair. In that moment, forty-two years ago, a conscious decision was made to author a book one day. What book was never clear. Not the topic or purpose or the impact I'd wanted to make on a particular target audience. I simply wanted to write a book, put my name on the front cover, and have a tangible legacy that would collect dust on bookstore shelves, mostly to satisfy my ego and say, "I did it."

Zip forward to adulthood and into the third decade of my professional career, and the desire to add "author" to an already-robust resume had really ramped up. I had built a thriving little empire in my private clinical practice and was respected within my professional community and well-regarded as an expert in my field. I had begun to feel that authoring a book would be a vehicle to modify and expand the services I had long-provided to children and families—a new business model that was exciting and that lit a fire in my belly.

This new business model would allow me to slough off the parts of the work that were exhausting me after more than twenty years of being in the trenches (and courtrooms) with angry, divorcing parents who were fighting custody battles and losing the war that matters—the one for their child's well-being. I had absorbed gallons of pain, hurt, and sorrow from thousands of suffering children (and their parents and the legal community); and I was tuckered out. Creating a preventative model, by serving in a consultation and coaching role, and getting back to my roots and true calling as a teacher seemed more fulfilling. However, the book was not actually getting written.

Truth is, I was too busy sustaining the perfect life I'd created. That is, until 2018 when I started to get the message that it was time for change. Lying in bed one evening, alone and crying, I said out loud to no one in particular,

"This cannot be it. There has to be more than this." That thought was immediately accompanied by shame because I had everything everyone told me a happy person has, and everything that I had prayed for as a little girl—a solid education and high-earning career, an upper-middle class home, a hard-working and good-looking husband, two healthy and amazing kids, successful and supportive friends, a dog, and two paid-for vehicles in the garage. To anyone looking in from outside these four walls, my life was truly perfect. But, living inside those four walls, there were secrets that I was keeping... even from myself.

Shortly after asking if this was it, an email arrived in my inbox from a local pie shoppe that hosted small business seminars. Normally, I did not have time to read this sort of email; but that morning, I took the time and noticed a book writing seminar advertised in the coming month. My workload had reduced to an unusually slow pace so I had time, but not a lot of expendable income. I impulsively signed up on a whim.

By the time the workshop rolled around, the pace of my usual rat race had returned and something had fallen through on my calendar, which meant I had no childcare for my eight-year-old daughter. I emailed the workshop leader (Amanda) and asked if it was appropriate to bring my daughter along, hoping she'd say *no* so I could stay home and knock a few more things off my big to-do list instead. Of course, she obliged and invited my sweet pea to attend.

In the coming days, multiple circumstances threatened to hijack our attendance but, at my daughter's insistence, we made it. After two hours of listening and enjoying a slice of homemade pie, it was clear that while I had more questions than answers, I absolutely knew I needed to work with

Amanda. She seemed harmless enough, and she liked my kid. I was ready to write a book, and there in my path was the avenue to make it happen.

Months passed as my busy life resumed and Amanda and I talked by email. Finally, I said yes to a writing retreat happening the first part of January 2019. It was a financial stretch and meant I would need to leave my children for a week, which I had never done before. They were nine and fourteen and I was the orchestrator of their lives, the helmsman of our ship, the gorilla glue that held our family secure. I was pretty sure this book would be authored in six-months tops and published within the year. This is what perfectionists do—we set unrealistic expectations of ourselves in an attempt to maintain the illusion because being real would require admitting the bumbling and unpolished mess we know ourselves to be.

Perfectionists like me love day-planners and organizers and calendars. We have label makers, color-code our closets, alphabetize our canned goods, rely heavily on sticky notes, make lists, and we are never-ever late, undone in public, or unprepared. That's why I had an anxiety attack on day one of the retreat when I realized I was late—a whole frickin' day late! How could this have happened? I had it on the calendar and the outline on my desktop, which I had checked often leading up to the day. Ducks in a row gal here. And when I realized this, I still had to get to the grocery store, prepare meals for the kids, get a pedi/mani, and pack my bag with all the new outfits I had bought and, and, and... I was a day late!

When I texted Amanda to acknowledge my failure, she replied to my frantic message with one word: "Breathe." Breathing was too time-consuming back then; not a practice I brought into my conscious world, but an unconscious function my body was responsible for managing. Moving forward with the day, I kept checking items off my list until it was time to pick up my kids from school. It was the same school where I had picked them up thousands of times before; but that day, I saw a sign by the entrance that had the word TRUST in painted white letters, on a wood base, with a little rusty butterfly attached. You probably know by now that Amanda's brand is based on the butterfly so I wondered, just briefly, if this message was meant for me.

Turns out this would be the first in a long line of signs and magical affirmations telling me that I was no longer in control and never actually was—that the universe was taking back the wheel (with force) and it was time for me to let go, look around, and start waking up to see.

On day two of the retreat, which was actually the first day we were scheduled to work together, I arrived at a full house because everyone else apparently read the memo correctly. I rolled up during "silent reflection time." Jesus, Joseph, and Mary—it was clear I was really being tested. This gal likes to talk. I spotted an overstuffed chair in the corner, plopped my rear-end down, and plucked *Chicken Soup for The Soul* off a nearby bookshelf, noticing that the silent attendees and Amanda herself were all dressed in comfortable loungewear. Looking down at my crisp new outfit and freshly-manicured nails, I realized I was fully outside of my comfort zone.

That first evening, we did an intuitive exercise which was designed for us to tell ourselves which st*ry was likely to keep us from moving our book project forward. I loved the intuition part, happy to finally know and connect with other people who got real gut feelings and signs before anyone else; but I was still unclear about how any of my personal stories would affect the book I was writing professionally.

When the exercise revealed that a story in my own marriage might interrupt my process of writing a book for parents in high-conflict divorces, I found myself wondering if I'd made a big mistake. The next day, it was time to start exploring the story, out loud, in this safe space, with total strangers. And it was then, seated in a wooden rocking chair in the cozy retreat cabin, that I finally shared a secret no one else had ever heard.

Amanda caught her breath and began asking grounding questions. I answered her questions as quickly as I could, wishing we could just move on to the next participant.

God, I should not have said anything at all. There were so many other stories I could have chosen to focus on—less embarrassing and painful... and actually related to my book!

I held a journal in my lap—the only journal left on the table after everyone else had selected theirs. It would not have been the one I would have chosen, but it might have chosen me. A message on the back read, "Do the difficult things while they are easy and do the great things while they are small. The journey of a thousand miles must begin with a single step." It was a similar message to the card I'd pulled earlier that morning: "Middle Earth shows up when conditions are favorable to your undertaking. Do not hesitate, move forward as heaven and earth are smiling upon you. The world is your playground and what would require great effort at any other time can be accomplished with ease right now." My mind struggled to understand the connections.

I need a break! I thought when we went to lunch. I told Amanda I was going to take a drive into town to get something, and I took off to... collect myself...

I Google-searched a cool-sounding store, entered the address into my GPS, and drove down the mountain. Somehow, I took a wrong turn and ended up in line for a toll bridge. I hate bridges—they terrify me!—but there was no way to turn around. I paid my two dollars and drove forward, clenching everything all the way across. I reversed course in a gas station, anxiety building about crossing back over. Then something happened. Half-way across that terrifying bridge, the majestic snowy mountain I had just descended was right in front of me. The winter sun was shining bright and reflecting like glass off the river below. A wave of pure joy and peace washed through me at that moment—all the clenching and over-firing nervousness gone, leaving only the sweet buzz of serenity left in its place.

Damn, how long have these scrumptious dopamines been dormant?

Driving into the town I had originally aimed for, it seemed there was only street parking and not much of it, except for one spot outside the huge glass window of a coffee shop with patrons packed inside. I looped the block hoping for another option—something less dangerous to my pride.

Nope, not today, Sister. Just do it, ya chicken! Parallel parking was never a skill I'd mastered and I was certainly not comfortable having an audience. All serenity from the bridge experience fled and anxiety ruled again. I held my breath and got busy. Success! Done like a pro, the perfect me on display. *Phew!*

Next to the coffeehouse was a gift shop I had not seen in my Google search. Something special for my kids was a must after leaving them for a whole week, so I went in and was greeted by a cheerful employee. I didn't feel much like talking—the recent adrenaline rush now fading and leaving a budding headache in its wake. However, at his insistence, we struck up conversation and I shared what I was up to at the retreat. I called myself an "author," even though one word had not been written. He was exceptionally curious and kept digging for more, so I cautiously offered a few of my ideas.

This dude is going to think I'm nuts!

The gift shop employee (Hood River Aaron, I named him) not only affirmed my ideas but related to the subject material after recently going through the process of divorce and sorting out child custody himself. He affirmed and encouraged me and added to my undeveloped ideas for the book. After purchasing a few gifts, I hurried back to my car and wrote everything down as quickly as I could.

Hot damn! No one is ever going to believe this!

Back at the retreat, an outline for the book showed itself—a very rough draft of what could be. Amanda introduced more exercises over the week designed to help each of us better understand our own st*ries and how they were intertwined with our books.

Obviously, she is speaking about them—not me. But whatever. I'm going to get this book done.

Seemingly out of nowhere, two very best friends from different seasons in my life (youthful, joy-filled seasons) appeared by text message and provided a reminder of my more authentic self—a younger, less stressed, and freer version of me. A conversation with my high school and college best friend reminded me of a time when we used to sneak into bars and nightclubs using our fake IDs. The name on my ID was Vanessa, which became an alter ego for my naughtier self as a young adult—the delicious kind of naughty. It only made sense that Vanessa would become one of the main characters in my story. Stunned by all of the affirmations suggesting that I was on the right path, I was fired up to work on my book.

After a full week, I left the retreat feeling refueled and pondering "The Messy Middle." These words came up often at the retreat and, while I had no idea what anyone was actually talking about, it seemed important. The day after re-entry to usual life, my daughter was supposed to be getting ready for school but was playing her piano instead. As I hurried her along, the name of the piece she was playing jumped off the page: "The Middle" by Zedd, Maren Morris, Grey—(Lyric Video). I hummed along to the song's lyrics while dropping my daughter at school and then I drove to work.

"Okay, Universe, I'm listening and looking. Show me what I need to see," were the words I spoke out loud this time while shaking my head in disbelief. I had no idea what I was asking for, but answers began to show up right away.

At my office, I sat adjacent to my administrative assistant and dear friend and filled her in on the retreat experience and how I had decided to write this book in a "choose-your-own-outcome" format. Her eyes widened as she looked at the wall on the other side of our waiting room that held a magazine rack. On the rack was a parenting magazine. On the cover was the picture of a snowy mountain with the words "Choose Your Own Adventure." She abruptly brought that magazine into view for me—one I had been walking past daily, multiple times, for months.

I gasped. Hood River Aaron had also affirmed the idea that I'd had to write a "choose-your-own-outcome" style story for parents navigating high-conflict divorce who find themselves stalled in litigation about the best decisions for their children. My life's work would be creatively proffered in a fun, useful, meaningful manuscript to help move families from crisis to healing... and thriving. Right after seeing this magazine, dated months prior (the same month I'd met Amanda at the pie shoppe—cue spooky music!), a new batch was delivered. For years, this free monthly resource magazine had been delivered routinely to my office, yet this one copy had sat for eight months without being replaced. Then like magic, a fresh delivery was waiting outside my office suite door the day after I finally saw the message on the old copy. It's the truth. You seriously cannot make this shit up!

I found myself juggling work, home, high-level perfectionism, and now, the process of authoring a book. Time was in short supply—sleep too—and grumpy was an understatement of my mood. One day, I needed to drive a distance for an assignment and decided to download an audiobook for the road trip. Quickly, I realized that the audiobook I was after was not the one that downloaded. Tech is not my thing, and I was pissed. I had paid $20 bucks!

"Fine," I scoffed. "I'll listen to whatever crap this is." It was Amy Poehler's book, *Yes Please*. At least I knew who she was and enjoyed her on SNL. I hopped in my car, connected to Bluetooth, and heard the first words Amy read in her ever-so-sweet "I'm annoyed at the world" tone: "Writing a book is fucking hard..."

Right on, Sister! I had to pull over to manage my huge belly laugh, cry, call Amanda, and reground before heading out. Over the next five hours, Amy and I bonded—me in my car and her delivering a message that seemed as if it were written especially for me.

Similar affirmations—these "magical moments"—began showing up all around with colleagues offering support and accolades and professional organizations offering unsolicited endorsements. I even "coincidentally" met a prominent legal professional in L.A. right at the time I started to believe that my message could serve more than the local community where I worked. She invited me to be a guest on her podcast—a platform to discuss and promote my message once it was finished.

I was beginning to understand that these supernatural affirmations had been there all along; I had simply not yet been able to see. But now, the universe with all of its grace had grabbed me by the shoulders, shaken me hard, and screamed, "LOOK! Look at what you have been walking past all this time—the treasures have always been here... in plain sight. Choose courage, young padawan, and discover the answers that you already know."

Unexpectedly and so randomly, undeniable confirmations were received that the universe and great co-author were really there for me—a secure foothold of support, the load bearing wall to everything that had been and all that was about to happen. Although I had heard these words before, it was with a new awareness and new context and clarity that I understood them: "Life does not happen to us; it happens for us." Go ahead, loop back, and read that sentence again. Those are some powerful words right there. All of this (the good, bad, and full extent of the shit show) was happening for me. Everything leading to this point had happened for me, to give perspective and teach lessons about the wide-ranging spectrum of my humanity. The neon flashing signs were everywhere, and I was no longer asleep and able to pass by them without seeing the messages so impeccably laid out along my path—the breadcrumb trail that would lead me home.

You'd think I'd be thrilled, right? Well, I was. But I could also feel the fu*#ing universe, the great co-author, threatening to disrupt my normal—the comfortable, controlled illusion of the secure and stable life I'd worked so hard to establish. It seemed like a mystical portal had revealed itself and my eyes were beginning to open and my other senses were waking up, too.

I continued marching forward into this emerging reality as a second retreat grew near. As a priority, I would assure a prompt arrival on the proper day. Having learned at the first retreat that everything is easier in community, I found myself stoked to see my sister-friends again—the ones who helped expand my field of vision and held safe space to do the required work. This time, we focused on family of origin st*ries that might be impacting our ability to complete our projects. We burned up old st*ries and useless childhood messages in a raging bonfire—complete with smores and lurking wildlife. At one point, Amanda caught me impersonating a family member and asked me to do more of that for all of the characters in my life. She reminded me that I'd had a dream about communicating my message through improv on big stages someday and said this might be another powerful way to process these stories.

As I acted out frustrations about my childhood, work, and marriage and the exhausting roles I had agreed to for so many years, I blurted out the words, "I am the fu*#ing universe!" in response to my husband's statement about how nicely the universe always lines things up (activities on our over-scheduled calendar, groceries and dinner every night, the kids' school, clothes, shoes, supplies, homework, healthcare, vacations and, and, and). It sure seemed, in that moment, that I had been carrying the equivalent weight of the universe. It felt good to admit my rage about it out loud, if only in the safety of this improv session among trusted sister-friends.

By the end of the second retreat, the book was moving along. I had direction and words were flowing out of me with the force of water over Niagara Falls. Main characters were busy establishing themselves—a husband and a wife, two kids, and the family dog. Mom and Dad were divorcing and each making choices about how they thought best to move forward through that process. The predictable consequences of those choices sometimes made me cringe and often made me laugh. Laughing was something I had not done much of lately, and it felt good.

It took time for me to look and eventually to see—to be present and to start feeling the continuum of human emotions that it seemed I had turned off somewhere along the way. But, when it happened, I welcomed this thawing of my soul. All the writing and accompanying retreat exercises had somehow cracked me open and allowed light to shine on the dark and lonely place in which my authentic self was trapped. I knew she was bound and gagged in there, and that she was frightened—scared shitless, actually—to step fully into the light, knowing this would require personal development, use of her big-girl voice, and uncomfortable helpings of change.

This way, Sister. Keep moving towards the warmth!

Six months after I started to write the book, an incident happened in my work-life that really unhinged my sense of safety, stability, and worth. It involved an aggressive attorney and a colleague serving as the attorney's "rebuttal witness." Both were disrespectful and belittling of my professional ethics and character while I testified in a courtroom trial. That's what I do for a living—I'm an expert witness. I testify often and have a solid reputation. This is the arena where I am able to be the strongest advocate for children. The incident I've described is not a common experience and the judge's ruling affirmed my sound recommendations; but the two men who attacked had pushed me over an emotional cliff.

Men… aggressive… disrespectful, belittling, challenging my sense of safety, ability, and worth—this theme was familiar, but I could not really place the intensity of it.

The courtroom experience triggered me so badly, I was not eating or sleeping well; and after a few days, it was obvious I needed professional help to work through this unsettling ordeal. I remembered a recent blog post from a "therapist who sees therapists" and went searching for it in my trash folder, at 3:00 a.m., because I was up and really suffering.

Geez, I must seriously be losing my mind!

Therapist of The Year was gracious and made time for me in short order. We quickly resolved the presenting issue and then he read back the words I had used to describe my "perfect" family—my husband, kids, and me—and, for the first time, I heard the lie. I saw the illusion I had painted for everyone else and chosen to believe myself. My family was a mess. I was unhappy and not even sure what was wrong. It seemed worth exploring at least, so we continued forward in our sessions.

With the strength of Hercules, Iron Man, and Thor, I resisted the truth of what was unfolding as the therapist and I began unraveling all the parts of my family dynamics. We dared together to pull back the veil and look behind the curtain of the polished, perfect life I believed to be the truth. It was arduous and painful work and, in no way, did I feel ready to walk down the path that was emerging before me. When he asked about the book and the characters in it, we started to connect the dots between the content and my own life.

My God, could those two main characters in my book possibly be me and my hubby? Is that what Amanda was trying to tell me with those exercises at the retreats?

Eventually, I came to terms with the fact that my marriage had suffered a major trauma over a decade earlier and never healed. I revealed to Therapist of The Year the same ugly story I had let out at that first book retreat—my big bad secret full of lies, deceit, and betrayal—and discovered that this trauma had morphed into a hidden force, a powerful toxic undercurrent, that saturated our household with negative energy over the last ten years.

The more I wrote, the more I realized the similarities and connections between the story I was writing for an audience and the real-life story that was flowing out of me. Authoring the book had become a conduit through which I was able to recognize and then start working to heal old st*ries. Sometimes healing happened alone while writing in a puddle of tears; many times, it happened with Amanda's expert help or in community with my sister messengers; and thankfully, it also happened in formalized psychotherapy with a trauma-trained professional.

Once I started seeing Therapist of The Year, it became obvious that the undertaking of writing my book would be much more than a six-month venture. So, I settled into a fresh rhythm—slowly letting go of control, surrendering to the larger agenda, flanked on all sides by new allies there to support me. I knew the only option was riding this tidal wave into shore.

It was right about then that the most curious thing to date actually happened.

It was time to write the "Gold Star Parent" chapter. I had saved it for last and really looked forward to writing this section, believing it would be the easiest and most rewarding to write. After all, I had coached parents for years about being their best selves and certainly, in my striving for perfection and with all that textbook and real-world knowledge, believed I was a gold star parent myself.

Not today, Momma!

Nothing would come out. I was blocked and blocked hard—start, stop, delete, start, stop, delete. This went on for a few weeks until my whole right hand cramped up; and by cramped up, I mean not one finger would extend and retract enough to type or hold a pencil. Nothing. I could not even tie my shoe! That sucker was frozen up and painful. An SOS went out to Amanda. "Breathe," she encouraged, hearing my panic.

All this breathing has got a girl hyperventilating over here!

I employed all the best self-care tactics I knew to relieve the pain and loosen the muscles in my hand; but it was only after Amanda asked me to work through several prompts with her that I achieved relief. The prompts focused on my relationship with my own mother. Having worked through family of origin issues at retreat number two, Amanda was familiar with the delicate dynamic between us. After spending time answering her prompts, I shook my head and said, "What? Are we actually talking about her or me? Are you saying I am her and she is me?!?"

No way! This cannot be the truth. I've worked so hard to generationally evolve!

After this breakthrough, the chapter wrote itself. My mother exited stage right and remained in the shadows until a critical moment, one and a half years later, when her words were the saving grace that fully cracked open the shell around my soul and allowed much-needed light to flood in.

My first writing contract with Amanda had expired and, knowing I was on the right course, I signed a second one, more confident in the process and the fiscal investment. Amongst the valuable components of her program, this second contract also included another retreat—an experience I knew was the salve for my weary and battered self. By now, no cost would have been too high for another retreat experience. I equated the prior two retreats to the heavens throwing a perfectly-tailored life vest down to keep me afloat through the stormy waters that started churning. I was in for any program that offered more of this mystical elixir.

Sign me up!

I continued in the writing process while managing all other aspects of my busy life—career, home, parenting, birthdays, holidays, births, and farewells. Knowing another retreat was on the horizon kept me focused in the "real world." We had placed retreat dates on the calendar but those fell through for one reason or another, and a second set of dates were selected. Beating a calendar into submission is one of my superpowers, so I arranged, rearranged, elicited help from others, and moved appointments around to make it work.

Then the bottom dropped out. In a casual conversation with Amanda and other messengers on our group call, she said we were not going on a fall retreat—that it was not the right timing and wasn't going to work out and that she would refund the hard costs of the lodging and food.

Excuse me, what?!?

I just sat there with my jaw dropped open, quiet, because the words brewing in my mouth were not fit for public. Over the course of my career, I'd learned it was sometimes best to just bite your tongue and, in this case, with enough force that I tasted blood.

Christ! How is this even possible? This is why I was willing to pay Amanda the big bucks. And she did not even check in with me—she just cancelled it!

I'd heard her say something about having an in-town retreat at a coffeehouse instead, which was WAY different for me than traveling to the mountain—not even close to packing up and leaving my usually overwhelming life behind. In-town meant I had to juggle all my usual responsibilities and try to make progress on the book. No way was I going to get much writing done that way.

Fuck! I knew this had been too good to be true.

In the coming days, I stewed, and ruminated, and got angry, but quashed that unwelcome emotion as soon as it surfaced. I was a pro at quashing anger—it was all around me—and mine did not feel safe to unearth. It seemed like Amanda was stealing money from my piggy bank and, more importantly, challenging the trust I had extended to her and the sisterhood of other messengers—the only people other than my therapist and my sister with whom I had ever shared my secret. Trust was not easy for me. I had long ago learned that trusting others was dangerous. The emotional roller coaster building inside of me had a familiar feeling—betrayal.

I knew it was too good to be true!

Despite our marital problems, I always confided in my husband—a reliable confidant and lifelong best friend who usually balanced me out. One afternoon, I told him about my upset feelings and disappointment with Amanda. He was quick to jump on the "breach of trust" bandwagon and quick to point out that, in my own naivete, this was a frequent theme I encountered in close relationships, suggesting something might be wrong with my judgment. It seemed he thought it best to cut ties with Amanda and find another way to finish the book.

That's weird. My knight in shining armor's words don't seem so shiny today.

The usual comfort my husband's words provided were not satisfying and instead settled on me like a wet blanket—a stinky, scratchy, wet blanket. Typically, in this situation, I would have made up a lame excuse why I was no longer going to write the book and would have ditched Amanda and her tribe of messengers and gone back to the safety of isolation. But that wet, scratchy, stinky blanket was bothering me something fierce, and I needed it off. So I wrote an email to Amanda, confessing what I would usually do in this situation (bail), and what I'd hoped to accomplish in our communication (repair).

God, I hope she does not tell me off, or that I'm too sensitive and crazy.

Amanda responded to my outreach nearly-immediately with assurance and a commitment to work this out and to repair the breach, which is exactly what we did and what two mature people do inside of a trusting relationship. We spoke our truths and listened, discovered common ground, and found a compromise that provided us a win-win.

Maybe there is something to this authentic-self BS and genuine value inside trusting relationships, where two people feel safe enough to show vulnerability and work through imperfection.

We continued on, stronger than before, having successfully navigated what could have ended our collaboration. Amanda and I got to it and pushed through the fall and into the holidays.

The first draft was fully written on New Year's eve of 2019—one year after I had started—and I was feeling really good about it, even after the tough feedback from one of Amanda's readers.

Apparently, I had created a real douche-bag of a male character who was aptly named Kenny. This first reader said it bordered on "male-bashing."

What? Really? Is this what Amanda was trying to say when she suggested removing some of these details? I was confused, horrified, and also grateful to have gotten that feedback before releasing my book into the world. I decided to rewrite Kenny's part during that coffeehouse retreat because I just couldn't wrap my head around this feedback alone. I was really going to have to focus.

Fortunately, as I sat in the coffeehouse, waiting for inspiration to strike, Mr. Hottie Pants walked into the cafe and sat down beside Amanda and me. We stifled a giggle when, over text, I pointed him out and told her that he was going to be my inspiration for rewriting Kenny and that he looked a lot more like a Luke. Right there and then, one of my main characters was redesigned.

I began writing the husband character in my book with this fella in mind rather than channeling the suppressed feelings about my own. Having made this conscientious shift, though not even close to making the real-life connections yet, I thought I'd slayed it.

Not quite...

The first group of readers included people who know me really well.

My sister's comments caught me off-guard: "Wow, there's a lot of your family in this story. Everyone okay over there?"

Uh, yeah, just fine, thanks. Geez, I only threw in a couple of my own stories where they seemed appropriate. What is she even talking about?

My husband's feedback was helpful in understanding the way men hear and perceive things—certain words or phrases that could be interpreted as sexual when not intended to be so.

Strike one.

My mother-in-law loved it. She thought it was terrific—male-bashing and all.

Strike two.

My friends scanned through it and those who are also high-achieving perfectionists (we run in packs) returned grammatical corrections and "Great job!" pats on the back. Others decided they just didn't have the time to read through it after all. "Sorry!"

Strike three.

My office manager and dear friend, a surrogate mom of sorts, delivered the truth in the way only someone who really loves you can. This thing needed more work, including the title. No way was that going to fly. *Crush Your Ex* was far too dramatic and just plain uncouth.

You're out!

I was the one left feeling crushed, defeated, a little bit ashamed of myself, and realizing I needed help—more help to work this thing through and deliver the message that I was intending for parents and families who really need it.

Back to the drawing board we went.

After taking time to consider and incorporate changes based on round one feedback, test readers in group two returned consistent constructive criticism. Apparently, they thought this sucker was *way* too long. This girl likes to talk, remember? Still unbeknownst to me, even in that moment, I was working through some deeply buried stuff—years and years and years of repressed sludge. Luckily, "slice and dice" is Amanda's specialty. "Cutting the fat," she called it. It's nerve-racking to trust someone else to cut your content—painful even. Thank God for Amanda and her patience and grace as I begged that she leave certain elements in my story.

Test readers in group three included a few members of the legal community in which I worked—attorneys and judges. Same deal. More work was needed but, thankfully, they all agreed that I had nailed the wise and poignant judge's voice. I laughed out loud. That was *my* wisdom shining through, not an actual judge's words, and my struggling ego insisted that I receive the credit.

Why can't I just be good enough for once!

Frustrated to be making more edits and just wanting to be done, the spring of 2020 provided yet another obstacle to completing my book—a global pandemic that ended life as we knew it.

The book stalled because my private practice with children and families exploded. What do you expect when everyone is locked up at home together? Conflict and mental health problems were front and center for all of us! Everyone and everything seemed to be falling apart. I was too busy to look at any of those things I had started to notice about my unhappy home; all those lessons learned in the writing process and therapy were sent to the back burner while I tried to keep myself and everyone else calm and moving forward. By fall of 2020, I told Therapist of The Year I didn't have time for therapy and needed a break. Of course, he reminded me ever so gently that therapy was a time of healing and value, crafted special for me, not something that should be looked at as an obligation on my calendar.

Whatever, Traitor! I thought you understood how busy my life is! Besides, you asked about a topic I'm not ready to discuss. You're always digging around in my brain, finding stuff before I'm ready to say it out loud.

By summer, the housing market had exploded, and we decided to sell our stunning "wow factor" home for a hefty profit—a home my husband had remodeled from the ground up, and the only home our children had known. We loved our home. Even in the chaos, those walls felt safe to the four of us. It represented everything good about the life we had built together. We moved during raging northwest historic wildfires and had a fire in our own backyard forest on the day of our closing. My world was literally set on fire but, even then, the flashing neon sign did not register.

After we moved, there were boxes everywhere for weeks and I was completely displaced—my perfect world upside-down at every turn. I needed to get my home office set up, as COVID was still in full swing and working remotely was a must. While unpacking, I came across a letter from my mother—something she had sent me fifteen years earlier. She never writes me letters, not before or since. This letter was a response to the Christmas Wish I had offered to her the year my son was born—a note wishing her "happiness and joy," accompanied by a ring that held both of our birthstones. The letter she wrote in return explained why she believed her happiness and joy had been depleted. Over five handwritten pages, she had shared her pain and her doubt in herself, her value, and her own worth.

Bigtime triggered, I crumpled up that note and threw it into the trash—the outdoor trash can. The big gross smelly one. For the rest of the day, garbage piled on top of it. Promptly at 3:00 a.m., I awoke (the sit-straight-up-in-horror kind) and, like a desperately hungry racoon in the darkness of night, I stuck my head into that can and dug it back out.

My God, I realized, re-reading my mom's letter under the moon and stars, tears streaming down my face. *She is me and I am her.* I needed to do something. I needed to figure this out. *My children deserve better—a gold star mother would make sure of it!* I deserved happiness and joy, too, and could feel that mine had also been depleted over all these years.

While breathing in the night air, words I'd recently heard popped into my head: "You can't wait until life isn't hard anymore, before you decide to be happy" (Jane Marczewski). It was in this moment that I realized happiness and joy were the lifelines that I needed—ones that I could choose—to pull me from the rubble of everything else that I could feel collapsing around me.

I was exhausted when Amanda announced a new program—Write to Right the World. It was launching in two weeks. I did not have time for it, but The Wind kept whispering, "Sign up!" If we brought a friend to the program, there was a discount. So, I phoned a friend, hoping she would say *no*. But she was in. *Damn it! One more thing to manage on my calendar!* We signed up together, and I was promptly asked to post a photo. There was one handy on my desktop that I had recently displayed on social media to commemorate my anniversary—a black and white photo of my husband and me, twenty years earlier, in love and smiling on our wedding day. I posted it as the framework for my thread of daily writing prompts and the self-growth work I would accomplish over the next ninety days. More messenger sisters had gathered and the next portal opened. (Amanda, have you thought about calling your programs Portals?)

Of all the aha's and affirmations and magical moments that had shown themselves since I had said YES to my message/story/book, the one that the universe was preparing me for—the biggest aha of my life—was pulling into the station and about to irreparably "right my world."

The universe knew the book was not ready because *I* was not ready and had not yet fully understood or finished writing my story—for "me" and the "us," not just for "them." The connections were not yet complete. The great co-author insisted that I dig deeper and embrace this next-level opportunity for healing that was only available in the rawness of truth.

About a month into our ninety days, the friend who said yes as my discount partner had picked up on something or some thing(s) I had posted and told me, "We need to talk." This was not only a friend but a colleague—a psychologist with specialized training. During our conversation and, with just a few questions, she told me in no uncertain words, "You have to look."

That word again: Look. The simple word with so much meaning that I had spoken out loud to my husband more than a decade earlier when I had told him that our marriage would be over if I ever had the slightest intuitive impulse to look for evidence that he was not actually going to change. Unknowingly, with that strong declaration, meant to protect my own heart and our family's stability, I had positioned myself, nose first, staring into a corner that it would take more than a decade to emerge from.

"Look" became one of those four letter words associated with pain and sorrow and grief. So, I didn't. In my perfectionistic way, I took this to a high-level task and I didn't look. Not for twelve years, until my friend who I'd invited to join the Write to Right the World group told me that I needed to, that I must, that I had to. And so I did, although not until after a panic attack like none before. A few days after she told me I had to look, and during an argument with my husband, the air was literally sucked from my lungs, I could not breathe, not even one breath. Nothing in, and nothing out. I thought I was going to die. This was absolute confirmation— an alarming medical event that ripped me from the corner where I had been paralyzed. The universe decided to shake me awake with a multisensory experience laced with terror. Finally, the universe had my full attention!

Looking, and finally seeing, was the beginning of a great awakening. A delayed process of deep sorrow, grief, anger, and rage began to ascend from every cell in my body. It was excruciating, though with absolute grit, lots and lots of support, and the formal disclosure of truth, this was the start of a healing journey for my entire family. Perfectionism, overachieving, overworking, overeating, hypervigilance, disassociation, compartmentalization, dysthymia, anxiety, and panic had all risen to the surface where these self-defeating coping strategies could now be seen. These had become the soul-depleting compensations I had relied on to survive my pain which, until that moment, I had refused to consciously acknowledge. It was from here forward that I became a witness to my story, rather than an actor in it. (Thank you, Ram Dass) I could now finally see rather than react and deflect and stifle and just barely survive. I could finally breathe.

The writing group had become another lifeline—a sisterhood who literally saved me from imploding while unraveling the illusion of my perfect life. They held steadfast as I leaned into a safe place to process and grow and center—to breathe. The same day that I looked (for evidence my husband had not actually changed), I had also sent an SOS to Therapist of The Year. Again, he was gracious and made time for me in short order. I could literally see and feel more of the army assembling around me, offering the safety net, the scaffolding of protection necessary for that first [intimidating] step on my journey of a thousand miles. I was finally ready, and beyond grateful for the community of noble allies who stood loyally at my side—each of them delivered with divine intention. Life, happening *for* me and *through* me, not *to* me. Amen.

Finishing up this chapter, I can see the closing of my story and the intricate weaving that pushed my message forward— my own experiences that might now serve as someone else's survival guide. The magical affirmations continue to show themselves now that I am fully and intentionally looking around, and open to seeing—no longer facing that dark and empty, lonely, and isolated corner.

It is three years since I said yes to the workshop facilitated by Amanda, who now sits among my most cherished and trusted inner circle. Every day, I am starting to feel more restored to factory settings. You really cannot make this shit up, although if I heard someone tell my own story, I may not even believe her. Alas, it is the truth—every last word shared in this chapter.

Here, right now, in this moment, at another retreat, staring towards the same majestic mountain on which I shared my secret for the first time, I am breathing freely, surrounded and supported by other soul-nourishing messengers whose collective energy fills up those places in me that laid barren for so long. I am free and I am at peace. My authentic self acquired what she needed to let loose of the shackles and walk into the light. And, my whole family is on the mend—saturated in truth and kindness, understanding, and grace. It is obvious to me, with the knowledge I have been gifted, that we really are all just walking each other home. (You slayed that one, Ram Dass.)

On this rollercoaster I managed to write a kickass book that exceeded my wildest expectations and accomplished exactly what I set out to create as a resource for children and families who are stuck in high-conflict domestic relations litigation. My legacy shall indeed sit dusty on bookstore shelves. Without any marketing at all, through the writing of my story, nearly fifty consultation and coaching clients just showed up—like magic! The associate who I envisioned hiring and training and leaving in my place, but never had the energy to look for, quite literally found me. A colleague offered up professional filming equipment which meant I could now produce the online curriculum that had been brewing in my mind—but was stalled because that kind of project seemed like too much to figure out. And then a dear friend, a professor and director of family studies at my alma mater, asked if I would like to create and teach a course at the University about families in change, effective models of co-parenting, and successful family blending post-divorce. Yes, please!

With the words of my story now on the page, more connected relationships have emerged with my clients and colleagues, children, family members, and friends— especially those people who have earned my trust and with whom I can mutually share and create spaces of safety and wellness. Whether or not my husband and I will build a new marriage, or create a different kind of relationship outside of one remains unclear; but he will always be the most consequential person in my life. I am steeped in gratitude for the poignant lessons that can only be learned inside a partnership like the one he and I have shared journeying to the greatest peaks and the deepest valleys. I discovered, while navigating through those journeys, that it is in the blinding valleys of darkness in which all things of power and majesty are born. In this divine birth (alarming, seductive, and painful birth), my soul was welcomed to thrive because regardless of my husband's choices, I had harnessed absolute confidence and conviction in my own.

The symbol you have seen throughout this chapter is a triskelion. It is a sacred symbol that represents journey and the change of life as it unfolds. It represents the tale of forward motion—circular and interconnected experiences that lead to understanding, advancement, wisdom, and choice. It showed itself to me at the start of the writing process, and serves as a grounding element of my book. The day after the book releases, it will be tattooed on my body—a permanent reminder that all we get are time and choices, and that we must be wise with both.

Would it surprise you if I told you that my attendance at the retreat where I am sitting now was nearly hijacked, same as my initial introduction to Amanda at the pie shoppe, and for the same exact reason? My daughter needed care over the weekend. "No worries. Bring her along," was the solution Amanda offered, same as three years before. And I was a day late to this retreat, too, although I saw it coming this time and remained calm, breathing steadily on my new foundation.

Oh, and you won't believe it. Or maybe you will by now. Remember that terrifying toll bridge I was forced to drive over? Getting to retreat number three required that I drive over that baby again—the only route to the Airbnb Amanda chose "accidentally." I was not nearly so scared this trip over because I had two sisters in the car with me. I had the gifts of love and joy and laughter to get me across. After a couple of days at the retreat, the weekend arrived and I needed to leave the Airbnb to pick up my little sweetpea. Another trip over that damn bridge. "Lean in. I've got you," The Wind whispered (the voice in my mind suspiciously similar to Amanda's). And I was instantly offered that same release of serenity that washed over me the very first time I had taken a "wrong turn."

There are no wrong turns. Just our unique paths, which lead exactly where the universe intends for each of us to be. The breadcrumb trail that leads all of us home. In the cracking open of these meaningful experiences—the ones that honor and anchor our authentic selves, not the illusive ones clothed in perfectionism—we are offered clues, affirmations, magical moments, and sometimes those huge blinking neon signs. Each of them is laid out for us, in plain sight, once we are brave enough, supported enough, and once we allow ourselves to become vulnerable enough that our divine souls have the courage to look, so that we can see the truth of what we already know.

Thank God that I asked out loud for clarity in 2018, that I opened the pie shoppe email, that my daughter made sure we got to the workshop, and that I said y-e-s to my childhood dream of writing a book. Thank GOD it was Amanda at the pie shoppe who brought the sisterhood of support without whom these words would not be on the pages you're reading. Thank GOD I learned how to breathe with my conscious mind, put my needs first in the least selfish way, and re-learned how to see and feel and connect, to release control and perfectionism, and to let others witness and know the messy, undone, anything-but-perfect and vulnerable me. Thank GOD I learned that courage is a choice and kept making them, no matter how terrified I was to see or make a mistake. Turns out that I do not have to be the fucking universe after all. The Universe—our great Co-Author—has proven to be steadfast and trustworthy, infinitely capable, and more than strong enough to carry the entirety of these burdens without any help from me.

Amanda's Side of the Story

"Amanda, you won't believe…" she started.

I listened as she shared the series of recent events that had led to a bittersweet breakthrough.

"I've been writing my *own* story and I didn't even know it!" she finished. Observing my face like the badass intuitive helping professional that she is, she gasped. "Did you know?!?!?!?!" Her eyes were tired from the tears but wide with wonder.

I nodded, remembering that first moment when I'd realized it, almost two years earlier.

"Why didn't you tell me?" Her eyebrows scrunched with confusion.

"Well… I did, actually…" I paused. "You just weren't ready to see it." She tilted her head and waited for me to proceed. "Remember that first retreat, when you shared your big secret?"

"Yes."

"I knew the minute you shared it that there was no coincidence that you were writing a story about helping children through high-conflict divorce and sitting on that secret for so long. Of course, I didn't know if it was a family of origin story, or if there was something you couldn't see in your marriage. Either way, I knew that you were writing this book for *you* first."

"Wow. From the beginning? Geez. How did you try to tell me?" she probed, searching her memory for a moment.

"Remember the second retreat you attended?" She nodded. "Well, there were two. The first was the invitation to use your stand-up chops to impersonate your mother. I'd heard you talk about your parent's relationship and wondered if that would help to break some awareness loose for you. When I tried to make the connection between their relationship and yours, you glazed over..."

"Oh... yeah... I do remember that..."

"Yeah, and then I was a little more direct when Kathy began coaching you around the voice and explaining how the way you were writing it wasn't going to work. Remember I told you that I wanted you to write it raw, without thinking about any of that style stuff, because I knew there was a therapeutic component to this?" Lori stared at me blankly. "Right, that's the look you gave me then and said, 'Amanda, I'm writing a choose-your-own-outcome book about two people who are going through a divorce.'"

"Wow. That's crazy."

"Yeah, and then when I read the first piece you wrote for Kenny and we got the feedback that confirmed it was a little too harsh, I knew it was about you and your hubby. And some of those details you put in that first draft gave me some indication about the details of your own story." I reciprocated her sheepish grin about Kenny and continued, "Lori, I was blind to the reality of abuse in my family for thirty-five years, and seven of those were spent in deep introspection, therapy, and healing spaces. My initial response to this awareness was shock and self-deprecation. How could I have been helping people escape similar situations and rewrite their stories for years, and not see this happening in my own life? But, after time, I realized that my awareness happened at the perfect moment—after I had witnessed the grace in my story, gathered tools and skills to navigate the rupture in a healthier manner, and been surrounded by allies who would hold and love and support me through that excruciating work." I paused. "I saw the same thing happening in your world. The incredible amounts of magic that happened with Hood River Aaron, the magazine affirmation, the emails that showed up in your inbox while we were talking about people. Then there were the inciting moments with the attorney, and then you found therapist of the year and shared that he was asking some of the same questions I was. When we had that huge miscommunication about the retreat and worked through it, I knew there was a reason I had failed to clarify details when I saw how deeply it rocked you. I hated that my miscommunication had triggered such deep pain and intense feelings, and I wondered if it was an opportunity for you to experience repair with someone you'd really let in. I just knew that your Co-author was preparing your heart and psyche for what was coming, and I didn't want to push the awareness on you before you were ready. Our psyches hide this shit from us for good reasons, and I believe it's better to wait until a person is truly ready to see than to force an awareness."

"I can definitely see that. Even the way the whispers came about Write to Right the World and the impulse to invite my colleague, and the way she saw and reflected what she did at the exact moment I was ready to see it... You really can't make this shit up."

I smiled and let the awe hang between us for a few moments before we finished our chat and said goodbye.

Lori, and all of the messengers who started their projects alongside her, entered my life at the perfect time. I'd just released my second book, *Upside-Down Messenger,* in which I'd tackled the topic of The Messenger Matrix and sought to inspire my readers to question their assumptions about success and its methods and requirements and tune into their own Sacred Code for *their unique approach* to living and sharing their message. Almost as soon as I'd finished that conclusion, my Co-author had decided it was time for me to surrender more of the belief systems and structures that I'd been leaning on for too long.

By the time her group started, I was challenging assumptions and old st*ries in my marriage (That's right—I am always asked to do the work before I facilitate it for others!) and finding myself in new territory in my business. I felt utterly unprepared for the first retreat she attended. Reviewing my old agendas, I somehow knew they would not suffice; and despite my best efforts, I had been unable to develop a solid agenda for the experience. In fact, my Co-author had only given me the first exercise for the first day, and then only gave me the first exercise of every day for the next six days. This was a huge departure from my modus operandi of hyper-organization and—preparedness, complete with beautiful PowerPoint presentations to guide the carefully-crafted experience. (Yes, Lori and I share the love of post-it notes and ducks in rows.) And, I believe that is one of the reasons that those two retreats were the most powerful retreats I'd ever facilitated. After ten years of this work, I'd finally digested my own message and was able to just *be* in and with the experience and witness it, rather than get ahead of it, drive it, and push it the way I thought it should be pushed.

When Lori responded to her husband's glib text "See, the universe always works this out!" with "I am the fucking universe!", it was the opportunity for my Co-author to drive the point home: *"Amanda, you don't have to figure it all out, hold it all together, and make it all happen. I'm going to keep giving you the next right step, and all you have to do is be true to yourself while taking it."*

Witnessing the incredible amounts of magical affirmations and divine interventions happening for Lori reminded me of my own perfectly-orchestrated journey and helped me to relax more deeply into another level of presence and trust in my personal and professional life despite the absolute chaos that ensued.

I mean, when I realized that I had booked a cabin with a view of Mt. Hood instead of booking it on the mountain itself for our most recent retreat to write these chapters, my immediate reaction was, "What the hell is wrong with me? Am I totally losing it?" And yet, I knew there had to be a reason. When Lori told me about her experience of picking up her daughter and realizing that was the same bridge she'd crossed the day of her biggest act of trust with me and our small community, I just knew that was the reason I'd booked it. It was the perfect story loop conclusion to our journey of ever-deepening trust that it's all happening *for* us and *through* us, not *to* us.

And yet, it wasn't the end.

As you'll see in the conclusion, our journey of healing our trust issues has not only continued, but pushed us both further than we ever imagined going.

Dawn Bennett, Founder of Touch Remedies, loves empowering individuals from all over the world to embrace powerful new ways to transform themselves and connect more deeply with themselves, others, and their communities through her Relationship & Intimacy Coaching. Her background as a Massage and CranioSacral Therapist, homeopath, Emotional Freedom Techniques Practitioner, and student of all modalities that help individuals and communities heal, combined with her experience of speaking, teaching college-level massage, building an award-winning massage business from scratch, and traveling across the world, has equipped her to help people move through challenges such as loneliness, disconnection from others, and anxiety or sadness.

Tapping Through My Story

Dawn Bennett

Y ou better have that book done before I come over
to Sweden!"

The text containing my mom's playful words made me
unreasonably, deeply angry in my core.

*She has no freaking idea, does she? She doesn't realize the
amount of work that has gone into this book already. She has
no idea what I've gone through, opening myself up enough
to tell these stories. Hell. She doesn't even know half of this
stuff happened to me. No one does.* I got up from the table in
the open, bright kitchen where I was cat-sitting and looked
out upon the Norwegian landscape. I could feel the roiling
depth of self-judgment coming forward. *I would love to finish
chapter five. All the other stories came out easily. Well, maybe
not so easy. But at least they came. I had no idea the amount
of work I'd have to do on myself to allow them to be exposed
on the page.* I strode into the mud room, put on my shoes,
grabbed the house keys, and escaped into the solitude of the
mountains, thinking about where this whole journey had
started three years earlier.

Touch Remedies

"You should write a book on touch!" The enthusiastic young
dark-haired Californian told me after my brief experiential
presentation. "I'm going to ask the people I see when I

do Meals On Wheels if they want a hug before I go!" The excitement shone in her eyes as she shared about all the ways she could increase touch in a positive way within her communities.

My heart warmed and I smiled at her while thinking, *Seriously? That's the third time I've heard that I should write a book in the last month. But what would I write about? I don't have enough content, experience, or knowledge to write a book on anything. What on earth would I say? Lots of people have shared their stories and experiences with me, but when it comes to touch—I am only a massage therapist. Sure, I help people heal their emotions and touch challenges on a one-to-one basis, but that's not book material. I'm not a touch specialist or anything.*

I touched her shoulder and said, "Glad you enjoyed it and can apply it to your life so quickly." I talked to a few other newly-inspired touch enthusiasts before heading out of the conference room.

I can't wait to go hiking. I love speaking, but it's time to immerse myself in the woods for a bit... and hide. A book! Why on earth do people keep saying that?

Ugh. Who knew that two months after starting, I'd be 80% done with my book and super stuck on the last 20%? I thought as I trudged up the mountain, remembering all of the other apparent confirmations that this was the right path. *First, my client brought me the New York Times article that got me speaking about touch. Then the women who insisted I should*

write a book after my speaking engagements. The final straw was getting denied the work permit.

I thought back to the conversation with Stefan, the head manager of my new job in Sweden, telling me the government wouldn't approve my work permit because they thought there were too many massage therapists already. He had relayed the information with frustration and anger in his voice, knowing that my skills far surpassed massage.

Suddenly, an unbidden thought came into my head, as if it were my own brilliant idea. *I should write a book! I already have the tickets back to Sweden to start the job, so maybe this is perfect timing.* As quickly and powerfully as the idea came in, I pushed it out. I didn't want to write a book and be vulnerable to criticism, judgment, and forcefully stated opinions. I didn't need that energy in my life.

But then there was Ursula's urgent response to my idea. "You NEED to talk to Amanda. She's AMAZING." As my former business coach and a best-selling author herself, I trusted her judgment and found myself looking at Amanda's website.

The program is probably too much—probably too expensive, probably too everything. But I wasn't about to waste my life trying to write a book and then have to edit it over and over. God knows I hate doing things more than once or twice. *Such a waste of time.* Six days later, I found myself talking to her, sharing my ideas, and listening to her validate the idea to write.

"Your personal stories will add to the research and make it something new—something that resonates with your audience's experience around touch," Amanda said simply, allaying my fears. "Plus, that's where your credibility around touch resides. The only thing to consider is that it might bring up some old stories that still have some pain in them."

She didn't even sell me on it. It was just what I needed
to do. What I was called to do. And suddenly, with the work
permit fiasco, I had the time, space, and freedom to do it. I
reasoned that I should be able to write a book in a month. I
was in tune with myself and my life. I did my healing work on
a regular basis and had for twenty years. *What would a book
change and bring forward that I haven't already explored? It
should be simple.*

Touch Remedies

By all accounts, it wasn't horrible until chapter five. I had
moments in which writing the story brought up nostalgia for
relationships and times long past, fear of what my life would
look like once I returned to the United States, and longing
for someone to understand me in a deeper way. Moments
in which I desperately missed touch and companionship,
even as I cherished the time with myself. I used Emotional
Freedom Techniques (also known as EFT or tapping) when
I ran into big emotions, so even though there were moments
of tears and tantrums, the words flowed out with a certain
amount of clarity and ease that felt impossible for the
last chapter.

But it's okay. I can still get this done, I assured myself as I
took my boots off and hurried to my computer for the group
co-writing session online. As soon as we'd debriefed as a
group, I asked Amanda if we could go into a breakout room to
discuss my stuckness.

"Maybe chapter five isn't coming because you have caught
up to your storyline and you have something more to learn
before you can write it." Amanda's words rolled simply

and easily out of her mouth and straight to my gut, which retaliated like a momma bear whose cubs were threatened, rising full height from the back legs and letting out a giant roar.

Are you kidding me? We already planned this book and not only has she cut a bunch of it out, but I have spent hours editing over and over and she's basically saying I can't finish it now. She's not listening to me at all. Here I am, paying her a shit-ton of money to help me get this done, and she's sitting there all calm and cocky, as if she knows better. As if all my goals don't matter and I should just happily comply.

I suppressed my temper and looked at her in what I hoped was a calm manner, pausing before I replied in the most even-keeled voice I could manage. "Well, I really need to get this done before I leave Norway. I cannot write while I'm with my mom, and then I will be on the move and taking classes; and I don't know when I will be able to work on it again."

Not to mention I want this book done before I return home in four months. There is no way I would be able to manage marketing and writing and rebuilding my practice all at the same time.

"Just trust. You've actually written this really fast. Pay attention to every interaction and see if there is something that you witness that will unlock this chapter." Amanda's calm voice did nothing to ease my internal deadlines or silence the internal critic telling me to just get it done.

What does she know? I shut my laptop to the group zoom meeting, stood up, and hustled out the front door again. *Thank goodness for midnight sun.* It was just past eleven p.m., and the landscape was perfectly lit as though it were a couple of hours before sunset. As I stomped up the road to

my favorite mountain path, I reconsidered everything I had
written thus far.

*Maybe this is just all a terrible idea. What is everyone going
to think of me? I've talked about my parents and my family.
What will happen with my business? How will people receive
this book? Even though I've combined stories of clients and
friends to get the point across while preserving confidentiality,
will people think I'm talking about them? Will they feel judged?
Will they judge me? Will I lose everyone's trust? Amanda has
no idea what is at stake here. Maybe I should just let this whole
silly thing go. Who cares anyway?!* My mind focused intently
on the steep, rocky path in front of me as I pouted like a five-
year-old child.

*Yeah, and what's everyone going to think of you when you
give up?* The other side of my self-critical brain jumped in.
*You told people you were going to write a book on touch. You
have posted on Facebook about it. People know. You can't back
out now. Your word is on the line. And what about all those
people you encourage to do their own healing work? To break
through their own shit? To give themselves grace and time and
patience? Why won't you do that for yourself?* The emotional
and logical sides of my brain kept battling as I stubbornly
puffed my way up the 1800-foot elevation and began to use
my tapping skills to address the voices that had been instilled
by societal expectations and pressures.

On the way down, I found some grace and some peace,
and had started considering ideas for a second book. *I am
seriously crazy. I should just go home and go to bed.*

Yet coming in the front door just after 1:00 a.m., I found
myself on zoom again with the writing group, furiously
typing notes and outlines for the ideas for yet another book.
Things that felt important to share but did not fit in this first

book. *How much more healing and upheaval do I have to go through before this is all done?* I rolled my eyes at myself while also excited about the possibility of helping people connect more deeply to themselves, their relationships, and their own community. Finally exhausted, I shut my laptop and headed upstairs to sleep for a few hours. And then, like it does so often, the universe reminded me why I said yes to all of this madness with a dream.

In the dream, my sister, Cathi, had jumped into the lake from the dock, grabbed a young girl who was struggling to resurface after a long period underwater, and started swimming her towards shore. Watching from ashore, I was horrified. Cathi hadn't asked for permission to touch the girl! What would the mom do? What kind of trouble would my sister get into? I looked over towards the mom to see if she had noticed. She just stood there watching, seemingly unconcerned that her daughter had almost drowned and was being embraced by a complete stranger in the deep cold water.

I woke with a start. *That was odd. Why would my sister get in trouble for helping? But it also felt like the mom would be angry at me as well. What is my subconscious trying to tell me?* I lay there pondering my societal training against cultural anomalies that had been exposed during my interviews with others.

Suddenly, it made sense. *Oh yeah. My dad told me about the woman who said she wouldn't touch someone else's kid, even as the kid was lying there hurt on the playground. My dad didn't want to help the poor girl either for the same reasons. What has happened to us? When I was young, adults hugged me back if I hugged them. If I got hurt, the nearest adult would rush to assist. If I was separated from my parents in a store, someone would hold my hand while we searched for them.*

I got up, a bit shaken, and headed downstairs to do yoga and eat before diving back into another round of edits on chapter two, which was all about intention and safety around touch. It's true. You can't make it up.

Rolling out the mat and dropping into child's pose, I wondered, *How many stories do I have to hear about people not being able to reach out in the most basic and human-like ways to connect and keep each other safe? Why can't teachers hug their students back? Why can't we help each other in times of need? Why can't we hug our friends without fearing someone will judge it as sexual? How did our first form of communication and deep biological need become such a source of shame in our society?*

After yoga I made coffee and considered, not for the first time, all the deep healing work I had to do around all the messages I'd learned through parental lecture, societal observation, social training, and personal experience. "Family members get to hug you whenever they want. It's not nice to say NO unless people are doing something really wrong. Cross-gender touch is only about sex. In fact, I am valuable only for sex. I don't get to ask for the type of touch I want or need. Women only touch other women if they are being fake. Touch is only okay when I'm being a professional."

It just goes to show how sexually-charged and woman-shame-focused the American culture is, that a book about non-sexual touch brought up all the unhealed crap around my role in both professional and intimate relationships as well as the mistakes and trauma I've experienced along the way.

I shook my head and refocused myself on what I needed to do for the day in order to be ready for my mom to show up in less than two weeks.

Touch Remedies

"I'm headed to bed, Dear." My mom gave me a quick hug and kiss as I sat staring at my computer before she ducked into the bedroom in the Swedish Airbnb.

Okay. I HAVE to get more written on this dang chapter. I just cannot relax, and it's throwing off this whole time with my mom.

I willed myself to come up with content, pissed off and restless and blaming the book for every miscommunication, every distraction, and every moment I couldn't be present with my mother. The book project was hanging over my head like a self-imposed guillotine. I glared at the screen, searching my brain for teaching moments around culture and community that would resonate with my story and inspire others. Nothing came. I stood up again and wandered to the bare fridge, searching for something to eat to distract me from the nagging emotions.

We've been together for almost a week now, and she's barely asked me anything about it. It's interesting to feel as if she's not trying to connect with me, when my energy is completely disconnected from her; all of my mental bandwidth is book-focused instead of connection-focused. She wants to have fun on vacation. I thought it would be playful and free like the last time we spent time together, yet I'm not taking the opportunity to practice my own teachings. I'm not asking for or getting the connection or the touch I need; I'm self-punishing because the book isn't complete. I'm letting my own mental timeline create a physical and emotional detachment.

I ate my apple and celery pensively and stared at my bare chapter, willing the content to write itself and put me out of my misery. I sighed forcefully and leaned back in the wooden chair, letting my mind drift until I relented and headed to bed.

I woke from another intense dream about communities and people being disconnected. Immediately, I realized my external feeling of disconnection was coming from deep within.

I was experiencing opposition in many areas of my internal life: the sudden desire for a partner on one side, while the other part of me relished and embraced being alone; the desire for touch and connection, even as I realized I was more touch-sensitive than I had ever been before; the desire to share experiences and be vulnerable so others can learn, while cringing as stories that no one knew came flooding out on paper; the frustration that there was no one, beyond my content coach, who understood or even bothered asking what I was stirring up during this writing process, even as I wanted to pretend I was strong and invincible.

I hadn't fully integrated two sides of me. The loving and open person who loves touch, loves community, and loves connection; and the one who is professional, put-together, detached, and has been shamed around touch in multiple arenas. Chapter five started structuring itself as I kept using my EFT tapping, reconciled my two sides, and chose to connect with my mother instead of pushing towards a fictitious deadline. I let go of fears that every story I had with a member of the opposite sex would create an assumption and judgment by the reader that these interactions were sexual in nature, or that people only connected with me because of my looks. That none of this connecting stuff was truly real.

I knew I needed to reconcile those parts of myself before others could heal from their own internal Touch Crisis. I refocused, let go of the book, and focused on the leftover time with my mom, trusting I'd get it done before returning to the U.S. in January, which had been my goal in the first place.

Touch Remedies

I met Armond at a cafe in the south of England shortly after my mom returned home. He was an elderly gentleman who seemed a bit lonely and wandered into the buffet-style café, curious and perhaps a bit confused. He chatted with women at their tables, engaged in conversation, and patted them on their shoulders as a goodbye. His intention was purely to get answers and connect; even ten years ago, no one would have thought anything of it. However, with the current anti-touch culture, no one wanted to give him the time of day—even though he was being completely respectful. I engaged with him enthusiastically, and after he decided to have lunch there, I swung by his table on the way out; and we had a lovely conversation about his wife. The culture around touch for his age group was completely different than my own, but he was doing the best he could. I wanted everyone who read my book to think about <u>that</u> when there were age, gender, socioeconomic, and/ or cultural differences involved. That reminder, on the heels of that experience with my mom, was just what I needed to quickly write chapter five!

Touch Remedies

"I haven't started yet," one of my test readers said, a few days after the deadline for feedback for the book so I could move on. *Seriously? Only two of the eleven people are done. I am never going to get this book out.* Three days of working on structuring signature speeches, workshops, and retreats for the future had me restless and unsure of myself again. So uncertain, in fact, that I was actually looking forward to doing final edits and sending the book on for endorsements and final pieces.

How frustrating! Now is the perfect *time to release the book. I originally wanted it released by January. Then I was saying April. It's almost May, and it will be a minimum of five more weeks after everyone finishes before this thing will be ready, according to Amanda. The people I'm interviewing are suffering either from a lack of touch or an inability to communicate their wants and needs around touch boundaries.* Frustrated and restless, I stared at my messages. *I only have two months left with my contract with her as well. If this damn thing isn't done by the time our contract is up, what am I going to do? I'm not paying more money to get this stupid thing completed. Plus, it's almost summer. Quarantine might be over soon. Everyone will get outside and play, and no one will want to buy this. Book sales are really high right now, and I've missed it. People are touch-starved and they have no resources. When we get back to "real" life, people are going to be scared and confused about how and when to touch because the virus is still running around. My book would have been perfect to be out now.*

August finally rolled around. "That's it." I looked at Amanda with determination. "I don't care anymore. I'm releasing it September 1st." By now, I had been speaking online about touch again, had done two full marketing rounds to get people excited about the book, and had yet to finally release it. "I didn't know we'd have to do so much editing for layout, and I am over the fact that people are going to judge me. Screw it all. I'm sick of it. If I'm going to create change, I also have to free up my energy around this book and move on. I'm tired of waiting."

And so it was. I started telling my networking groups, friends, and family of my intent to be a best-selling Amazon author. I uploaded the book, created an author page, and set the release date. I prepped and scheduled automated emails asking and reminding people to purchase September 1st. I got support from other best-selling authors. And I waited for this process to be over.

When the day finally rolled around, I was ready. About 8 a.m., I jumped online, coffee in hand, and started posting live videos, DMing friends, and stalking the Amazon charts and my Kindle Publishing rating. *How long should this take? A few hours? If everyone buys at once, I may hit bestseller quickly, so I can relax.* I was watching three categories: New Releases, Interpersonal Relations, and Communication and Social Skills. *It's not updating hourly! How frustrating. What a day for Amazon to be having problems!*

My mom called around 12:30 pm. "How's it going? Have you hit number one yet? I bought a bunch for friends and family. You'll have to come sign them all."

"I'm stuck at number four in New Releases: Communication and Social Skills behind some guy named Trey Gowdy who holds the first three places," I said, completely unaware yet that he was a New York Times Bestselling Author. "And number two in New Releases: Interpersonal Relations. Amazon isn't updating sales regularly." I knew this because I was also monitoring the number of books sold, and the number of people who told me they had made purchases far surpassed the number I was seeing on my screen. *I'm so nervous. What if I don't make it? Why does it matter to me so much that I do now? Is it because I was so cocky about it? Because I've worked so hard that I feel I need that level of outside validation? Or have I turned it into some sort of popularity contest in my head?*

Touch Remedies

Three o'clock. Still at number four and number two. *I'd just be done now if people weren't reaching out so fervently to support me.* I was getting tired of being on my computer. Tired of stalking Amazon. And honestly, almost sick of drinking coffee to keep myself engaged and energized.

"I'll set up a Facebook live with you." Travis Sims, the owner of Accelerated Global Connections and best-selling author, offered. "You can do this!"

"I just got off work and have been contacting all my family and friends to remind them," my friend Lisa texted. "You've got this! I love you!"

"I have been posting in all the groups I know," my friend and business coach Les exclaimed. "I bought 20 books myself. What else do you need from me? How can I support you?"

All this time, I thought people didn't really understand or care how big of a deal this book is for me. I marveled at my own blind spots. *It was my own ego in the way... again.* I was overwhelmed by the amount of energy and the time others were putting into helping me. *Okay. Here we go. I can give it one more push.*

Touch Remedies

Six-thirty. I have to be done. I have to just let it go and trust. I had processed my emotions, realized where my fears and ego had become too wrapped up, and took care of myself by doing some tapping, conceding to one last post, closing my computer, and taking a deep breath. *I've become so agitated, it almost feels it would be anticlimactic instead of exciting if I did hit number one. Time for a walk, another breath, and dinner with a friend.*

My belly full of steak and brain relaxed by great conversation under the balmy evening sky, I reflexively refreshed my Amazon page as my friend ducked inside for a moment. "AAGH!" I shrieked, stunned. "I hit number one." I took a quick screenshot, even as I realized that I wasn't attached anymore; although it was a fun achievement, it wasn't the original purpose.

I shared something amazing that will help hundreds of people. I wanted it to have the same impact as my speaking engagements—to help others feel inside themselves, learn to communicate, and create connection. The same way I felt connected today by the outpouring of support. Community. Isn't that the point? That we let go of our attachment to outcome and the rigid belief systems that subtly influence multiple areas of our lives? Our relationships? Content yet exhausted, I said goodbye to my friend and headed home, reveling in the peace of a project complete.

"I read your book and you are right about one thing. I had a lot of big feelings."

The extremely critical and nearly-cruel email was sent from my website contact page; her years of pain and suffering evident from the words, and projected directly at me.

Isn't it fascinating that this was my biggest fear—that someone would be triggered by the ideas, stories, and invitations in my book? I did everything I could to prevent it, yet here it is. No matter how trauma-informed I am, no matter how many licensed therapists and abused women have read the book and offered suggestions, there will still be individuals who experience pain via the words I write.

Taking a deep breath and tuning into her anguish, I wrote a gentle reply, acknowledging her words, knowing it had nothing to do with me. *It's not my job to tell her what I've been through, how she can heal from this, or that perhaps something bigger is giving her this nudge to resolve her abuse. Hopefully she finds that for herself.*

An engaging email from another person balanced out the energies. "One thing that strikes me, walking around local towns and cities. People seem more likely to touch (pet; stroke; handle gently) a dog than a human... Now, I'm ageing and starting to take life on a deeper level more seriously, but a society of humans not touching? Is that what we have become? I get the strong sense your book could be more important, if not urgent, than I first imagined."

This email asked me to think closely about my next book on relationships.

I was already in the process of recording ideas. People were sharing their relationship and touch challenges from Covid, and my subconscious was writing their answers as I slept. I'd wake one or two nights a week, frantically grabbing for my phone to voice memo the ideas and inspirations vividly presented in my dreams before they became lost.

Why do I want to be in this place again with Amanda? Because I know the message and the story is healing to the messenger and the receiver in ways I can never plan. I know that even though I became frustrated with the process and projected it onto Amanda, the support and guidance she provided allowed the content to flow onto the page in the most authentic and gentle way possible. She encouraged and allowed my own healing on the way, and that alone was invaluable. I believe my soul purpose is to connect people to each other and to love. I still screw up. I still struggle. For all of you reading these lines—releasing your message to a broader audience could be the most impactful decision you will make. Congratulations.

Touch Remedies

My next healing journey has started. I am working on my second book; this one an archetypal book about relationships, intimacy, and healing. Of course, this book started as I am finishing my relationship and intimacy coaching certification. Now, I am upside-down again, paused in my writing to create my new website, my expanded business, and my new living situation. I have come to the realization I really do want to find a soulmate—a partner with whom to share time, passion, and energy. I'm doing my healing work with myself and others, and noticing where I am stuck in my writing process.

I am confident it will all start moving again shortly. By the time this book is released, my practice will be in full swing, I will be working on the road as a digital nomad, and the next few books that are already in my heart and somewhere in my brain will come to fruition. Until then, I continue to navigate the tricky terrain of relationships, touch, and healing. I'll see you on the other side.

Amanda's Side of the Story

"Amanda, I'm really upset..." My heart jumped into my throat and my pulse raced as I read the text from my newest client. Her frustration oozed from every word, and I found myself caught between a creeping sensation of shame that I had failed her and my inner coach's growing awareness that her st*ry had been triggered for a reason. Dawn was upset because she had sent me multiple emails and requests, and I had not responded in my promised timely manner. Quickly, I reached for my laptop to figure out why this had happened. It didn't take me long to locate the problem: Every single one of Dawn's emails had bypassed my inbox and landed in my Trash folder.

That has never happened before, I thought as I picked up the phone to call her, explain what had happened, and help resolve the upset. Half-way through the conversation, she confirmed my suspicion, "I guess I've grown accustomed to your quick responses and this just triggered all of my 'feeling unheard' stuff. Thank you for calling to help me understand what happened."

Immediately, my mind flashed to the scene in her book that had tugged at my heart and made me giggle out loud. Grown-up Dawn gets caught up with some work and when she comes back to the living space to hug her parents goodnight, she finds they have gone to bed. Upset, she trudges to the kitchen... And I couldn't help but see the extra details of a childlike response: slumped shoulders, a pout, and a little kicking of ground.

I realized, of course, that I was projecting details from my personal life, but from the opposite direction.

Over the years, I've discovered that *most* of my clients and I share similar backgrounds and tendencies that tend to emerge from similar types of trauma and experiences. For example, lots of my clients grew up with narcissists and so we share the tendency toward codependent fixing and preventing. Many of them are also empathic and highly-intuitive, so we tend to overdo and burn out to help others. Those of us who share similar religious or marital backgrounds find lots of intersections of perspective, pain, and power. And every once in a while, my Co-Author finds it important to teach me something important through the eyes of someone who sees and experiences the world very differently.

Dawn is one of those clients. Her life experience couldn't be more different than mine, especially around her message. As you'll see reading her book, she is what she calls "high-touch," meaning that she craves and requires it more than someone like myself, who she would appropriately label "touch-averse." Because of my childhood, traumas, and probably my extreme empathy, I not only shy away from touch but it doesn't naturally occur to me that I fail to give healthy and appropriate amounts to the people in my life.

Fortunately for me, I got some education in physical and emotional needs at the university while training to become a teacher and knew enough to try to prevent some serious damage with my son when he was born. When he was teeny, I spent a lot of time snuggling him; but as he got older and started moving around, I realized that I wasn't snuggling him as much and needed to empower him to ask for the touch he needed: "When you want a hug or a back rub, please come ask Mommy for it."

Unfortunately, this messaging and empowerment didn't work as well as I'd hoped with my husband. (You can laugh.) When Dawn entered my world, I was right in the middle of recalibrating my relationship with my husband. Thanks to that cohort in which intimate relationships were the source of the st*ry that would hold everyone back, I too was neck-deep in the down-and-dirty work of trying to make my marriage healthy again. It sucked! And I do believe that Dawn's presence in my life—our at-least weekly interactions—were my Co-Author's clever way of keeping the importance of affection and intimacy at the center of my world.

It also helped me to understand myself and my needs and release a lot of the judgment around myself, as I'd felt "broken" for many years when it came to this topic. And, maybe more importantly, it helped me to release judgment of "high-touch" people who I had previously perceived to be too needy for most of my life. Geesh! Those conditioned ruts run deep.

Even though our backgrounds are different, Dawn and I do share the "Why isn't anyone listening to/hearing me?" st*ry and that was seriously up for me in so many of my relationships during the time she and I worked on that book. Family of origin. Husband and son. Clients. Coaches. Even my closest friends seemed to not hear me when I shared. Of course, our practical circumstances also set us up perfectly to push each other's buttons in all the right ways. She was in Europe and I was in Oregon, so the time zone difficulties were real. Plus, I was completely overwhelmed with several legal battles that were taking every second of extra time and way too many of my brain cells. And of course, I was working through the "consent and communication" chapters with her when my legal ally helped me realize that every area of my life could experience healing with the truth that "If you don't object, you consent." (YCMTSU!) With her emails going to my Trash folder, this was all quite the setup for regularly facing opportunities for frustration (or growth) for both of us.

Fortunately, we chose growth and were able to lean into it and even find our sense of humor about it. And, only after our commitment to getting this project right for readers, I'm certain that it was our love of all things salt and chocolate that kept us on track and connected through all of the dances we were invited to do.

The first dance was sorting out the balance of personal story and science. She'd been researching for years and was eager to get the important pieces into the book without positioning herself as a research expert, while I was certain that personal story was the way to connect with the reader before informing them. It took us a while, but I think we nailed that dance. Of course, there was the "you're not hearing me" dance, which we eventually sorted out; and then there was that final comma dance during the editing phase. Whew, that miscommunication added time and frustration for both of us.

The trickiest dance of all was the impatience dance. Many clients arrive imagining that they can write their book in a month or two, and some do, but most of them realize that six to nine months is more reasonable. Dawn wasn't having it. After flying through the first several chapters, she stalled on chapter five and didn't love my regular reminders that this often happens and usually means there's something else that needs to be seen or healed or included that just hasn't arrived yet. Unfortunately, she struggled the way most authors do through those times—getting way too hard on themselves. It was difficult for her to move through and difficult for me to watch because there was simply nothing I could do to propel her forward. (I knew better than to try to get in the middle of whatever her Co-Author was trying to help her see.) We celebrated hard when she "got it" and wrote chapter five in very little time; and we celebrated even harder when she launched her book and made it a bestseller (though I'm still confused that she tried to get through that day without a stash of chocolate and wine).

I'm excited about the second book we're working on because it's definitely the book I wish I had early in my marriage and I know it will help couples with this conversation. And that third book for parents... well, let's just say I am knowing that more parents will have the opportunity to experience what I did last year the week Dawn was launching her book...

My seventeen-year-old son had left the room and when he didn't come back for a long time, we assumed he'd fallen asleep; and so we went to our room, closed the door, and began to get ready for bed. When I heard the knock on the door, I opened to see a young man with a childlike expression on his face, "Mom, I'm here for my hugs." When he left, I looked at my husband and said, "Our seventeen-year-old son just insisted on a hug before bed. I think we're winning."

I truly believe that the touch crisis is one of the biggest crises we face on this planet. Truly, climate issues, political and social issues, and even economics matter little if we do not quickly learn how to have tough conversations around consent and begin nurturing ourselves and those we love with the physical touch we *all* desperately need to stay healthy and happy. And yes, that means this "touch-averse" girl is actually enjoying touch a lot more now after working through all of this alongside Dawn. I'm so grateful for what her message has made possible in my life and to be helping her bring this conversation to the world.

As a writer and emerging entrepreneur, Aaron Johnson is passionate about helping people uncover and unleash their infinite potential into the world by building relationships and communities that facilitate deeper learning, necessary conversations, and transformation personally and collectively. He founded Caterbuilder because of his love of community and experience with technology. At heart, he's a detail-oriented visionary with a knack for messaging, storytelling, and cultivating joy and growth in communities.

"I'm Having a True To Intention Client Moment"

Aaron Johnson

" **F***ck you and your healing-through-writing bullshit."
    I sent the text and blinked the tears back as a wave
of emotion crashed against old wounds of the past. I knew
she would probably cry while reading the part of the chapter
that had brought me to tears and then laugh at my tongue-in-
cheek, only-half-serious jab.

I'd been listening to her stories about clients healing their
lives for my whole life, and I'd had a few YCMTSU moments
while writing my part of our collaborative work, *A Religion
of Story*; but I hadn't experienced it until now... at least, not
consciously.

*Who knew that this was so needed? Maybe she did... no, she
definitely did. That's so like her.*

In fact, when we had begun writing the book, I was
resistant to the idea of incorporating real stories from my
past. For a while, I didn't know why—it felt like an invisible
wall that I wasn't allowed to question. And oh, how my mom
tried to convince me that it was the right thing to do; but I
didn't listen.

She saw what I couldn't (or refused to) see: old st*ries
that were ready to be rewritten.

Everyone has them. I wasn't oblivious to that fact, but
I thought that maybe I was different. I knew that I wasn't

nearly as messed up as a lot of kids are—by far—so there's no need for me to write about that stuff, right?

So naive.

One of the goals of our book is to show families how stories, through universal truths and archetypes, build our moral compass and inform our choices in the real world. Hence, *A Religion of Story*. To that end, my first impulse was to approach the writing with a purely logical and highly-structured perspective. Which TV shows or movies relate to this chapter's topic? What did I learn from them? What did this character show us? Why did their choices result in __? How does this lesson relate to the real world?

This approach worked for a little while. Let me tell you, the first chapter I wrote—chapter four—was a *breeze*. Not only was I using my favorite story of all time (*Harry Potter*, of course!), I was motivated and excited to be sharing in this way, articulating concepts about friendship I had known but never explored in such a methodical fashion. New *aha's* and awareness greeted me at every paragraph as I reunited with familiar stories of my childhood.

Chapter five (we went out of order because, you know, why the hell not?) was harder, but I pushed through. It took longer and a lot more planning to tackle the topic of Redemption and villains. Yet, the original plan was still working, so there was no need to give it another thought.

Chapter one slapped me in the face. The planning process became dreadful, and my desire to paint the page waned. Our scheduled writing time quickly became resented and unproductive, pushing me into a mindset defined by confusion and frustration; confusion as to why I had all-of-a-sudden lost my writing drive, and frustration from that. Suddenly, my thoughts were filled with questions like, "What's wrong with me?" and "Do I really want to do this?"

After a couple weeks of progress slowing to a crawl, I decided that I'd had enough.

The discouragement hit me all at once while I was sitting upright on my mom's futon couch, laptop in lap, and earbuds in place. My fingers rested on the keyboard, occasionally brushing the keys with boredom. To no avail, I had tried listening to music to forget the fact that I couldn't write a damn thing. I let the annoyance at my failure to do something that usually came so easily to me boil; and eventually, it came out all at once. Ripping the earbuds from their sockets, I exhaled, "Mom, I can't do it. I'm stuck."

She swiveled in her desk chair with concern. The reflection in her blue light glasses made it hard to see her eyes, but the stature of her eyebrows made it clear that she was surprised by this outburst. "Happens all the time. You want to talk about it and maybe it'll get the juices flowing?"

"No, it's not like that. It's... well, I don't know what it is." I folded my arms and looked off into space. "I'm just not motivated to write this anymore. It doesn't *feel* right."

She didn't respond right away. Instead, she pursed her lips and crooked her mouth to the side as she does when she's problem-solving. *Sometimes I really hate it when she does that.* Raising her eyebrows, she cautiously suggested, "I know it's not your favorite idea ever, but what if you used personal stories?"

Not again. I told her when we started this project that I didn't want to do that. I tried lying to myself by thinking that I was resistant to the idea only because I thought the analytical approach would be better overall. But, no. It was more than that. The idea of sharing some of those stories—opening up to the world and becoming vulnerable in that way—was the real repellant. Wasn't this just a guidebook to get families to think about the stories they consume?

Right...

I had finally opened up to her about my dilemma, and she insisted that I consider it. She believed that using personal examples would inspire me to connect with the teachings (and therefore the readers) on a deeper level and, overall, offer a more fun and motivating writing experience.

Lucky for me, our "writing" time ended and I brushed off her suggestion once again, yet something in me had warmed up to the idea a little more.

The next Sunday, I came right back and sat on the futon couch with my laptop in my lap once again. *Shit. Still blocked.*

At that point, I threw everything I thought I knew out the window and decided to browse our notes. I scrolled until I found the section for chapter two and my gaze fell to the "Personal Stories" bullet point where my mom had written down the ideas for how our real-life stories could connect to the themes of the book.

She's right. This would be so much better if I included my personal stories.

And so I got right to it. It was slow to start, and I was skeptical—at first. But it didn't take long for the words to flow like a river and for the keys on my keyboard to play their sweet story melodies. After about twenty minutes of writing, my mom came into the office. I met her eyes as she did, grinned, and let out a small sigh. "You were right."

"I know."

It was a cute jab and a reminder of who the expert is.

Writing resumed at a quickened pace. The writing "flow" hadn't been this strong since the beginning, even though it contained some of the hardest content I've ever put to paper. Personal stories flew out of my fingertips, making me chuckle to myself regularly, for two or three chapters.

But then, I'd hit another wall.

Chapter five is about villain tells and redemption, and while there are many good examples of villains and their opportunities to redeem themselves on TV, the dilemma I found myself in was choosing which real-life story to connect to such a touchy topic.

I sat down to brainstorm, but my search came up empty-handed. The gravity of the question made me realize it was time to discuss it with my mom.

"Hey, Mom." She took a moment to finish typing and swiveled to look at me. "I can't figure out any good stories to use. I don't know of any 'villains' in my life that would make sense in the context of the rest of the chapter."

"Oh. Yeah, that is difficult." She crooked her mouth to the side again. "What about Gramma?"

Gramma?! My stomach churned and the voice of morality inside my head quivered. By writing about someone in my life—my great-grandmother, no less—who I perceived as a "villain" at times, would readers then assume her to be "bad" or "evil"?

That's not okay. That's not true. How can I avoid that?

I didn't say any of that out loud, but my scrunched face and wide eyes must've done the talking for me because my mom continued in an effort to quell my apparent concern. "She would be the perfect one to talk about because you can see all of her—the woman that you loved and who was your buddy through early childhood, and the traumatized person who acted like a villain in the end."

What if she can be both? Fun at times and in pain at others, always loving yet sporadically villainous with her words? Maybe "villains" aren't one-dimensional...

Yeah, my brain sort of broke at that moment. And nearly so did my keyboard. Even though I'd already written that insight into the analytical part of the chapter, bringing that awareness into this particular relationship did something at a deeper level inside of me.

After that epiphany, I got straight to writing, but I did so in the privacy of my room this time. Never had a chapter been this easy and so hard to articulate at the same time.

At the rate that I was typing, I got to the rough part pretty quickly. Emotions welled up inside of me, but I kept pushing through.

"She became the manipulative Mother Gothel to our Rapunzel. We knew she loved us, and we loved her, too. But when it came time to live our lives—to seek adventure and pave our own path—we became her villain. As hard as it was to accept, she, too, had become an unexpected villain of my story. And I wanted to rewrite it."

"F*ck you and your healing-through-writing bullshit."

The more that I experience writing as an outlet for processing all of life's sh*t, the more that I can see that my mom is really a therapist. Asking the big questions, never giving away the "answers," and holding space for growth. Recently, she helped me see how inevitable this moment really was when she said, "What's funny to me right now is that the title of the book (*A Religion of **Story***) indicates the necessity of story, and yet this is what you were resisting." You really can't make this sh*t up. She showed me how to engage story from an analytical lens, and now I've used that to guide me to an introspective one.

That doesn't mean that it was easy. The resistance was *real*!

In the end, I was able to let go of the negative emotions surrounding my relationship with my great-grandmother. It's easy to appreciate the good times in spite of the bad, and most importantly, I see that it all happened *for* me, not *to* me.

And, of course, I was able to truly experience what it feels like to be a True To Intention client, especially because the book has emerged at the same time as a bunch of other opportunities.

It's never *just* the book, is it?

I've completed my high school journey, started a business, and moved 1,200 miles all within seven months. Looking into the future, we're launching our book, I'm jumping into a project to deliver a community learning environment for families, and I have a whole new world to explore right outside our new home. I know that I'm doing exactly what I'm meant to be doing because I have witnessed the ways in which my life is being orchestrated in incredible ways.

And yet, every day, I still find myself at war with the "little things"—the frustrations when it doesn't seem to be going the right direction, the doubts when it seems to be taking too long, and the anxieties about the uncertain future.

Fortunately, exploring and writing about personal and collective stories always brings me back to the same place: It seems that, no matter what life throws at us, the war with the "little things" is there to remind us that it's time to grow, to become someone new, and step further into who we are destined to become. Whenever something bad happens, we can't go back and stop it from happening. (Even our favorite time-traveling characters don't seem to be able to do it.) But we can make sure that it doesn't make us someone we don't want to become.

When we truly accept that life is happening *for* us and not *to* us, we have more agency in our life to choose who we want to become. We can make the conscious decision to become someone better rather than let the world make us someone worse.

That's why I really think our book can help other families realize that they can be the hero of their stories, not a spectator or a villain. Engaging story is the first step to rewriting our own. Once we start to see patterns on the screen and the page, and consider the possibility that those patterns are just a reflection of the themes in our own lives, we can begin to experience life asking this big empowering question:

If life can happen *for* our favorite characters, why can't it happen *for* us, too?

Mom's Side of the Story

"How was Human Spark class today? What did you all talk about?" I asked seventeen-year-old Aaron once we were on the road home.

"Well, my teacher believes that, in my lifetime, I will have the opportunity to choose immortality—that they have found a way to stop cell degeneration."

"Wow. What would you take into account to make that decision?" I wondered out loud, to myself and to him. When he looked at me curiously, I continued, "I mean, would you choose immortality if the world was still being run by bad guys, or if these climate issues were bound to happen, or...?"

"Mom, I think it's more a question of morality..." he gently interrupted my direction.

"I'm sorry... what?" I asked, caught completely off-guard.

"To choose immortality is to go against Nature." He said it so matter-of-factly, it made my head spin. It was time for me to look at him curiously and keep us safe on the road as he continued, "Well, Mom, how many stories like *12 Monkeys* and *About Time* do we have to watch to really understand that Time is a gift, and that having a finite amount of it makes us appreciate and savor it? And how much of that is really just a conversation about trying to control what isn't ours to control?" Again, matter-of-fact.

I decided to play devil's advocate: "Some would say that Nature is responsible for evolution and our desire and capacity to evolve even further—maybe toward immortality?"

He shook his head with certainty. "Nope, I think it's dangerous to ignore the laws of nature. I wouldn't do it. Every story we've ever watched has warned against it."

We have spent most of our time together watching movies, television series, and videos and discussing writers' intentions, human development, relationships, and why such messages might be emerging at particular times in our personal and collective history, so it didn't surprise me to hear him referencing them. What did surprise me was hearing him use them as reference points for his own worldview. Soon after this conversation, there was another moment when we were watching a tv show together, he said something that told me he had arrived at some important answers about God inside himself, and that his answers were not only a lot healthier for him at seventeen than mine were for me when I was that age, but they were also really his.

A tear slipped down my cheek as I recognized the feeling I was experiencing. It wasn't just momma pride. It was the same feeling that I had when he was three years old and corrected his angry great-grandmother when she was scolding him: "I'm not bad. I just made a bad choice, and I'm sorry." It was one of those moments in which I witnessed a generational st*ry matrix heal.

While this young man exudes all of the best qualities of those who have come before him, this process of working through stories together has allowed him to free himself from the unhealthy generational patterns, and choose the role he wants to play in his personal story and the bigger collective story.

After that conversation and those that followed in the next few months, as he connected the stories we had experienced with the information in some of his classes and on the news in conversation with me, I realized that our story needed to be told and this idea of raising a child on the religion of story might help other parents raising a child in a world that, as I write these words, is facing some of the toughest challenges in our history—a global pandemic, racial unrest complete with peaceful protests and violent riots, and the infringement on personal constitutional freedoms.

So, I pitched the idea and he jumped right in. The book quickly revealed its amazing framework of story-based themes (Uncertainty, Self-Knowledge, Training, Camaraderie, Redemption, Destiny, and Leadership) and we began collaborating to identify which stories we would use and how we would organize our contributions.

I knew that I wanted to start each chapter by bringing the reader into our living room during various conversations we've had over the last seventeen years so they could eavesdrop, be inspired, and maybe discover a few tricks for facilitating these conversations. And I also knew that some of these conversations seriously triggered me, and I would need to help parents recognize that this will likely happen to them too and why, and then how to navigate those moments with their children. Of course, that meant that I would be sharing my very personal stories, and I wondered out loud if Aaron would share his. Having already written one book about our journey together, I knew that it would be easy to show how he and I always seem to be "in the same theme at the same time." But that was a hard NO for him, and we worked together to find a way that felt safe for him to get started. (Yes, I was still hoping that at some point, he would write his stories!)

Navigating the tender spaces between Mom, Collaborator, and Coach became the most important task before me. I knew I would write my parts quickly because I could already see them all, and I knew that he would take longer because he was about to begin articulating his entire worldview and establishing exactly how it was shaped. That's no small task for anyone, let alone a seventeen-year-old!

I encouraged him to start with chapter four (Camaraderie), since the most important story used is his favorite of all time, Harry Potter. I thought it would make it easier for him to wrestle with just the writing process, rather than content as well. I was right. He soared through that chapter quickly, and then really seemed to enjoy working through the chapter on Redemption. We had a lot of fun, and

I loved everything that was flowing out of him onto the page. And I was sad when it stopped.

There were lots of times that our levels of enthusiasm for the project didn't match and, truth be told, many moments when I felt frustrated as a collaborator; but as a coach, I knew there had to be something else happening beneath the surface. It wasn't like him at all to simply let scheduled writing times slide by without so much as an acknowledgment. It wasn't like him to be stuck in a writing process at all. It wasn't like him to be so irritable about something that he genuinely loved to do.

I tried to keep the lines of communication open and support as much as I could with ideas for shifting the energy or the direction of the content, but he was stuck; and there was nothing I could do about it but wait for our Co-Author to intervene. (Cuz you know I wasn't about to try to manipulate the laws of nature!)

The first intervention happened when my sister launched her non-profit fundraiser and asked me to lead a workshop. Less than two weeks before the 2020 election, and closing in on six months of a global pandemic, the purpose of her fundraising event became supporting people (who would become sponsors) through those crazy times while raising money for the orphans she had visited in Africa. Having just completed my portion on the theme of Uncertainty, and some serious personal discovery around how my childhood stories shaped my tolerance and approach to Uncertainty, I asked Aaron if he would be willing to co-facilitate with me. He said YES and we had so much damn fun that night. I think it rekindled the desire to work on the project as well as sparked my desire to co-facilitate workshops on all of the themes with him.

Mock trial competitions and holidays provided more reasons to put off the writing, and then we found ourselves at the beginning of 2021 with another inspiration emerging. Sometimes these "new inspirations" are distractions and ways for messengers to procrastinate, but sometimes they are very important "detours" that end up leading to a better end. His was the latter.

One of our mutual clients asked him to help her build an online community for her network, and he absolutely fell in love with the experience. He loved the strategy, the design, and the work so much that he decided to launch a business to help other entrepreneurs develop similar online spaces that support the people they serve.

When he told me he was going to call the business Caterbuilder, I knew exactly what was happening with the delays on the book project. He described a logo that would be the word Caterbuilder but the "C" would look like a caterpillar's head, complete with antennae. "I mean, I've been signing my name like this since I realized I was your little caterpillar. Just seems like..."

"Destiny," I finished the sentence for him and he smiled in agreement. I don't know if he made the connection that I did, but I could see how he was just getting ready to live the last two themes of Destiny and Leadership (He was inspiring all of us with his work as a leader of the Youth Advisory Council!) before writing about them. That's when I knew for sure that he would end up sharing his personal story... but how would I convince him to do it, especially in the middle of this inspired phase of creativity and building? He was ON FIRE with inspiration and it was so fun to watch him build a website, work with his aunt to design elements he couldn't figure out on his own, and write sales copy that made this messaging mom proud.

With the website complete, and a few clients under his belt, he came to two quick conclusions: The first was that it would be awesome for us to work together, so I could help his clients develop powerful content for their online communities, and the second was that it was time to try writing the book again.

It didn't take long for him to realize that telling his personal stories was the path to unlocking the writing again, and I LOVED watching him smile and laugh as he wrote the first story about being a maniacally-competitive five-year-old who learned how to navigate uncertainty during a particularly challenging Uno game. He's such a freakin' amazing writer!

Toward the end of that chapter, he began writing about the move from his childhood home and his family to another state and school and I could see him crunching through the emotions of it. He popped his earbuds in to keep his energy up and moving, and about an hour into the writing time, he exclaimed, "Mom, this is a crazy story loop! Here I am writing about the move to Oregon and how it turned me upside-down, at the same time we are talking about moving to yet another state and I'm having all the big feels about leaving my friends here, and a song that I've never heard before comes on... and it's all about MOVING and UNCERTAINTY! You can't make this up!"

I'm excited to finish A Religion of Story, and I am confident that Aaron's healing and growth through this project have all been part of the bigger plan coming together for both of us... and so many others. The delay in the writing opened up space for inspiration for working together to help other messengers and to co-facilitate workshops around the themes we discuss in our book, and it also was my first step into my own next level of Collaborative Leadership in my business and this book.

Writing is such a challenging opportunity to reveal things to ourselves that we have long suppressed or ignored. Collaborative writing is like doubling-down on the opportunities (read: messy miscommunications, misunderstandings, and moments of utter mayhem) to uncover what is just below the surface, begging to be seen and known. From making the decisions about which content to include and how to organize it, to setting timelines and work sessions, to staying accountable to each other and keeping safety and love at the center, to gently pushing and nudging each other to go a little further even when we don't think we can—it's all tender work. And I have to tell you, I'm really glad I learned what I did with Aaron—the safest person in my world—before I got the idea to launch this book. Talk about a disaster waiting to happen without all of these lessons already learned!

"I'm lost in divinity
Between pages and ink,
Shaking the hand of God
In every stranger I meet.
I've kissed heaven so many times
I write to see it bleed
And when my pen runs dry,
I dance to hear Love speak.
So if time be my salvation,
Then fear be my enemy,
And if my tongue forgets to pray,
All I have to do is breathe."

Alyssa Noelle Coelho

Conclusion

Next-Level St*ry Collisions, Healing, and Wholeness

This book is set to launch almost two years after the initial "rabblers" rallied to collaborate on it. And I have to say, I'm really proud of us. The book turned out even better than I dreamed. The next-level healing people experienced while writing chapters was beautiful to witness. And two years isn't bad, given the fact that we survived (and even grew) through a global pandemic, political upsets, and social and economic ruptures, not to mention some major st*ry collisions among us.

As you have seen, deciding to write one's own book is like opening a portal to transformation. Doesn't it only make sense that having twenty-ish people writing their stories and working together to create one offering would crack that portal open even further and intensify the experience?

At the beginning of our first meeting, I shared my intuition that we would experience some challenges in the collaborative process. I offered that I had done my best to mitigate the potential issues I saw, but that we would need to stay committed to ourselves, each other, and the healing process this experience would activate. I knew there would be some collisions, but I couldn't have planned more epic ones than those we experienced.

Of course, there were the common experiences and big feelings that happen during any group project. You remember those from school, right? There are some ambitious few who jump right in and finish their part right away. Others get distracted and delayed and struggle to complete their part. And of course, there are those who realize the project isn't a good fit and kinda fade to the background or leave it completely. Add a global pandemic to the mix, and it's easy to understand why several folks decided to leave the group or renegotiate their level of engagement. Those changes always impact the group dynamics, and so we all had to grieve the initial vision and the people who left and continue on together.

Then there are the inevitable communication challenges that come with this large of a group compounded by the external stressors of what was happening on the world stage. Due to the pandemic, we met less frequently than originally planned, but I stayed connected to everyone individually. I knew the collaborators who were really struggling to keep their businesses and/or their well-being above water, and I renegotiated timelines for them. Unfortunately, I did a terrible job of communicating these renegotiations to the larger group, so there were some upset feelings experienced by those who had completed their chapters quickly.

When we finally were able to meet in person, we had the extra step of uncomfortable conversations around Covid safety measures among a group of people with rather diverse perspectives of what we should do. I think we handled that one alright, but we all felt the impact of the absence of those unable to attend for one reason or another.

Of course, there were the "opportunities" that always come when almost a dozen people stay in the same home together for several days in a row. It creates quite the perfect little storm for us to see the st*ries that are lurking just under the surface; and somehow, the environment always seems to be coordinated perfectly.

For example, Dawn was dealing with a significant experience of her st*ry of "no one is listening to me" before she even showed up to the retreat. Then, for days, she felt like she was talking and we were not hearing her or, worse, were ignoring her completely. We could tell she was upset, but there was resistance when we tried to engage. When she shared her heart with everyone present the last night, I started laughing out loud and then stopped abruptly when I realized I probably sounded like a jerk. "Oh my goodness. I had no idea this is why you were upset. Do you think it's a coincidence at all that we have been in a home with the worst acoustics and I haven't been able to hear even what the person standing next to me is saying?" They all looked at me stunned, but it was true. An old st*ry had been sparked for me the first day of the retreat by an object that was handed to me, but all I knew at the time was that my nervous system felt like it did in 2015 and all of my tools for calming it down weren't working. Thus, I had been managing serious audio overload (and anger) the entire time at that home because I had to work so hard to hear what people were saying, let alone coach and collaborate. You can't make that shit up! As soon as we realized that there were other factors and we all owned our parts in the st*ry, the big feelings dissipated a bit and we went back to enjoying each other's company (as much as you can in a house that makes it hard to hear each other).

A few months later, another collision happened. Lori Bonnevier had been in the final phase of editing her own book and was feeling very unsettled about the publishing process. I had explained the publishing options, but her emails about considering looking for a publisher and then deciding to self-publish with my team's support had stopped

for some time. Thinking she was working on the final edit
of her manuscript, I left the conversation for a future time.
Then, one day, after enjoying breakfast together and catching
up on life, she started to squirm. "Uhhhh... Amanda. I wanted
to talk to you about something..."

As she told me the story of feeling terrified that her book
was garbage (everyone feels this way during this phase),
finding a new small publisher online, and sending her
manuscript to "see if it was any good and if the publisher
would be willing to publish it," I could feel the color leave my
face and my heart start to race. The clencher was that this
publisher was one of my colleagues—someone I'd introduced
her to the year before who had already breached my
coaching relationship with Lori with some well-intentioned-
but-not-what-she-needed coaching. I held my breath and
tried to stay calm as she shared how she had gone behind
my back (*because she thought I wasn't trustworthy?*) to a
colleague of mine (*who also hid this whole exchange from
me?*) to have her determine whether the book that we had
poured our time and tears into was any good (*I thought she
was happy with the work we had done together?*). As she
shared from her heart, mine worked hard to identify and
digest all the feelings: hurt, anger, sadness... betrayal. Just
as I articulated that last feeling to myself, she confirmed it,
"Amanda, I feel like I cheated on you and I'm sorry..."

In that moment, my world started to right itself again
as I realized that she was using language that captured the
theme of her own wounds—the ones her book had helped
her to confront and begin to heal. You really can't make this
shit up. As a coach, and a recovered survivor of betrayal
myself, I knew this was an opportunity for another layer of
healing: When we see our capacity to wound another in a

similar manner, even if it is to a much lesser degree, it helps us to write truer stories about ourselves, our villains, and our world. I also knew I was far too emotionally overwhelmed in that moment to make that connection for her as a coach and decided to bring it up later before I leaned into the uncomfortable space as much as I could. Assuring her that my truest intention is the absolute best path for her and her book, I told her that if she felt this publisher was the right choice, then I would support her in any way she needed, even if that meant shifting from coach to cheerleader. Before we left, we talked about the possibility of her hiring my team to get her business ready for the opportunities the buzz and the launch would bring, rebranding the business and website, and developing online courses that would provide an opportunity for a larger audience to get high-level support. This would also create the space for her to increase the cost of her traditional services to something more in line with the value she actually provides and with her desires to reduce her workload and spend more time with her amazing kiddos while they are still at home, and under her care.

In the end, this collision turned into quite the opportunity. Not only did Lori land a publisher with wide marketing reach to foster her message, but we are also testing out a collaboration that could provide huge value for my future clients. Plus my team has been able to develop their skills and portfolios while supporting my colleague's efforts. That's right, my colleague was just beginning to realize she needed to find a team quickly when I pitched the collaboration. It truly became a win-win-win for everyone. What if all st*ry collisions, even the painful ones dressed in betrayal, hold the possibilities for everyone to come out better, stronger, and more whole on the other side?

And then there was the most epic collision of the entire project.

Torey had been struggling to find her flow with her chapter. She knew the theme was owning her story, no matter what other people thought or felt about it; but there was a bunch of resistance happening and she wondered out loud to me if it was because she wasn't really excited about sharing her message anymore. After looking at her first rough draft, I was concerned about her statement that "a perpetrator was now in office" and the implication that Kavanaugh was one as well. I knew a lot of people might agree with her, but I also didn't want her extremely important message to be lost on readers who disagreed and really needed to hear her story. I knew there had to be a way for us to communicate the level of impact these events were having on her, sparking her own stories of being dismissed and even shamed, and showing the YCMTSU messiness of it, *without* polarizing and losing a good portion of the readers unnecessarily. I knew I would have to lean into a very tough conversation with her and I asked Theddee to take a look to help me figure out a way to maintain the integrity of Torey's experience and feelings without stating her feelings and opinions as facts.

Theddee wasn't able to look at it for days and, after a very personally challenging weekend, she decided to take a look at the chapter right before the team meeting where she was going to present her approach to maintaining a healthy culture among team and clients at True To Intention. Really, you can't make this up. Ready?

Ten minutes before the meeting, I get a text from Theddee that says something like, "I hope that rant wasn't too much. I had a weekend full of dealing with false accusations and

Torey's chapter lit me up." I looked in my inbox to review her rant and my heart dropped when I realized that Torey owns the Google Doc. That meant that Theddee's rant, which was intended solely for my eyes, went directly to Torey's inbox. Oh no!

I went over to the chapter to see how bad it was and gasped. It was bad! The concern I had about losing readers was confirmed. Theddee's perspective was that accusations aren't always true because she had been falsely accused and so had her husband, and so she wasn't sure that a perpetrator was in the White House. And it didn't just turn her off from reading Torey's story, it hit an old wound and she had expressed some deep and dark feelings about women who had falsely accused someone she loved. Of course, I've been coaching her for years to bring these hidden wounds into the light so they can be seen and released and was happy to see her "go there" and allow her own healing to happen. Unfortunately, because of the broken system with the Google Doc ownership, her wound was now visible in the wrong place and primed to collide with Torey's wounds around not being believed, and being shamed and called awful names, when her accusations toward her perpetrator were true. And it was intense. In fact, I don't think I've ever heard Theddee use such cruel language or express such ugly sentiments in more than ten years of being close friends. Shit.

Quickly, I sent a text to Torey and told her that she had something in her inbox that was probably going to seriously upset her. I explained that Theddee had some personal wounds that she was working out with my help, or so she thought, and apologized for the failed system that led to this hot mess. I also told her I would be available that whole day if she wanted to talk or scream or cry.

Then, we started the team meeting on Culture. Theddee was in tears, somewhere between rage and shame; and so instead of talking about Culture, we co-created it right there. Safety. Unconditional Love. Truth. Personal Responsibility. Communal Healing.

By the time the meeting was over, I had heard from Torey and she was definitely upset. When we talked, she shared that this reaction was the exact reason why she had stalled in sharing her story and speaking to audiences. There were many times when she would be sharing and the room would go hot or cold, or both. She couldn't figure out how to tell her story without upsetting folks, and she didn't want to do that.

What a st*ry collision! Because of Theddee's experience, she tends to question accusations; because of Torey's experience, she tends to believe them because she knows what it takes for victims to come forward.

Suddenly, I saw how, if they were willing, this whole YCMTSU st*ry collision could be the pathway to a new experience and maybe even some additional healing for all of us. But it wasn't going to be a walk in the park to get there. Theddee sent me an email she wanted me to forward to Torey. It was an apology, an explanation, and an invitation to talk. Torey agreed and we all met online to work toward resolution and healing.

I was grateful to be in the company of two women who are more committed to Truth and Love and Healing than being comfortable. I believe Torey experienced a safe space to be heard and supported, and Theddee was able to clarify that it wasn't Torey's story that set her off—it was the statement of feelings as facts that got her because she had just dealt with a very similar situation that weekend. In fact, she told Torey how important she believed the message of *No*

Big Deal is, and shared personal experiences of being a victim herself and supporting other victims in healing. Together, we discussed the lines between sharing personal stories, perspectives, and feelings (which no one can ever argue with) and depicting any of those as facts… and how when we cross those lines, we lose our connection to our audience by polarizing them on details that aren't even necessary for us to get our message across.

It wasn't easy, and I'm deeply sorry for the personal upset that happened for both of these ladies, but I really do believe that we are all better, stronger, and clearer after that perfect st*ry storm. Torey's chapter is extremely powerful and won't lose a portion of the readers who really need to hear her message. Theddee experienced healing. And I am feeling more confident as a leader, having co-navigated this extremely tender situation.

And that's important because, as I shared in my introduction, I believe that's the true reason for the inspiration for this project: We have all been called to our next level of collaborative leadership. And, for me, this was one intense course in Leadership School and has provided the pathway of healing that I needed for what this project has catalyzed in my business and my personal life.

In early 2021, while we were busy working on our chapters, I received the same message in three different conversations with three different people who do not know each other. (This is how my Co-Author gets my attention when I'm busy!) The message was, "It's time to expand." Really? Right when I was just starting to enjoy the flow? Of course! But I knew it was the right direction. There were some services my clients needed but I didn't offer, and I could not find a trustworthy service provider for them. That usually

means it's time for me to create something. But how was I
going to do that during my busiest year ever in business and
one in which my family and I were moving to another state?

That answer came, again, multiple times from multiple
sources: "It's time to build a team and let them create these
new offerings." As soon as I heard that message, I laughed out
loud. The team had already gathered for a few of my clients.
My son, Aaron, was masterfully managing admin, systems, and
online events; Alyssa, my youngest sister, was designing book
covers and visuals for podcasts, curriculum, and marketing
content; my other sister, Ciara, was creating amazing videos
that told the story of events and brands; and two of my client-
turned-readers were helping me with editing projects because
I'd run out of time. Come on. That's hilarious!

As soon as I pitched the idea of more intentional strategy
and growth as a team, they all jumped at the opportunity
and started taking ownership of new offerings they wanted
to create and manage in the business. Alyssa is taking the
lead in public relations and creating a fiction department in
addition to expanding our product development to oracle
decks and promotional products. Aaron quickly set up the
new podcast (Sips of Story 'n Sanity) and is developing more
efficient systems for collaboration and serving our clients
in addition to bringing some of our tech-averse clients into
the 21st century (their words!). Theddee and Lori Giesey
are excited about the children's book department we are
going to create. And Ciara is helping us with community
events because no one facilitates parties and games like her.
Oh, and the best part is, they all want to co-facilitate st*ry-
healing events (which we will now call portals, thanks to Lori
Bonnevier!) with me for our community and beyond. How
fun is that?!?

But there was one big question on my mind: What about my bandwidth for the part that only I facilitate? The content development and messenger st*ry-healing?

The answer to that big question came during our in-person retreat for this project. Everyone began to share their first drafts of these chapters; and when I opened the floor for feedback, my two sisters blew me away with the questions they asked and the suggestions they made. Just as I was marveling at it (and wondering if I was really seeing it), I got a text from Theddee who was listening online: "Amanda, who is that talking? Which sister? She is like a mini-Amanda! What an incredible coach!"

I responded, "It's both of them," set my phone down, and let the tears fall.

It's already been built. While I've been focused on serving my clients and family members over the last few decades, I've unknowingly been cultivating a team—a family—of people who I know, love, and trust... who love this work and are devoted to it because it has changed their lives... and who do not have to be trained because they have been living in this experience for years. Is it possible that we were all inspired at the just-right time to find each other to heal the st*ries and then fall in love with the work and share the experience with others?

It's just another bit of evidence that these inspirations we have to go out and change the world with our messages are really, truly, divine conspiracies to help *us* become true to our original intention... to crack open the opportunities for us to witness our st*ries and reclaim the parts of us that were abandoned, shamed, and repressed... to invite us back to wholeness. But it doesn't stop there. Our Co-Author seems to be masterfully weaving all of our storylines together at the perfect moments, so that our story-sharing and st*ry collisions can accelerate and deepen the process for our individual and collective healing.

The gift of all of us saying YES to the inspiration, and doing the grueling work of st*ry-healing so that we can serve others, is that our own healing happens more quickly and easily... *if* we are aware and refuse to back out or away from the work when the inevitable st*ry collisions happen.

Years ago, when I read Neale Donald Walsh's words in his book, *Happier Than God*, I could feel their truth and had a small handful of stories that could validate it. But now, after more than ten years of witnessing *our* stories and certainly at the end of this incredible project, no one will ever be able to convince me that this is not the truth:

"Now comes a *huge* part of the 'mystery formula' for how life works... *The Multiplier Effect.* By focusing on yourself you limit the amount of energy that you output, because *there is only one of you.* Yet by focusing on others you *multiply* the amount of energy you output by the number of others with whom you do so... Until I understood this and began working to heal all others, I, myself, would be slow in healing... Until I understood this and sought earnestly to remember all others as Who They Really Are, I, myself, would be slow in remembering Who I Really Am..."

Those of us inspired to create and contribute and change the world have the astounding opportunity to experience this truth every single day. The journey is not for the faint of heart, but I hope by now you can see how worthy an adventure it is. Saying YES to the initial inspiration is the beginning of your journey home to *you*; and if you say YES to helping others, and you stay present to how the st*ry collisions are unfolding in divine order for everyone's highest good, then we will all get home sooner.

About Amanda

 Amanda Johnson helps aspiring and seasoned change agents write truer individual and collective stories. She partners with divinely-inspired souls to craft messages for maximum impact on their audience, brand, and bottom line AND heal their st*ries, so they can change the world without compromising their health, sanity, or soul. After years of engaging, clarifying, and helping others develop powerful messages [as a Student, Teacher, and Master Writing Coach], Amanda uncovered her own. The decision to share it launched her on a journey of transformation that quickly made her personal and professional life unrecognizable.

Realizing how powerful a Message can be—not only for the audience, but for the Messenger—Amanda integrated everything she'd learned from some of the world's most outstanding educators, transformational coaches, and heart-centered business experts, and grew a dynamic, profitable brand around her Butterfly Approach to Writing, Speaking, and Training in just a few short years. She has facilitated dozens of books from Inspiration to Impact, and several of those to Amazon Bestseller and award-winning status. She has also been blessed to co-generate paradigm-shifting, systemic-change-catalyzing curricula that is improving the lives of tens of thousands of teachers, parents, and children.

Five years after Amanda wrote, published, and launched her first book *[Upside-Down Mommy]* as an Amazon Bestseller in less than 3 months, she wrote *Upside-Down Messenger* to make The Messenger Matrix visible to messengers struggling to change the world on their own terms.

A Special Invitation for You

After reading these stories, you may be realizing that if you are going to complete that creative project or move that coaching business forward, you are going to need more than the inspiration you've experienced while reading these pages.

You're going to need new tools, skills, guides, and allies.

Most importantly, you're going to need a Cocoon in which you can dissolve the st*ries that stand between you and your intention.

That's why we want to invite you to join us in **CocoonU**—the online community where we provide all of these and more for creatives, messengers, and entrepreneurs like you who are tired of trying to figure it out (and do it) all alone.

Try it for 30 Days for FREE and ENJOY:

Writing Days (Weekly)
Co-working sessions with allies will move your project forward!

Portals (Monthly)
Mini-workshops will launch you into new possibilities
for your messaging, st*ry-healing, and more!

Community Play (Monthly)
Game nights will make it fun for loved ones
to join you on the creative journey!

Group Innerlight Sessions (Monthly)
Energy balancing sessions will help you release old st*ries and
create pathways for new ones to be written on all levels.

Saved By Story (Monthly)
Story-focused and chocolate-filled discussions will
accelerate your st*ry-healing and increase your wonder.

Discounts on Other Quests, Retreats, and Services
If you want to dive deeper, discounts will make it more doable.

Value = $290+
Regular Monthly Investment: $29/month

Go to www.TrueToIntention.com/CocoonU
and find the support you need today!

Made in the USA
Las Vegas, NV
22 January 2022

41997429R00273